The Student Struggle Against the Holocaust

The Student Struggle Against the Holocaust

by

Rafael Medoff & David Golinkin

Foreword by Aryeh Rubin
Introduction by Irving (Yitz) Greenberg

David S. Wyman Institute for Holocaust Studies
Jewish Theological Seminary
Schechter Institute of Jewish Studies
Targum Shlishi, a Raquel and Arye Rubin Foundation

Jerusalem
2010

ISBN 978-965-7105-67-2

Distribution:
The Schechter Institute of Jewish Studies
POB 16080, Jerusalem 91160 Israel

Tel. 02-6790755
Fax 02-6790840
Email: schechter@schechter.ac.il
Website: www.schechter.edu

Produced by Leshon Limudim Ltd., Jerusalem
Tel. 02-5372212 Email: leshon@netvision.net.il
Printed in Israel

TABLE OF CONTENTS

Acknowledgments   vii
Foreword by Aryeh Rubin   ix
Introduction by Irving (Yitz) Greenberg   xiii

Chapter 1:   American Jewry and the Holocaust: The Setting   1
Chapter 2:   Retribution is Not Enough   27
Chapter 3:   The Sefira Campaign   67
Chapter 4:   Epilogue   107

Symposium: Reflections on Three Remarkable Students   115
    David G. Roskies: A Story That Must Be Told   117
    David Golinkin: Why Noah Golinkin Fought   121
            to Save the Jews of Europe
    Mishael Tziyon: A Letter from Rabbi Moshe "Buddy" Sachs   128
    Jonathan Lipnick: Jerome Lipnick's Two Black Ribbons   132
    Abe Golinkin: Vision, Activism and Courage: 137
            Indispensable Attributes of the JTS Students
    Haskel Lookstein: The Rally That Almost Wasn't   141
    David Ellenson: Lessons for Jewish Leaders   148
    Rafael Medoff: Writing the Student Activists Back   154
            into History

Appendices   157
Abbreviations Used   215
Notes   217
Bibliography   237
Photo Credits   246
Index   247

ACKNOWLEDGMENTS

The authors are deeply grateful to a number of friends and colleagues for their assistance.

For their aid with various aspects of the research, the authors thank Ruth Tonkiss Cameron and Michael Boddy of the Burke Library at the Union Theological Seminary; Sarah Diamant, Yevgeniya Dizenko, Ellen Kastel, and Rabbi Jerry Schwarzbard of the Ratner Center for the Study of Conservative Judaism, at the Jewish Theological Seminary; Pearl Berger and Shulamith Berger of the Yeshiva University Library, and Rabbi Elly S. Krimsky of the Yeshiva University Alumni Office; Simone Schliachter of the Central Zionist Archives; Christopher Brennan, the Gardner A. Sage Library Director at the New Brunswick Theological Seminary; Kate Skrebutenas of the Princeton Theological Seminary Library; Bonnie Falla of the Moravian Theological Seminary Library; Patrick Slaven of St. Mark's Library at the General Theological Seminary; Suzanne Estelle-Holmer of the Yale Divinity School Library; Julien Simon of the World Council of Churches Library & Archives; Genie Abrams of Temple Beth Jacob (Newburgh, NY); and Ms. Sheryl Hoffman. Prof. Jeffrey S. Gurock read early drafts of the manuscript and offered many important suggestions. Dr. Euan Cameron of the Union Theological Seminary provided helpful insights and assistance. Photographs were kindly made available by the families of J. Herbert Brautigam, Jr., Ivol Godby, Earl Shay, Noah Golinkin, Jerome Lipnick, Moshe "Buddy" Sachs, Rabbi Joseph Lookstein, and Abraham Zuroff, as well as by Dr. Russell Gasero of the Reformed Church in America Archives, Bonnie Clarke, librarian at the Sarasota (FL) Temple, Judy Weidman, librarian of Congregation Beth Israel in Houston, TX, and Joel Elliot, executive director of Temple B'rith Kodesh, in Rochester, NY.

The authors are grateful to Donny Finkel and the staff of Leshon Limudim for typesetting the book. We are also grateful to Linda Price and to Stephanie & Ruti Design for their design of the book cover, and to illustrator and School of Visual Arts faculty member Sal Amendola, who beautifully re-created the "Jewry's Crisis Calls for

Justice" poster from a faded 1943 image of that document, for use in the cover design.

Finally, the authors are pleased to acknowledge the generous financial assistance they received to support the writing and publication of this book, provided by The David S. Wyman Institute for Holocaust Studies; Targum Shlishi, a Raquel and Aryeh Rubin Foundation; the Schechter Institute of Jewish Studies; Dr. Alan Cooper and the Publications Committee of the Jewish Theological Seminary of America; Rabbi Jonathan Lipnick and Susan Scheuer; Rabbi Haskel Lookstein; the family of Rabbi Moshe "Buddy" Sachs; Rabbi Richard Plavin; and Mr. Henry Gerber.

Rafael Medoff and David Golinkin
Washington, D.C. and Jerusalem
27 Tishrei 5771, 5 October 2010

FOREWORD

Shortly after graduating from college, I bought a car in Paris and traveled across Europe for six months, not in the tradition of the European Grand Tour, but as a very personal exploration of a destroyed world. It was 1974-75 and I felt compelled to retrace part of my parents' escape routes from the furnaces of Hitler's Europe, to visit eleven former concentration camps, and to familiarize myself with devastated Jewish communities behind the Iron Curtain.

At that time, my endeavor was practically unheard of; it was long before the March of the Living made such sojourns commonplace. In fact, the Holocaust was not a major topic of discussion among American Jews.

The community simply had not yet found a serious and consistent means of integrating knowledge of the Holocaust into its consciousness or into public discourse. As a consequence, most American Jews, whether members of the general community or officials of Jewish organizations, generally steered clear of Holocaust-related topics. When I was educated at Jewish day schools and yeshivas in the mid and late 1960s, the Holocaust was never mentioned in any formal sense, even though we were aware that many of our teachers were survivors. At Yeshiva University, my alma mater, the subject matter was so novel that there was no course explicitly dedicated to it – instead, the pioneering Rabbi Dr. Irving (Yitz) Greenberg taught one of the first university-level courses on the Holocaust in the United States, under the rubric of a seminar on totalitarianism and ideology. A further indication of the lack of American Jewish interest in the subject was that in some of the shtetls I visited during my travels, I was told that I was the first Jew to visit since the late 1940s and early 1950s.

If American Jewry's response – or rather evasion – even thirty years after the Holocaust was puzzling and disturbing, its lack of action during the Holocaust was nothing short of devastating. In *The Student Struggle Against the Holocaust*, Dr. Rafael Medoff and Rabbi Prof. David Golinkin do us the great service of introducing an exception to the rule, and it is a striking exception. In this important book, we learn of the remarkable actions of three young rabbinical students at the Jewish Theological Seminary who *did* act, despite the collective lack of will of the larger community. In the story of Noah Golinkin (the father of co-author David Golinkin), Jerry Lipnick, and Moshe "Buddy" Sachs, we find much to admire. In learning of their activities, readers may experience both hope and despair: hope because their story shows us that action *is* possible, despite great odds, indifference, and outright hostility; despair because if there had been more like them who were willing to take a stand and act on behalf of Europe's Jews, perhaps collectively they could have made an even greater difference.

The months I spent traveling through post-Holocaust Europe had a profound effect on me. The psychological trauma and emotional stress I experienced as a consequence of visiting the sites of atrocities, and the cities and villages that had once been home to vibrant Jewish communities, helped shape the direction of my life, my philosophy, and my thought processes. At the time, and certainly since then, I have increasingly believed most of American Jewry to be guilty of silence and deserving of criticism. That the world let this happen is inconceivable. That American Jewry was generally silent is a travesty.

There is no question that American Jewry could have done more. *The Student Struggle Against the Holocaust* clearly shows us this; in reading about the accomplishments of three young rabbinical students, it is impossible not to imagine all that might have been accomplished if the larger American Jewish establishment had stepped up to the plate.

There could have been frequent mass protests. If ever in our history civil disobedience was justified, it was in response to the Roosevelt administration's abandonment of the Jews of Europe during the Shoah. Perhaps widespread protest efforts would have had only a limited impact; perhaps restrictions on quotas for entry of Jews to the United States would have not been lifted; we do not know if a massive outcry would have prevented the turning back of the *S.S. St. Louis* and its doomed passengers; nor we can know if organized action such as shutting down the major traffic arteries of New York, Chicago, Detroit, and Los Angeles would have convinced the United States government to bomb the railway tracks leading to Auschwitz. But American Jews could have tried, and if they had, they would have left a very different legacy. Their actions would have set a very different example, and the tone and precedent of righteous protest would have established a basis for an appropriate communal response to the existential problems facing world Jewry today. As Rabbi Haskel Lookstein wrote in his 1985 book, *Were We Our Brothers Keepers?*, "The final solution may have been unstoppable by American Jewry, but it should have been unbearable to them. And it wasn't." Instead, for most American Jews, life went on as usual at all levels: at the institutional level, at the communal level, and at the personal level. The Jewish organizations held their annual dinners, the synagogues held their dances, and the people held their wedding and bar mitzvah parties during the decimation. Life went on; Europe was a world away.

Many American Jews claimed not to have known what was going on during the early stages of the Holocaust. While that in itself is difficult to believe given the widespread press coverage of the massacres, certainly by 1944 when Hungary's Jews were being rounded up for deportation to Auschwitz, and the Allies were stepping up their bombing runs to Germany and Poland, the American Jewish community should have, at the very least, pushed and screamed for the bombing of the railroad tracks leading to Auschwitz. That did not happen.

Given the tenor of the times, the fact that Noah Golinkin, Jerry Lipnick, and Buddy Sachs did in fact rise to the occasion is notable. These students could not adhere to their daily routine while their brethren were being gassed in Auschwitz, massacred in the forests of the Ukraine, or waging a desperate rebellion in the burning buildings of the Warsaw Ghetto.

The Student Struggle Against the Holocaust demonstrates that a few individuals with conscience, grit, and determination can make a difference. They took on the establishment, they challenged the indifference of their countrymen, and they countered the sad apathy of their co-religionists.

I believe that if a victim from the Holocaust could rise up from one of the mass graves and speak, he would ask three questions: Why didn't the Jews of the world move heaven and earth to stop the massacre? Why wasn't more done to bring the Nazis to justice after the Holocaust? Why didn't we as Jews make a serious effort to find the mass graves, to discover where and how the Jews were killed, and to say *Kaddish*? We have no adequate answers to these questions. I am ashamed of the legacy of inaction we have left for future generations.

Many consider it impolitic to judge the Jews of that era. Our tradition teaches us to refrain from judging another person until you stand in his or her shoes. And we are all aware that it was a different time, a silent time, a time rife with antisemitism promoted by the likes of Father Coughlin. Yet the scope of the catastrophe negates all other factors. I believe that American Jews, their leaders, and their institutions made an insufficient effort to raise the alarm as one-third of world Jewry vanished in the crematoria of Auschwitz.

The story of these three individuals provides a sliver of light in a densely dark epoch. Whatever misgivings they may or may not have had regarding the success of their mission, they could at least face the rest of their lives knowing they took action, and they left for their children and grandchildren – and for us – a model not of inaction, but of caring, concern, and compassion, a model of being proactive. At a time when most of American Jewry went about their daily lives, with some tangled up in bickering with each other and intensifying the disunity among the various factions of Jewry, these three young rabbinical students tried to rally Jews and Christians alike to speak out against the destruction of European Jewry.

Had the Holocaust not occurred, today the worldwide Jewish population would be thirty-two million strong, according to demographer Sergio Della Pergola, of the Hebrew University. Instead, we number thirteen million. And yet today, even with these reduced numbers, the Jewish people face severe threats. There are regimes that threaten Israel with military destruction, terrorist groups that strike at Jews from Tel Aviv to Buenos Aires, boycott movements that seek to undermine Israel's economic well-being, and propagandists who try to undermine its legitimacy. Israel's army can stand up to the guns, tanks, and bombs; world Jewry must respond to those who use other means to assault the Jewish State.

It is my hope that as we read of and applaud the heroic actions of these three young rabbinical students, we just may become inspired to rally the Jewish masses of today so that the errors of our past are not repeated.

Aryeh Rubin
Aventura, Florida, Isru Ḥag Sukkot 5771/2010

INTRODUCTION

In the final days of November 1942, two months after the Nazis had completed their mass deportation of more than 250,000 Jews from Warsaw to their deaths in Treblinka, Jan Karski arrived in London. Karski, a courier from the Polish underground, had just returned from a dangerous secret mission to report on the anti-Nazi underground in Poland and its efforts. In the course of his mission, he was smuggled into the Warsaw Ghetto and rode on the rail lines to the extermination camps, reaching a transit camp near Belzec. He saw the box cars and the hideous trail of the dead and dying along the way. The trip so seared his conscience that he spent the rest of the war trying to convince American, British, Polish, and Jewish leaders that an unbelievable mass murder was underway and that they must do something to stop it.

In London, Karski met with Shmuel Zygelboim, the Jewish Bund's representative on the Polish National Council, affiliated with the Polish Government-in-Exile. He delivered to Zygelboim a message from the Warsaw Ghetto that he had memorized, for fear that if it was written down and he was caught with it, it would endanger his life:

> Tell [the Jewish leaders] that we feel hate for those who were saved there because they are not saving us... they are not doing enough. We know that there in the humane and free world, it is absolutely impossible to believe what is happening to us here. Let them do something that will force the world to believe... We are all dying... Let them lay siege to Churchill's government and others, proclaim a hunger strike; let them even die of hunger rather than budge until they believe and take measures to save the last remnants who are still alive. We know that no political action, no protests or proclamation of punishment *after* the war will help. None of them make any impression on the Germans. (Israel Gutman, *The Jews of Warsaw, 1939-1943: Ghetto Underground Revolt*, Bloomington: Indiana University Press, 1982, 362-63)

When I heard Karski's personal account, given at the United States Holocaust Memorial Museum in Washington, D.C. at a conference in the 1980s, I found him to be electrifying in his intensity. His account was so riveting and devastating that I felt that his narrative could literally melt a heart of stone. Yet the decent, civilized people whom he met – from President Franklin Delano Roosevelt and British Foreign Secretary Anthony Eden, to the Polish Government-in-Exile (cf. p. xv) and Jewish leaders in England and the United States – did not respond as they should have. Whether because of the heavy burden of daily responsibilities, or the presence of antisemitism in themselves or their fellows, or the desire for respectability and not to be seen as one who rocks the boat, or by sheer routine and other priorities – they did not drop everything and insist on doing something to stop the most total criminal enterprise of all time. In truth, I cannot get my mind around it.

Post-mortem, we know from Helen Fein's book (*Accounting for Genocide: National Responses and Jewish Victimization During the Holocaust*, New York: The Free Press, 1979) that the key to Jewish survival rates during the Holocaust was the behavior of the bystanders: Jewish survival rates varied from over 95% in Denmark to 40% in France to 10% in Poland. The Nazis' behavior did not change the survival rate – in every country, they sought to murder all the Jews. Jewish behavior throughout Europe – that is, trying to live under the blows, striving to maintain culture and values, and trying to survive – hardly varied. At the very end, when it became clear that all were doomed, a small percentage tried armed resistance. None of these patterns had significant effect on the final outcome. Where the bystanders approved, participated, raised no obstacles – Jewish survival rates plummeted. Where the bystanders withheld approval, objected, helped save Jews, resisted, Jewish survival rates rose. What outside governments with armies, military supplies, strong commercial sanctions, power would have done to reduce Jewish deaths is beyond calculation – but we will never know.

The vaguely addressed, toothless words of condemnation jointly uttered by the Allies on December 17, 1942, and the later halting, only partly approved rescue efforts launched by Jewish groups had little or no deterrent effect on the Nazis and few actual survival results. Direct outside attacks on the death camps and the rail lines to them were never undertaken. No one took the drastic steps needed to make the Allies believe, let alone act seriously to stop the mass murder. The only one who dropped everything to protest was Shmuel Zygelboim who heard the message directly and immediately from Karski. Unable to get action from the Polish Government-in-Exile or his fellow Jews, Shmuel Zygelboim committed suicide in protest at the utterly inadequate response of world leaders to the genocide.

This background explains why this book, *The Student Struggle Against the Holocaust*, is so important and valuable. True, the story it tells is how three young rabbis-in-training tried, with only limited success, to arouse the conscience of America's Jews and of Christian religious leaders to take adequate action. But the model is important. The Torah tells us at length how Joseph's older brother Reuven wanted to save him from death or being disposed of. Although he never openly spoke about his desire to save Joseph and although by the time he returned to the pit where his younger brother initially was held, Joseph was sold and gone – still the Torah recounts the story. Why? Because at a time when the conscience of all the bystanders failed, he understood the need to do something. Conclusion: We need to know about the saving moral minority, and we need to know so we can imitate their behavior the next time a parallel situation emerges. By recounting their efforts and remembering their names, we educate the next generation and we raise the odds that more good people will act the right way and mount a successful effort to get life-saving action.

Student action can make a difference.

In the 1960s, Soviet Jewry was cut off from world Jewry. Oppressed and denied its cultural or religious heritage, it appeared to be lost and about to disappear. Then a handful of Soviet Jews decided to reclaim their rights and identity. Then the State of Israel and the Six Day War aroused a flood of identification. Still, the movement could not have become successful either in gaining the right to emigrate or to reconnect to its heritage without the help of world Jewry, Israel, and various democratic governments, the United States first and foremost. When their fate hung in the balance and when world Jewry appeared to be sleeping and ready to fail its brothers by going on with business-as-usual, the Student Struggle for Soviet Jewry was born. This time, the students organized more widely and began to focus media and world attention on the cause.

xv

We owe an historic debt of gratitude to Jacob Birnbaum, founder of SSSJ, who dedicated his whole life to using the student lever to move Jewry, then the American government, then together with Israel to move the other democracies to help bring about a miraculous release of Soviet Jewry. Of course, SSSJ caught the winds of Soviet Jewish awakening and America opening up to a new pluralism and a media that was ready to highlight the cause of the downtrodden everywhere. It is also true that the memory of the Holocaust and the continuing consciousness of the awful failure then operated to arouse conscience and action now. Still, without the student efforts, the critical mass of action, attention, and intervention would have never occurred.

Therefore it is essential that the record of the 1940s be put before the public and the redeeming example of the 1960s–1990s as well, to prepare us for whatever action will be needed in the next looming crisis. This is not a theoretical statement. The existential threat to Israel of Iran obtaining nuclear arms is months – or, at best – only years away. Personally, I do not see the infrastructure of adequate action being put in place at this time. Thank God, we have Israel now to protect us, but that is not enough. This book is to be blessed for again putting before all of us the choice and the need to act. As the Torah says: "I [God] put before you today, life and good, death and evil... Let Heaven and Earth witness that life and death I have placed before you, the blessing and the curse. Then choose life – in order that you and your children will live" (Deuteronomy 30: 15, 19).

This book puts before us the three students who chose life but were foiled by the failure of that generation's leaders to respond adequately to the magnitude of the unfolding catastrophe. It should be put alongside the student choice that moved the world and succeeded – in order that this generation understand that it must choose again – and that it dare not fail. We pray that this book will impact on the hearts and minds of Jewish leaders everywhere and on the students who will face the inevitable crises to come. May its readers – and all Jews – be inspired by the memory of the actions of the righteous in the 1940s to rise to the challenge of the next century, of the Jewish journey toward *tikkun olam*.

Yitz Greenberg
Founding President, Jewish Life Network/Steinhardt Foundation, 1995-2007
Chairman, United States Holocaust Memorial Council, 2000-2002
Vice Chairman, Student Struggle for Soviet Jewry, 1964-1991
Jerusalem, Sukkot 5771/2010

Chapter 1

AMERICAN JEWRY AND THE HOLOCAUST: THE SETTING

The Jewish Theological Seminary in the 1940s.

Every morning, at the conclusion of the prayer service at the Jewish Theological Seminary in New York City, the rabbinical students would walk over to the campus cafeteria for breakfast. And every morning in the autumn of 1942, Noah Golinkin would make a detour. He would walk down Broadway two blocks to a newsstand at 120th Street, and buy two newspapers: the *New York Times* and the Yiddish-language *Morgen Zhurnal*. As he walked back to the Seminary, Noah would hurriedly scour the papers for news about

1

the plight of the Jews in his native Poland, from which he had escaped just four years earlier.[1]

On November 25, 1942, a typically crisp autumn morning in Manhattan, Noah was thumbing through the *New York Times* as he approached the corner of 121st Street. What he saw on page ten made him stop in his tracks. "HIMMLER PROGRAM KILLS POLISH JEWS," a headline announced. The sub-headline added: "Slaughter of 250,000 in Plan to Wipe Out Half in Country This Year Is Reported." An additional sub-headline declared: "Officials of Poland Publish Data – Dr. Wise Gets Check Here by State Department."

The article reported that at the instruction of Gestapo chief Heinrich Himmler, Jews throughout Poland were being rounded up and taken away in sealed train cars, allegedly to be "settled" somewhere to the east. "Wherever the trains arrive half the people are dead," according to a report released by the Polish government in exile and quoted by the *Times*. "Those surviving are sent to special camps at Treblinka, Belzec and Sobibor, in Southeastern Poland. Once there, the so-called settlers are mass-murdered."

An estimated 250,000 Jews were already dead, and "half the remaining Polish Jews must be exterminated by the end of this year," according to the report.

Golinkin, his eyes wide with horror, read on. At the bottom of the article, the *Times* editors appended a six paragraph item from Jerusalem, quoting information received by Jewish leaders there. They provided additional ghastly details: large numbers of children murdered "wholesale within a few minutes by machine-gun fire"; "concrete buildings on the former Russian frontiers used by the Germans as gas chambers in which thousands of Jews have been put to death"; and "trainloads of adults and children taken to great crematoriums at Oswiecim, near Cracow." Oswiecim was the Polish name for Auschwitz.

Noah Golinkin in the 1940s.

After that, the *Times* staff had tacked on another small item, five paragraphs long, headed "Wise Gets Confirmations." Rabbi Dr.

Stephen S. Wise, the foremost leader of the American Jewish community, had announced at a press conference in Washington that the State Department "confirmed the stories and rumors of Jewish extermination in all Hitler-ruled Europe." About two million Jews had already been murdered, Wise said. [2]

If there was one figure in American Jewish public life whose word was considered beyond reproach by his co-religionists, it was Stephen Wise. Over the course of his nearly half-century in Jewish public life, Wise had founded and for many years

Rabbi Dr. Stephen S. Wise

led the American Jewish Congress and the World Jewish Congress (which he still co-chaired), served as president of the Zionist Organization of America, and as chairman of the United Palestine Appeal and the Emergency Committee for Zionist Affairs (a position he still held in 1942), all the while serving as spiritual leader of New York City's Free Synagogue (est. 1917) and president of the Jewish Institute of Religion (a non-denominational rabbinical seminary, est. 1922, which would later merge with Reform Judaism's Hebrew Union College). He was also well-traveled in the wider social and political world: he co-founded the National Association for the Advancement of Colored People (1909) and the American Civil Liberties Union (1920), actively participated in battles for union rights and women's suffrage, and enjoyed a personal and political relationship with Franklin D. Roosevelt, which gave him far greater access to the White House than any other Jewish leader. When a man of Wise's stature publicly vouched, in November 1942, for the reports of systematic mass-murder, there could be little doubt as to their authenticity.

Throughout the previous year, Noah Golinkin had read the news from Europe with mounting anxiety. Undoubtedly, the Germans had committed atrocities against Jewish civilians in occupied regions on a scale far more severe than the random acts of cruelty one might normally associate with a world war. The gradual accumulation of

3

President Franklin D. Roosevelt and his cabinet in 1938.

news reports, quoting apparently reliable sources, made that clear. But a systematic, deliberate campaign to annihilate millions of Jews, with gas chambers and crematoria built in camps designed for the purpose of mass murder – this was something far beyond what anyone could have imagined. His heart racing, the newspaper clenched tightly in his trembling hand, Noah hurried back to campus, to share the news with his closest friends, Jerry Lipnick and Moshe "Buddy" Sachs. Noah knew that something must be done – but what?

Persecution and Response

What the JTS students and most American Jews could not know was that despite Rabbi Wise's vaunted friendship with President Roosevelt, and his fulsome public praise of FDR, Wise privately was frequently torn between his strong admiration for Roosevelt's policies and his frustration at the president's unwillingness to take meaningful action to aid the Jews in Hitler's Europe.

As early as April 1933, just one month after Adolf Hitler became chancellor of Germany, Rabbi Wise privately expressed anguish that President Roosevelt, anxious to avoid irritating U.S.-German relations, had not publicly commented on the mistreatment of German Jews by the Nazis. "President [Roosevelt] has not by a single word or act intimated the faintest interest in what is going on" regarding the Jews in Germany, Wise confided to a friend. Despite numerous reports of Nazi persecution of German Jews, FDR refrained from any public comment on their plight. In June, after returning from Washington, Wise wrote to a colleague that "as far as the German situation is concerned... we could get nothing public out of the President."[3]

Other Jews of prominence likewise were unable to get anything out of Roosevelt regarding German Jewry. Longtime FDR friend and soon-to-be cabinet member Henry Morgenthau Jr. and New York judge Irving Lehman visited the White House in September 1933 to request a statement about the plight of Germany's Jews. FDR told them he preferred to make a statement about human rights abuses in Germany in general, without focusing on the Jews. Ultimately, however, he made no such statement.[4] "FDR has not lifted a finger on behalf of the Jews of Germany," Wise wrote to a colleague the following month. "We have had nothing but indifference and unconcern up to this time."[5] In the eighty-two press conferences FDR held in 1933, the subject of the persecution of the Jews arose just once, and not at Roosevelt's initiative. It would be five years, and another 348 presidential press conferences, before anything about European Jewish refugees would be mentioned again. Although personally discomfited by Hitler's treatment of the Jews, Roosevelt was unwilling to strain American-German relations by publicly complaining about such human rights abuses.[6]

Roosevelt's indifference presented Wise with agonizing dilemmas. If he were to publicly criticize the president, would that lead to a change in U.S. policy – or would it lead to Wise losing access to the White House? On the other hand, what was the value of such access if he could not influence the administration's position regarding German Jewry? How would the American public react to a Jewish outcry over a European matter at a time of isolationism and deepening economic depression at home – would it engender sympathy for Hitler's Jewish victims, or would it lead to increased antisemitism in the United States?

The subsequent radicalization of German policy, from anti-Jewish discrimination and occasional violence in the 1930s, to organized mass murder in the 1940s, confronted Wise and other Jewish leaders with an entirely new situation. Noah Golinkin and his friends, reading the newspaper report about Wise confirming that terrible news in November 1942, hoped to see a forceful response by American Jewish organizations. But as they would soon learn, much to their surprise and frustration, the leadership's response would become mired in an array of political and other considerations.

Different Strategies for Responding

American Jewish strategies for responding to the rise of Nazism reflected, in part, the cultural divide in the community between Jews of central European origin and those who traced their roots to eastern Europe.

The first major waves of Jewish immigrants to the United States, numbering about 250,000, came from Germany and elsewhere in central Europe in the mid and late 1800s. Wealthy German-born Jews established the first U.S. Jewish defense organization, the American Jewish Committee, in 1906. Its purpose was to serve as a respectable representative of the Jewish community in its dealings with the non-Jewish public and to ensure that communal power would not fall into the hands of more nationalistic elements whose behavior, they feared, might stimulate antisemitism. The AJCommittee's preferred method of political action was backstairs diplomacy, or *shtadlanut* – quiet intercession with political figures and modest requests that would not ruffle feathers. This approach was shared by another major Jewish organization, B'nai B'rith, a fraternal order which later also acted as an advocacy group.

The next waves of Jewish immigration came from Russia and its environs: between 1891 and 1914, approximately 1.5 million east European Jews came to the United States, fleeing pogroms and discrimination. They were less eager than their German brethren to shed Old World ways and generally slower to achieve economic success in the new world. They spoke Yiddish, embraced Jewish folkways, and supported Zionism. Less Americanized and typically found in the lower economic strata, they tended to be less concerned than German-born Jews about how they were viewed by non-Jews and more inclined to advocate publicly for Jewish causes. Resenting the elitist, self-appointed leadership of the AJCommittee, east European immigrants in 1918 organized the rival American Jewish Congress, which embraced Zionism, spoke out more aggressively than the AJCommittee for Jewish interests at home and abroad, and claimed to represent the sentiments of grassroots American Jews. Rabbi Wise, as the Congress's leader, came to be known as a Young Turk who symbolized the ethnically assertive attitude of American Jewry's new majority.

Having been raised in old world communities where religious observance was common, east European immigrants were more likely than their German predecessors to affiliate with Orthodox synagogues. Conservative Judaism, for its part, began to emerge in the United States in the late 1800s. Its rabbinical seminary, the Jewish Theological Seminary of America (JTS), was established in New York City in 1886, initially as a response by Americanized Orthodox rabbis and intellectuals to the radical tendencies of 19th century Reform Judaism. Over the next several decades, the Seminary gradually distinguished itself as the home of a separate denomination of Judaism. In 1913, the United Synagogue of America was established to serve as an umbrella for synagogues that opted to identify themselves with the Conservative movement. Measured in synagogue memberships, Orthodoxy was the largest of American Judaism's denominations until World War II, with Conservative Judaism second and Reform third.[7]

A fairly common set of sociological circumstances brought young men to JTS during the 1930s and 1940s. Typically their parents were east European immigrants whose level of religious observance had declined from the Orthodoxy of their home towns but to whom Reform Judaism seemed radical, almost Christian. As the products of semi-observant homes, where Jewish practices were warmly embraced if not always punctiliously fulfilled, these future Conservative rabbis gravitated towards the denomination that mirrored their own theological and ritual station in life.[8]

The families of Noah Golinkin's closest friends, Jerry Lipnick and Buddy Sachs, fit a similar profile. Lipnick's mother came from Russia in 1904, married an American-born Jewish businessman, and settled in Baltimore. They belonged to an Orthodox synagogue most of their lives, but were not Orthodox in their personal lives.

Sachs's father came to the U.S. from Lithuania at the turn of the century, married an American-born Jewish woman, and settled in Baltimore, where he became active in the local Zionist organization. Although he felt compelled by economic pressures to work on the Sabbath, he preferred to worship in an Orthodox synagogue.

Moshe "Buddy" Sachs in the 1940s.   Jerry Lipnick in the 1950s.

Eventually, however, the slight of not being called to the Torah because of his Sabbath violations convinced the elder Sachs to establish his own small synagogue, which followed Orthodox rituals but welcomed the religiously nonobservant. Buddy, whose interest in the rabbinate as a profession began at age ten, felt most comfortable in the movement whose ideology best reflected his own family's position midway between old world traditions and radical assimilation.

Golinkin trod a different path to the halls of the Seminary. His father, Rabbi Mordechai Ya'akov Golinkin, served as the unofficial chief rabbi of Zhitomir, rabbi in and around Vilna, and rabbi of the Free City of Danzig, on the Polish-German border, until the eve of the Nazi occupation, in 1939.[9] Noah reached the United States by himself in June 1938, having been admitted to Yeshiva College (later the undergraduate division of Yeshiva University); his student visa enabled him to enter the U.S. outside the regular quota restrictions.[10] He then worked energetically to obtain visas for his parents to come to the United States. They arrived in May 1939, less than four months before the outbreak of World War II, with the aid of a Newark (NJ) synagogue, which helped satisfy the visa application requirements by offering Rabbi Golinkin its pulpit. They subsequently relocated to Worcester, Massachusetts, where the elder Golinkin served as an Orthodox spiritual leader and kashrut supervisor. Noah then labored diligently to obtain visas for his sisters Rachel and Rivka, who ultimately reached Worcester on June 22, 1941, the day the Germans invaded Soviet Russia.

During this period, Noah began moving away from his Orthodox upbringing and chose to enroll in the JTS rabbinical program. At that time, a substantial minority of JTS rabbinical students came from Orthodox homes, sometimes simply because they were seeking a level of professional training not yet offered in Orthodox institutions. In subsequent decades, the theological and practical differences between Conservative Judaism and modern, or Americanized, Orthodox Judaism would become much more pronounced, but in the late 1930s and early 1940s there was still enough of a gray area between the two that many young men from Orthodox homes could attend the Seminary without fear of being ostracized by their families.[11]

Speaking Out vs. Keeping Quiet

When they read Rabbi Wise's confirmation of the mass killings, Golinkin, Lipnick, and Sachs hoped for a loud, public response from the organized Jewish leadership. Such an outcry would have been entirely consistent with the norms of American political culture, in which U.S. Jews generally have felt comfortable expressing their views publicly, even if they often have disagreed among themselves on tactics. As far back as the mid-nineteenth century, attempts were made, both through public protest rallies and behind-the-scenes lobbying, to bring about U.S. government intercession on behalf of Jews persecuted abroad, even when American interests were not clearly at stake. Jewish protesters secured U.S. intervention against a planned expulsion of two thousand Russian Jews from their homes in 1869 and against the mistreatment of Jews in Romania during the late 1800s and early 1900s. Jewish lobbying led to the U.S. abrogation of the Russo-American Commercial Treaty in response to the persecution of Russian Jews in the early 1900s.[12] These efforts accustomed the Jewish community to speaking out against persecution overseas and helped cement the concept of Jewish advocacy as a legitimate part of American political life. By the time of Hitler's rise to power in early 1933, the American Jewish community had the advantage of many decades of experience in the art of public advocacy.

For all its experience in the political arena, however, American Jewry was also saddled with deep divisions, both substantive and stylistic, among its leaders as to how to respond to overseas crises. Broadly speaking, the American Jewish Congress and other groups that were either Zionist or at least ethnically assertive favored publicly protesting against Nazi outrages. They believed that such protests might influence the Nazis to reconsider some of their more extreme policies. They were also optimistic that a significant portion of American public opinion could be persuaded to sympathize with Hitler's victims. The AJCongress and its allies felt confident that they could present Jewish concerns in the public arena in a way that would be considered acceptable in American political and cultural discourse. The Conservative and Orthodox movements generally adhered to this perspective and allied themselves with the political positions taken by the AJCongress and the Zionists. Most JTS students in the 1930s and 1940s likewise favored public Jewish advocacy and supported Zionism.

Yet a substantial segment of the Jewish leadership felt otherwise. The American Jewish Committee and the Reform movement opposed Zionism, fearing it would call into question American Jewry's loyalties. They – and, to a certain extent, B'nai B'rith as well – regarded a high Jewish profile as an invitation to antisemitism. In their view, downplaying Jewish distinctiveness was a virtue, emphasizing it a vice.

Such concerns about antisemitism were rooted in the reality that anti-Jewish prejudice reached record levels in the late 1930s. Polls found over half of the U.S. population perceived Jews as greedy and dishonest, and about one-third considered them overly aggressive. Surveys between 1938 and 1941 showed that between one-third and one-half of the public believed that Jews had "too much power in the United States." Approximately 15% of those surveyed in the late 1930s or early 1940s said they would support "a widespread campaign against the Jews in this country," and another 20-25% would have sympathized with such a movement; only about 30% indicated they would have actively opposed it.[13] These trends were even felt on Capitol Hill on occasion. A small but vocal number of congressmen exhibited fierce xenophobia, occasionally crossing over into outright antisemitism. An anti-Jewish outburst by Rep. John Rankin of Mississippi actually caused a Jewish congressman to suffer a fatal heart attack on the floor of the House of Representatives in 1941.[14]

These high levels of antisemitism were closely connected with the insecurities and fears brought on by a decade of economic depression. Anxieties resulting from years of widespread unemployment led many to search for explanations, to ask who was to blame. The underlying negative image of Jews, deeply ingrained in Western society over the centuries, offered an answer to many Americans. By 1940, more than one hundred antisemitic organizations were on the scene. The antisemitic Catholic priest Father Charles Coughlin published a weekly tabloid, *Social Justice*, that had more than 200,000 subscribers, and his Sunday radio broadcasts were heard regularly by 3.5 million listeners, along with an additional ten million who tuned in at least once each month.[15]

To Boycott or Not to Boycott

The differences between the AJCommittee's approach and that of the AJCongress were readily apparent in the weeks following Hitler's rise to power. The Congress quickly organized an anti-Hitler rally at Madison Square Garden; the Committee opposed public protests, fearing the non-Jewish public would be irritated by noisy Jewish demonstrations. The Congress supported boycotting German goods; the Committee opposed the boycott, fearing American Jews would be accused of dragging the U.S. into a conflict with Germany.

At the same time, however, Rabbi Wise was showing signs of preferring a more cautious approach. It was Samuel Untermeyer's ad hoc activist group, the American League for the Defense of Jewish Rights, not Wise's AJCongress, that initiated the boycott movement.[16] At Wise's insistence, the AJCongress declined to join the boycott movement during its first six months. He believed "the sanction of our government" should be obtained before proceeding.[17] Pressure from its membership compelled Wise and the AJCongress not only to endorse boycotting but to assume the leadership of the boycott movement, with its women's division taking on a particularly active role in such tasks as letter-writing and picketing businesses that carried German products.[18] Because of his reluctance to take positions contrary to the Roosevelt administration, Wise opposed a plan by Utah Senator William King in 1933 to introduce a resolution expressing sympathy with German Jewry. According to Wise, such a resolution would imply the administration was not sympathetic to the Jews under Hitler.[19] Although the AJCongress did sponsor several large "Stop Hitler Now" rallies in 1933, the speakers focused on condemning Hitler and avoided even implicitly criticizing U.S. policy towards Germany. In the years to follow, the AJCongress scaled back such mass protests, typically holding at most one such rally in New York City each year, with smaller events in some other cities, depending on the initiative of local activists.

Obstacles to Immigration

Although many German Jews hoped to escape Hitler by fleeing to the United States, immigration was severely restricted. America's traditional open-door immigration policy, which had permitted the unfettered entry of millions of newcomers, was reversed by the Johnson Immigration Act of 1921, which created a system of quotas based on national origins. Public and congressional support for immigration restriction was fueled by a number of factors. The 1917 Soviet revolution in Russia sparked anxiety about Communism and the danger that European radicals would import it to America. The changing face of American society as a result of the influx of European immigrants provoked fears of foreigners in general, especially Catholics and Jews. Prominent anthropologists contributed to the public's growing racism and paranoia by promoting theories that non-Caucasian races were corrupting Anglo-Saxon society. These sentiments, combined with racial tensions related to the post-World War I movement of many African-Americans from the south to northern urban areas, contributed to an upswell in support for the Ku Klux Klan, which at its peak, in the early 1920s, boasted a membership of more than four million.[20]

The immigration law passed in 1921 stipulated that the number of immigrants from any single country during a given year could not exceed 3% of the number of immigrants from that country who had been living in the U.S. at the time of the 1910 national census. A strong indication of the antisemitic sentiment that helped motivate the legislation was the fact that the original version of the bill was submitted to Congress with a report by the chief of the United States Consular Service characterizing would-be Jewish immigrants from

Poland as "filthy, un-American, and often dangerous in their habits... lacking any conception of patriotism or national spirit."[21]

In 1924, Congress tightened the immigration regulations even further. The percentage was reduced from 3% to 2% and, instead of the 1910 census, the quota numbers would be based on an earlier census, the one taken in 1890. This sharply reduced the number of Jews and (predominantly Catholic) Italians, since the bulk of Jewish and Italian immigrants in the U.S. had not arrived until after 1890. In 1930, the Hoover administration restricted immigration further by instructing American consuls abroad to scrupulously enforce the requirement that each prospective immigrant prove he or she was not "likely to become a public charge" after settling in the United States.[22]

Strong congressional support for restrictionism, backed by polls showing overwhelming public opposition to immigration, intimidated American Jewry. During the 1930s, no major Jewish organization called for liberalizing the quota system and few sought ways to increase Jewish refugee immigration even within the existing laws. A resolution introduced by Rep. Samuel Dickstein (D-NY) in early 1933 to loosen the visa requirements for "children and aged and infirm relatives of naturalized United States citizens" – from any country, not just Germany – was opposed by the AJCommittee because, as its spokesman, Max Kohler, complained to Dickstein, "You create a situation where it will be charged with force that American Jews want to sacrifice America's obvious and essential interests on behalf of their German Jewish co-religionists!" Kohler urged the congressman to "let your resolution die a natural, quiet death." He did.[23]

Not everyone in the mainstream Jewish leadership felt likewise. At the May 1933 convention of the (Conservative) United Synagogue of America, for example, chairman Hyman Reit urged the delegates to press Congress "to show some interest in saving humanity," and president Louis Moss called on American Jewry to appeal to Congress and the president "to open the doors of immigration to those in Germany who have endured oppression."[24] But the notion that Jews should lobby to open America's doors to refugees from Nazism was never embraced by the largest and most influential Jewish groups. Nor was it taken up even by the Conservative movement itself, despite the statements made by its leaders at the 1933 United Synagogue gathering. Instead, Reit and Moss were the first in what was to become a long line of lone voices for rescue, voices that more often than not would be ignored. Ten years later, the three JTS rabbinical students would face a similar uphill battle, although, as we shall see, with considerably more success.

Labor Secretary Frances Perkins, the only active pro-refugee voice within Roosevelt's cabinet in the early and mid 1930s, was willing, in 1933, to utilize a legal but little-known bond guarantee procedure that would have permitted more refugees to enter within the existing quotas, but Jewish organizations were reluctant to support the Perkins initiative, fearing the arrival of a large number of immigrants would stimulate antisemitism.[25] Jewish groups also feared that attempts to bring in more immigrants would provoke restrictionists to tighten the laws even further. Numerous such proposals were floated in Congress during the 1930s.

American Jewish attitudes toward the immigration issue were complicated by another factor: the very concept of mass immigration troubled some Jewish leaders, because of its implications for the status of Jews around the world. Rabbi Wise, for example, in a 1936 essay, warned against mass Jewish emigration from Poland on the grounds that it "might well become the 'locus classicus' for groups in all lands seeking to rid themselves of their Jewish populations... France, Czecho-Slovakia, or England might conceivably propose a conference on Jewish emigrants and refugees, without exciting suspicion with respect to their purpose."[26] During Wise's meeting with the Polish ambassador to the United States in April 1938, the ambassador repeatedly asserted Poland's interest in mass Jewish emigration, but Wise adamantly rejected the very concept.[27]

Palestine offered another potential haven for European Jewish refugees. The British had pledged, in 1917, to facilitate the establishment of a "Jewish national home" in Palestine. Shortly afterwards they conquered the region from the Turks, and in 1920 the League of Nations granted England a mandate to rule the Holy Land. Jewish immigration began in earnest and continued, more or less undisturbed, until 1936. A wave of Palestinian Arab rioting that year prompted the British to begin restricting Jewish immigration. American Jewish leaders, while troubled by the policy, declined to initiate a public campaign against England's Palestine restrictions. The AJCommittee warned that "notoriety and over-conspicuousness" by American Jews on the Palestine issue might provoke antisemitism in the United States. Rabbi Wise refused to take part in what he called "anti-British propaganda," arguing that everyone should "march shoulder to shoulder with England in the war against fascism, even if the Zionist cause suffered."[28]

The Palestine conflict in 1936 does, however, offer a lesson in the potential for exercising leverage on the Roosevelt administration. Shortly after the violence erupted, the British government was poised to suspend all Jewish immigration to Palestine. Rabbi Wise's private plea to FDR for American intervention was well-received by the president and his advisers, who thought a gesture regarding Palestine would help ensure Jewish support in the president's forthcoming reelection campaign. Seeing political gain and little risk, the administration decided to lean on London. The British, for their part, were anxious to keep Anglo-American relations in good order, and responded to Roosevelt's request by postponing the planned suspension until after the completion of a forthcoming Royal Commission study of the Palestine problem. During the lengthy delay until the study was finished, another 50,000 Jews reached Palestine.[29]

The German annexation of Austria in March 1938, with its attendant brutalization of Austria's Jews, cast a fresh international spotlight on Nazi barbarism. Accounts in the American press described the spiraling rate of suicide among Jews in Vienna and harrowing scenes of storm troopers forcing Austrian Jews to scrub the streets with toothbrushes. "Overnight," the *New York Times* reported, Vienna's Jews "were made free game for mobs, despoiled of their property, deprived of police protection, ejected from employment and barred from sources of relief."[30]

Facing mounting pressure from some members of Congress and journalists to aid the Jews, State Department officials, led by Secretary of State Cordell Hull, Undersecretary Sumner Welles, and Assistant Secretary George Messersmith, decided to "get out in front and attempt to guide" the criticism before it got out of hand. Welles proposed to Roosevelt the idea of holding an intergovernmental conference, in Evian, France, to discuss the refugee problem. FDR assented – but made it clear in his March 24 announcement of the gathering that "no nation would be expected or asked to receive a greater number of emigrants than is permitted by its existing legislation."[31]

Roosevelt's warning about immigration limits was actually something of a red herring, particularly in the case of the United States. This was because many German Jews could have found shelter in the U.S. even within the existing quota for Germany (25,957), had the quotas been administered in a reasonable fashion. In 1933, only 5.3% of the German quota places were filled; the corresponding figures for subsequent years were 13.7% (1934), 20.2% (1935), 24.3% (1936), and 42.1% (1937).[32] Out of a total of 129,785 German nationals who could have been admitted during those years, only 26,930 actually entered the United States. In other words, the German quota was 79% unfilled during the first five years of the Hitler regime.[33] Thus, nearly 103,000 German Jews could have been granted haven from Nazism without any liberalization of U.S. quota laws. They were kept out because the State Department directed consular officials abroad to use the strictest possible criteria in determining if a would-be immigrant was "likely to become a public charge" and therefore should be disqualified. Breckinridge Long, who in 1940 became Assistant Secretary of State in charge of immigration matters, characterized the department's approach in these blunt terms: "postpone and postpone and postpone the granting of the visas."[34]

Jewish leaders greeted the president's announcement of the Evian conference with lavish praise and high hopes. Rabbi Wise called it "a great act of faith and generosity."[35] Wise was also delighted to be invited to join the President's Advisory Committee on Political Refugees (PACPR), which FDR initiated in April 1938. Its ostensible purpose was to facilitate the implementation of the refugee

Assistant Secretary of State Breckinridge Long.

16

resettlement plans that would emerge from the international conference or other sources. In practice, however, Roosevelt paid the committee no mind and invariably sided with the State Department when it clashed with the committee. In one instance, Roosevelt assured Breckinridge Long that when PACPR chairman James McDonald complained to him about the State Department's refugee policies, Roosevelt had told him not to give him "any sob stuff."[36]

Wise considered attending the Evian conference, but in the end decided against it. The reasons for his absence foreshadowed some of the factors that would handicap his response to the European Jewish crisis in the years to follow. The first was the argument by his PACPR colleagues that the attendance of prominent Jewish leaders would call too much attention to the Jewish nature of the refugee problem. They believed that downplaying the Jewish identity of the refugees would make their entry to various countries more palatable. Their committee's very name reflected this approach.[37] The Roosevelt administration likewise sought to minimize the Jewishness of the victims, ultimately taking this attitude to such an extreme that a conference of Allied foreign ministers in Moscow in 1943, at the height of the Holocaust, would issue a statement decrying the Nazi persecution of various nationalities, but did not even mention the primary victim, the Jews.[38] Far from making Jewish refugees more acceptable, hiding their Jewishness undermined public awareness of their plight and undercut the pressures for rescue.

There were two other factors in Wise's decision to stay away from Evian, both of which would also affect his actions in the years to follow. One was his prior commitment to participate in a Zionist convention in Detroit the weekend of the Evian conference. Wise's wide-ranging interests and involvement in a long list of Jewish and secular organizations inevitably distracted him from focusing on rescue. The other factor was the problem of his deteriorating health. In June 1938, he began X-ray treatments for an enlarged spleen, one of several ailments that further slowed the 64 year-old Wise.[39]

In the weeks preceding Evian, American Jewish leaders helped the administration fend off advocates of increased immigration, especially Jewish members of Congress whom Secretary of State Hull worried were "going off halfcocked in the way of legislative proposals regarding immigration, quotas and the like."[40] In response to the German annexation of Austria, Representatives Emanuel Celler (D-NY) and Samuel Dickstein (D-NY) announced they would introduce legislation permitting the unrestricted entry of victims of persecution. The Celler bill was "so bad that it almost seems the work of an agent provocateur," Wise confided to a colleague. He and other Jewish leaders lobbied the congressmen to drop the legislation on the grounds that "it may interfere with the government's plans in connection with the international conference [at Evian]."[41] The congressmen relented. Meanwhile, AJCommittee officials learned, to their dismay, that Louis Gross, an activist-minded Reform rabbi who edited the weekly *Brooklyn Jewish Examiner,* was engaged in what they characterized as "agitation to increase the United States immigration quota so as to enable more refugees to come in... carrying on this agitation not only in his weekly publication but also by sending private letters to prominent personalities." An AJCommittee representative paid the rabbi a visit and convinced him to suspend his efforts.[42]

The Evian conference, which was held from July 6 to July 15, 1938, fell far short of Jewish leaders' hopes. One speaker after another reaffirmed their countries' unwillingness to accept more Jews. The Australian delegate announced that "as we have no real racial problem, we are not desirous of importing one." The British refused even to discuss Palestine as a possible haven. *Newsweek*, noting the appeal by the chairman of the U.S. delegation to the attendees "to act promptly" in addressing the refugee problem, noted: "Most governments represented acted promptly by slamming their doors against Jewish refugees."[43] Golda Meir (then Meyerson), attending Evian as an observer from Palestine, concluded that "nothing was accomplished at Evian except phraseology." At a press conference afterwards, she asserted, "There is only one thing I hope to see before I die, and that is that my people should not need expressions of sympathy any more."[44] Another critic pointed out that "Evian" was "Naive" spelled backwards. The problem, however, was not naiveté so much as it was calculated indifference.[45]

American Jewish leaders tried to put the best face on a bad situation. Rabbi Jonah Wise, who attended Evian on behalf of the American Jewish Joint Distribution Committee, found it "heartening" that the conference "did not deteriorate – as it might have – into a public discussion of the undesirability of Jews as immigrants or settlers." An AJCommittee publication reported, in a remarkable case of understatement, that "No nation seemed fully willing to open its doors." Rabbi Stephen Wise claimed that "American generosity and British caution" was the theme of the conference. In private, however, Wise told a colleague that Evian had turned out to be "a gesture which means little," from "an administration that pretends sympathy."[46]

Kristallnacht and its Aftermath

The persecution of Jews in Germany intensified suddenly and dramatically when the Nazis dispatched mobs of storm troopers to carry out the nationwide pogroms of November 9 and 10, 1938, known as Kristallnacht ("Night of the Glass" – a reference to the vast amount of plate glass shattered in attacks on Jewish property.) About 100 Jews were murdered and 30,000 more were sent to concentration camps. Nearly 200 synagogues were burned down, and more than 7,000 Jewish-owned businesses were destroyed. President Roosevelt strongly condemned the pogrom, recalled the U.S. ambassador from Germany for "consultations," and extended the visas of the 12,000-15,000 German Jewish refugees who were then in the United States as visitors. FDR made it clear that liberalization of America's immigration procedures was "not in contemplation." The administration did, however, permit the German and Austrian quotas to be filled in the months to follow, the only time during the entire Hitler period that all of the quota places were utilized. The respite was brief. By 1940 and throughout the rest of the war years, those quotas were again woefully underfilled.[47]

American Jewish organizations hesitated to challenge either the administration's policy or the prevailing public mood, which, according to the polls, continued to oppose large-scale immigration. Three days after Kristallnacht, representatives of the General Jewish Council, an umbrella group representing the four largest Jewish defense organizations, resolved "that there should be no parades, public demonstrations or protests by Jews" and that although "on humanitarian grounds, mass immigration of German Jews could not be opposed... at least for the time being, nothing should be done with regard to this matter."[48] When FDR queried his closest Jewish adviser, Samuel Rosenman – a prominent member of the American

Jewish Committee – as to whether he thought more Jewish refugees should be allowed to enter the U.S. in the wake of Kristallnacht, Rosenman opposed such a move because "it would create a Jewish problem in the U.S."[49]

In the wake of Kristallnacht, Senator Robert F. Wagner (D-NY) and Rep. Edith Rogers (R-MA) introduced legislation to admit 20,000 German refugee children outside the quota system. Supporters of the bill included prominent church figures, labor leaders, university presidents, 1936 Republican presidential nominee Alf Landon and his running mate, Frank Knox, and former First Lady Grace Coolidge, who announced that she and her friends in Northampton, Massachusetts would personally care for twenty-five of the children.

Nativist and isolationist groups vociferously opposed the Wagner-Rogers bill. Typical of their perspective was a remark by FDR's cousin, Laura Delano Houghteling, who was the wife of the U.S. commissioner of immigration: she warned that "20,000 charming children would all too soon grow into 20,000 ugly adults." FDR responded negatively to a private appeal to him by First Lady Eleanor Roosevelt for his support of the bill. He did tell Eleanor that he would not object if she endorsed it, but she did not do so. An inquiry by a congresswoman as to the president's position was returned to his secretary marked "File No action FDR." Mindful of polls showing most Americans opposed to more immigration, Roosevelt preferred to follow public opinion rather than lead it. Without his support, the Wagner-Rogers bill was buried in committee. Ironically, when *Pets Magazine* the following year launched a campaign to have Americans take in purebred British puppies so they would not be harmed by German bombing raids, the magazine received several thousand offers of haven for the dogs.[50]

A dramatic demonstration of the refugee crisis was provided in May 1939, when the German ship *St. Louis*, carrying 930 Jewish refugees with entry visas to Cuba, was turned away by the Cuban authorities. Hoping for haven in the United States, the "saddest ship afloat," as the *New York Times* called it, hovered off the coast of Florida, prevented by Coast Guard patrols from coming too close to the shore. A cable from the passengers to President Roosevelt pleaded, "Mr. President help the nine hundred passengers among them over four hundred women and children." But no asylum was offered by the Roosevelt administration. Eventually, a deal was brokered to send the passengers to a number of European countries which, tragically, lay in the path of the soon-to-be advancing German armies. Hitler's press scornfully highlighted the dramatic contrast between America's verbal criticism of German policy toward the Jews and its refusal to take in the refugees.[51]

American public opinion during the 1930s strongly opposed any significant U.S. action against Nazi Germany. A 1937 poll found 71% of Americans thought America was wrong to have entered World War I; many believed the U.S. had been tricked into the conflict by greedy weapons manufacturers. The hardships of the Great Depression further intensified the view that domestic concerns required America's full attention and that the country could not spare any resources for overseas matters. While most Americans found Hitler's totalitarian ways distasteful, only about one-tenth were willing to go to war for any reason other than to fend off an invasion of the United States itself.[52]

Many American Jews felt differently. They hoped the U.S. would take action against Hitler, not only because of the Nazis' persecution of the Jews, but because they realized Hitler was a threat to the entire free world. At the same time, they feared being perceived as warmongers. In numerous public statements, Jewish leaders tried to reassure the public of Jewish disinterest in military action against Nazi Germany. "No Jew on earth has asked any nation to take up arms against Hitler," Stephen Wise asserted in 1941.[53] Jewish concerns were exacerbated by the activities of extreme isolationists such as Charles Lindbergh, the widely admired aviator. In September 1941, he publicly accused "the Jews" of "pressing this country toward war" and complained about what he called "their large ownership and influence in our motion pictures, our press, our radio, and our government." Lindbergh also implicitly threatened American Jews, declaring, "Instead of agitating for war, the Jewish groups in this country should be opposing it in every possible way for they will be among the first to feel its consequences. Tolerance is a virtue that depends upon peace and strength. History shows that it cannot survive war and devastation."[54]

What They Knew and When They Knew It

In the wake of the September 1939 German invasion of Poland, information about the suffering of Polish Jews began reaching the American Jewish press. In addition to the expected news of Jewish communities hit by German bombardments or other war-related damage, there were soon reports of atrocities targeting Jewish civilians. One news report circulated by the Jewish Telegraphic Agency described how "Nazis entered the Polish town of Ostrovie near Warsaw, forced all the Jewish men to dig a large pit and then lined them up before the ditch and shot them down from behind with machine-guns so that their bodies fell into the newly-dug grave." A week later, the JTA reported that "400 Jews had been massacred in the Polish town of Lukov and several hundred in Kalushin."[55] In January 1940, the JTA described mass sexual assaults against Polish Jewish women by German soldiers and officers; in March, the New York Yiddish daily *Der Tog* reported the punishment of "such mutilation as removal of an eye" inflicted upon Jews who tried to escape into the Soviet-held part of Poland.[56]

Mobile execution squads, known as Einsatzgruppen, accompanied the German army as it invaded the Soviet Union in June 1941. In town after town, they took hundreds, sometimes thousands, of Jews into nearby forests or ravines, compelled them to dig mass graves, and then machine-gunned them into the pits. Ultimately between one million and two million Jews were murdered in this fashion. As early as July, there were sporadic reports in the U.S. Jewish press about massacres in Nazi-occupied western Russia. By the autumn, the reports were multiplying: on October 2, 1941, the JTA told of thousands of Jews being "simply mowed down by Nazi machine-guns"; on October 23, a JTA dispatch reported that 10,000 Jews had been slaughtered in the Kamenets-Podolski region. On November 16, the JTA described how "fifty-two thousand Jews, including men, women, and children, were systematically and methodically put to death in Kiev following the Nazi occupation of the Ukrainian capital" and that "similar measures, though on a small scale, have been taken in other conquered towns."[57]

A *New York Times* report on October 26, 1941, provided a detailed description of some of the summer's mass killings. "Reliable sources," quoting "letters reaching Hungary from Galicia" and "eyewitness accounts of Hungarian officers" returning from the front, described "massacres of thousands of Jews deported from Hungary to Galicia and the machine-gunning of more thousands of Galician Jews" in August. There were between 10,000 and 15,000 victims, some of whom were "machine-gunned as they prayed in their synagogues," according to the *Times*. "The deaths are reported to have been so numerous that bodies floated down the Dniester with little attempt made to retrieve and bury them."[58]

In the dormitory rooms at the Jewish Theological Seminary, Buddy Sachs read many such reports in the local Jewish press, but he assumed the killings were spontaneous outbursts accompanying the tragedy of war, rather than part of a systematic plan of annihilation. Part of the reason Sachs did not regard the reports as severely as he might have was that he was also an avid reader of *Hashomer Hatzair*, the monthly journal of the Marxist-Zionist youth movement of the same name. In February 1941, the journal published an extensive account of Zionist youth activities in Nazi-occupied Poland, which emphasized the persistence of Zionist culture despite the hardships of German rule. Later that year, Hashomer Hatzair published a small book, *Youth Amidst the Ruins*, which featured first-person accounts from Eastern Europe that stressed the same themes. Based on such reports, Sachs believed "that things were not as bad as we feared – that there were still all kinds of cultural opportunities, even under the Nazis."[59]

The intention of the editors of *Hashomer Hatzair* was not to downplay Nazi savagery, but to inspire their followers with stories of their comrades' bravery and to guard against suspicions that a central part of their movement was being wiped out. One may detect a somewhat similar motivation in the decision in 1941 by Dr. Solomon Grayzel, editor-in-chief of the community-funded Jewish Publication Society of America (JPSA), to turn down two book-length manuscripts, one describing the Nazi concentration camps at Dachau and Buchenwald, the other concerning the persecution of Jews in Vienna, because he feared reports about the atrocities in Europe were "terrorizing" American Jewry and "eroding the community's self-confidence."[60] While the editors at *Hashomer Hatzair* and the JPSA were well-intentioned, the effect of their actions was to help dull the American Jewish community's response to the plight of Europe's Jews.

In the case of Buddy Sachs, however, another important source of information soon overcame any doubts he may have harbored concerning what was happening under Hitler's heel. In the summer of 1942, Sachs found himself sharing a dormitory room with Rabbi Max Gruenewald, one of a number of German refugee rabbis housed at JTS during the war. Gruenewald, formerly president of the Jewish community of Mannheim and a member of German Jewry's major national organization, the *Reichsvertretung der deutschen Juden*, worked for the World Jewish Congress on refugee matters. Each evening, he returned to the JTS dormitory and relayed the latest ghastly news of Jewish suffering in Europe. Sachs was "stunned" to learn of the extent and severity of Nazi atrocities against the Jews.[61]

Throughout 1942, increasingly shocking reports continued to reach the Western press. In March, a European representative of the American Jewish Joint Distribution Committee reported that in the Russian city of Borisov, "the Nazis had ordered Jews to dig a communal grave, into which 7,000 men, women and children – some shot to death, others only wounded – were thrown and covered with earth," and because of the "the living breath of those interred," the field was "heaving like the sea." In May, the JTA disclosed how "in Vitebsky, the Germans rounded up several thousand men, women and children and loaded them into leaking boats which were towed to the middle of the Dwina River... When the boats reached midstream, the Nazi soldiers turned a murderous stream of bullets upon the Jews, killing thousands of the prisoners and leaving hundreds of others to drown when their leaking craft sank."[62]

In June 1942, members of the Jewish Socialist Bund in London released a report from their Polish comrades asserting that the Germans had "embarked on the physical extermination of the Jewish population on Polish soil," and had already murdered an estimated 700,000 Polish Jews. The Bund provided the names of many towns where the Einsatzgruppen had carried out mass killings, as well as the dates of the slaughter and estimates of the casualty tolls. The report also contained the first information about the use of poison gas to kill the Jews, describing the mobile death vans that were employed by the Nazis in the Chelmno camp in late 1941 and early 1942, before the gas chamber technique was perfected.[63]

In August 1942, a telegram to Rabbi Wise from the World Jewish Congress representative in Switzerland, Gerhart Riegner, reported

that "in Fuhrer's headquarters plan discussed and under consideration according to which all Jews in countries occupied or controlled
Germany numbering 3½–4 millions should after deportation and
concentration in East be exterminated at one blow... the action
reported planned for autumn methods under discussion including
prussic acid..." Riegner added that his informant's reports had been
"generally speaking reliable." In this case, the informant, German
industrialist Eduard Schulte, had again proven reliable, except of
course that the plan he thought was under consideration had already
been adopted and was well underway.[64]

As per wartime routine, the Riegner cable was first routed
through the State Department, where officials considered it
unbelievable and declined to pass it along to Wise, fearing he would
use it to press for U.S. action to aid the Jews. But Riegner also had
addressed a copy to British MP Sidney Silverman, who in turn
forwarded it directly to Wise. Wise immediately contacted Under-
Secretary of State Welles, who "tried to be re-assuring," claiming that
"the real purpose of the Nazi government" in rounding up and
deporting Jews "is to use Jews in connection with war work both in
Nazi Germany and in Nazi Poland and Russia," even though that
theory did not square with the numerous reports the State
Department had received about large-scale massacres by the
Germans of Jews who could have been used for slave labor instead.
Welles asked him to withhold public comment on the Riegner
telegram until its veracity could be investigated. Wise complied,
aware that by doing so, he was, as he wrote, "accepting a great
responsibility if the threat [of mass murder] should be executed."[65]

Long weeks passed as Wise anxiously waited to hear from
Welles. The weeks became months. "I haven't been able to sleep
since [receiving the Riegner] cable telling me that the plan is to kill all
the Jews in Hitler Germany," he wrote to a friend in September.[66]
Soon there was more such news, including a telegram from rescue
activists in Berne that the Germans had recently murdered 100,000
Jews in Warsaw and used the corpses in the manufacture of soap and
fertilizer. Wise agonized over the atrocities and his own sense of
helplessness. "I don't know whether I am getting to be a [*H*]*ofjude*
[court Jew]," he wrote to a colleague, "but I find that a good part of
my work is to explain to my fellow Jews why our Government
cannot do all the things asked or expected of it."[67] There was
something of a paradox in Wise's thought process: he wondered in

25

his private correspondence why Pope Pius XII had failed to "use the mighty ban of his Church [against the Nazis]" and he referred to Pius as "a politician first and a churchman second." Yet when it came to Roosevelt's failures, Wise found excuses. "Roosevelt cannot intervene, because Hitler will rightfully do nothing for him," he wrote to one friend in September. When the telegram about the 100,000 victims in Warsaw arrived, Wise consulted with colleagues over whether to ask Treasury Secretary Morgenthau "to put it before the Chief, just that he might know about it, even though, alas, he prove to be unable to avert the horror." Wise's loyalty to FDR was so unshakable that he seemed to automatically accept whatever position the Roosevelt administration took – in this case, the position that rescue was impossible until military victory was achieved – instead of subjecting it to the kind of critical questioning that he applied to other issues of the day. Asking Roosevelt to pressure Nazi satellite regimes for the release of Jewish refugees or to urge the British to open Palestine, or to take any other step specifically to aid Europe's Jews, meant breaking with a mindset that, by the autumn of 1942, had become deeply ingrained in American Jewry's foremost leader.

Wise's correspondence does contain an occasional wistful remark about U.S. apathy toward European Jewry. "If only those food boats [bringing provisions to Greece] might be permitted to bring refugees back. I wonder!," he wrote on one occasion. On another, having been told that FDR sent him regards, Wise wrote to his son, "If only he would do something for my people!" Yet such sentiments seldom rose to the level of practical action on Wise's part to change the policies he privately bemoaned. Throughout September, October, and most of November 1942, Wise "kept the thing out of the press," as he put it – not only keeping the Riegner telegram secret, as Welles requested, but going further and withholding other information he received about mass killings, such as the cable about Warsaw, even though arguably he might have publicized that particular news without violating his pledge to Welles about the Riegner cable.[68]

Finally, in late November, Welles confirmed the accuracy of Riegner's report. Wise then made it public, together with other reports he had received about the mass killings, at a November 24 press conference in Washington. That was the press conference that Noah Golinkin read about in the *New York Times* as he walked back to the JTS campus that fateful morning.

Chapter 2

RETRIBUTION IS NOT ENOUGH

Noah Golinkin showed his friends Buddy Sachs and Jerome Lipnick the day's newspapers. They compared the latest revelations with earlier reports of Nazi massacres, and discussed the information with other students as well as Rabbi Gruenewald. They pondered the wisdom and feasibility of a handful of rabbinical students organizing another committee or organization amidst the welter of Jewish political and religious groups already in existence. For all their doubts and organizational inexperience, however, the trio were driven by an overwhelming sense that the response of the American Jewish community to the catastrophe in Europe lacked urgency and direction.

Golinkin was the eldest of the three and their unofficial leader. When he began his studies at JTS in the autumn of 1942, he was 28, having already completed a degree in Polish law at Stefan Batory University in Vilna and a Master's in American history at Clark University in Massachusetts. On a personal level, Golinkin was the most closely connected of the students to the situation in Europe, having reached the United States in 1938 and still bearing traces of

Noah Golinkin in the 1940s.   Moshe "Buddy" Sachs in the 1940s.

Jerry Lipnick (left), and Moshe Goldblum, in Utica, NY, in the 1950s.

his native Polish-Yiddish accent. He was the one who constantly prodded and galvanized his friends to action. Lipnick and Sachs entered the Seminary a year earlier. Lipnick, 23, had already earned degrees at Baltimore City College and Johns Hopkins University, as well as a certificate from the teacher's training institute of Baltimore Hebrew College. Sachs, 21, studied at Baltimore Hebrew College and the University of Maryland, where he earned his Bachelor's, prior to beginning his rabbinical studies. The tall and lanky Lipnick, a popular figure on the JTS campus, was especially articulate and naturally stepped into the role as the trio's spokesman to the Jewish community and beyond. "Jerry had the gift of gab," Golinkin later said. "And unlike me, he didn't have an accent."[69]

The activist group that took shape in those urgent discussions in the JTS dormitory in late 1942 was not exactly a sophisticated political operation. The name they chose for themselves, "European Committee of the Student Body of the Jewish Theological Seminary," was unwieldy and vague; they were not trained in the language of public relations or snappy acronyms. The group's budget consisted of whatever spare change the students happened to have at any given time; they did not register as an official campus organization and received no funding from the JTS administration. Their "staff" consisted of one volunteer, Lipnick's roommate Moshe Goldblum, who offered to serve as their typist since he was one of the few students who owned a typewriter.[70] A handful of other students helped out from time to time. Strategy sessions took place wherever the students found spare time: in the JTS cafeteria during lunch, in the hallways between classes, late at night in their dormitory rooms. It was, in short, classic ad hoc campus activism: long on idealism, creativity, and dedication, short on funds and office equipment. "I had never before seen the dedication that I experienced then," classmate Wilfred Shuchat later wrote. "[It was] a dedication made all the more awe-inspiring by the skepticism and cynicism of all of their colleagues who did not give them the support that they deserved."[71]

The committee's initial agenda was quite modest and required few material resources. During the last week of November and first weeks of December, they inserted a special passage in the morning prayer service at JTS asking for Divine intercession on behalf of Europe's Jews, and recited extra chapters of Psalms in the campus Sabbath services. They buttonholed students between classes, in the library, and in the cafeteria, to acquaint them with the latest news from Europe. Many JTS students later credited the European Committee for opening their eyes to what was happening to the Jews under Hitler. When the major Jewish organizations proclaimed a community-wide day of fasting for Hitler's Jewish victims on December 2, the European Committee members pressed fellow-students to participate and donate their meal money to the Joint Distribution Committee for overseas relief. They also organized a memorial service at the Seminary for Jewish victims of the Nazis, which students and faculty attended. A minor controversy arose over Golinkin's inclusion in the public readings at the service of Ḥayyim Naḥman Bialik's famous poem about the 1903 Kishinev pogrom, "In the City of Slaughter." After the service concluded, Saul Lieberman, professor of Talmud at JTS, privately reproached Golinkin for using the Bialik poem, because of what he considered its negative attitude toward traditional Judaism.[72]

The Jewish Leadership's Restrained Response

The JTS students expected the confirmation of the mass killings to be met with a national Jewish outpouring of protest, and at first a

29

vigorous reaction did seem to be in the offing. A coalition of American Jewish leaders declared the slaughter of Europe's Jews "the greatest calamity in Jewish history since the destruction of the Temple" and proclaimed December 2, 1942 a day of prayer and fasting. Mourning services and memorial rallies were held in Jewish communities throughout the U.S. and abroad. In New York City, some radio stations observed several minutes of silence, and forty-six councils of the CIO and AFL labor unions, representing 400,000-500,000 workers, agreed to stage a ten-minute work stoppage.[73]

The fast day provoked some rumblings of dissent from those who regarded it as insufficient. A columnist for the Yiddish daily *Der Tog* asked, "We have fasted, that is some of us did, but is that all we can do for the Jews in Hitler-land as they walk in the valley of shadows?"[74] An editorial in the monthly *The Reconstructionist*, titled "Fasting Is Not Enough," questioned "the desirability of fasting and prayer when unaccompanied by any suggestion of an outlet in action for the emotions evoked." It chided Jewish leaders for failing to prepare a "program of action" along with the mourning rites. Reconstructionism was a recent breakaway from Conservative Judaism and its journal, which addressed a range of Jewish communal concerns, was read widely at JTS. Noah Golinkin, for one, took particular note of the "Fasting Is Not Enough" editorial, which mirrored his own budding concerns about the community's response to the Holocaust.[75]

In the meantime, Rabbi Wise asked President Roosevelt to meet a small delegation of Jewish leaders to discuss the mass killings. "I have had cables and underground advices [*sic*] for some months telling of these things," Wise wrote to FDR. "I succeeded, together with the heads of other Jewish organizations, in keeping these out of the press." But now that the State Department had confirmed the news, Jewish leaders wanted to "present to you a memorandum on this situation" and "hope above all that you will speak a word which may bring solace" to American Jewry.[76] The president agreed to see them on December 8, 1942.

The delegation consisted of Wise; Rabbi Israel Rosenberg, president of the Union of Orthodox Rabbis; Henry Monsky, president of B'nai B'rith; and Adolph Held, president of the socialist Jewish Labor Committee. After the meeting, Wise told reporters that the president was "profoundly shocked" by the Nazis' mass murder of European Jewry. According to Wise, Roosevelt said "the American people will hold the perpetrators of these crimes to strict accountability," and the president promised that the Allies "are prepared to take every possible step" to "save those who may still be saved." In a note to presidential adviser David Niles the next day, Wise exulted: "We ought to distribute cards throughout the country bearing just four letters, TGFR (Thank God For Roosevelt), and as the Psalmist would have said, thank Him every day and every hour."[77]

Adolph Held's account, however, offered a very different perspective. Held privately reported to his Jewish Labor Committee colleagues that FDR began the meeting by joking about his choice of Governor Herbert Lehman, a Jew, to head the postwar administration in Germany. Wise then spoke briefly about the Nazi atrocities. Roosevelt replied that he was "very well acquainted" with the massacres but it would be "very difficult" to stop them since Hitler was "an insane man." The president cautioned them against "mak[ing] it appear that the entire German people are murderers or are in agreement with what Hitler is doing," since, he confidently but errantly predicted, "There must be in Germany elements, now thoroughly subdued, but who at the proper time will, I am sure, rise, and protest against the atrocities, against the whole Hitler system." FDR asked the Jewish representatives for their suggestions. Four of them spoke, but Roosevelt "made no direct replies to the suggestions." Nothing in Held's private account corroborates Wise's public claim that FDR promised to take steps to "save those who may still be saved." The portion of the conversation in which the other Jewish leaders spoke "lasted only a minute or two," Held wrote. "The President then plunged into a discussion of other matters." Of the 29 minutes the delegation spent with the President, "he addressed the delegation for 23 minutes." As soon as FDR finished speaking, he "pushed some secret button, and his adjutant appeared in the room" to usher the Jewish leaders out. Held did not make his account public. The American Jewish community never learned that Roosevelt spent 23 of the 29 minutes telling jokes and commenting on subjects other than Europe's Jews.[78]

Other accounts of meetings with Roosevelt on refugee matters during the 1940s indicate that this tenor was the rule rather than the exception. In October 1940, James McDonald, chairman of the President's Advisory Committee on Political Refugees, together with

31

several colleagues met with FDR to plead for more visas. Henry M. Hart Jr., assistant to the Solicitor General, who was present, later recalled how "a very cordial Roosevelt spun a succession of stories. Whenever McDonald tried to confront the President with the refugee issue, Roosevelt would be reminded of something else and another anecdote would result. This entertainment continued until the half hour was up and 'Pa' Watson came in to mention that the next appointment was due. Then followed a few rushed minutes of trying to present the problem before the group left."[79]

Nahum Goldmann, co-chairman of the World Jewish Congress and Washington, D.C. representative of the Jewish Agency, gave a similar account when he briefed David Ben-Gurion and other Agency leaders in Jerusalem in 1944. Reporting on American Jewry's relationship with the president, Goldmann expressed frustration that "It takes six months just to get an appointment with the president. He spends the first ten minutes telling you anecdotes, and then he expects you to entertain him with anecdotes, and all that leaves is ten minutes to discuss serious issues. It is impossible to have serious political impact under these conditions."[80]

A Fateful Meeting

The JTS student activists, reading Rabbi Wise's description of the December 8, 1942 meeting in the Jewish press, were troubled by what seemed to be an emphasis on postwar retribution, with no specifics regarding immediate rescue action. They called Rabbi Wise's office to ask if he would meet with a delegation of Conservative, Orthodox, and Reform rabbinical students to discuss the situation in Europe. Wise agreed to meet them on December 17.

The idea behind having Orthodox student representatives, from Yeshiva College, and students from Wise's own Jewish Institute of Religion,[81] along with the JTS men, was to demonstrate to Wise that there existed a broad consensus among Jewish students, all across the religious spectrum, that American Jews needed to respond vigorously to the news from Europe. One of the JIR student representatives was Herbert Weiner;[82] one of the Yeshiva College students was apparently Irwin Gordon,[83] a YC

Irwin Gordon

senior and vice-president of the student body;[84] the names of the second JIR and YC delegates are not known. Golinkin and Lipnick represented the JTS student committee. Lipnick did most of the speaking.[85]

The meeting began with a brief discussion of the plight of Jews in Hitler's Europe. Rabbi Wise repeated the main points of the information he had presented at the November 24 press conference. In reply to the students' inquiries as to ways in which the organized Jewish community might respond to the European situation, Wise pointed to the December 2 day of fasting, the meeting at the White House on December 8, and unspecified steps which, he said, he and other Jewish leaders were taking behind the scenes but could not yet reveal.

Points of tension soon flared. Wise bristled when Lipnick spoke of the need to "evacuate" the Jews from Poland. "We don't evacuate human beings, we evacuate cattle," Wise interjected. This is Jabotinsky talk!" He was referring to Vladimir Ze'ev Jabotinsky (1880-1940), founder of the militant Revisionist Zionist movement, who had stirred controversy in the Jewish world in the 1930s with his calls for emergency "evacuation" of the European Jewish masses to Palestine, to escape what he predicted would be a tidal wave of antisemitism. Wise, in common with most mainstream Zionist leaders, favored a more gradual approach to the settlement of Palestine, with priority given to young immigrants trained in agriculture. Wise's strong attachment to the principle of equal rights for Jews in the Diaspora further militated against his acceptance of the concept of speedy mass emigration from Europe to Palestine. The rabbinical students had no connection to Jabotinsky's movement, but their unwitting choice of a term that Wise and others associated with Jabotinsky inadvertently provoked the Jewish leader's ire.

Rabbi Wise also took strong exception to their suggestion of the Virgin Islands and Alaska as possible havens for Jewish refugees. Wise cut Lipnick short, insisting that the Virgin Islands were "too hot" for Jewish settlers and Alaska was "too cold." [86] In fact, as we shall see, there was much more to Wise's opposition to those potential havens than the weather.

The Search for Havens

The rabbinical students were aware in general that the Virgin Islands and Alaska had been mentioned in the Jewish press as possible sites of refuge, but they did not realize that by the time they raised the subject with Wise, in December 1942, both possible havens had been long since buried by the Roosevelt administration. The Virgin Islands attracted interest from refugee advocates because as a territory rather than a state, its immigration policy was not restricted by America's quotas. In 1938, shortly after Kristallnacht, the Legislative Assembly of the Virgin Islands adopted a resolution welcoming European Jewish refugees. But State Department officials persuaded the president that "all kinds of undesirables and spies" would enter the Islands disguised as refugees, and from there proceed to the United States. "I have sympathy," FDR told Interior Secretary Harold Ickes, a prominent supporter of the Virgin Islands as a haven. "I cannot, however, do anything which would conceivably hurt the future of present American citizens."[87] Rabbi Wise declined to support the Virgin Islands proposal. He told a colleague in the

Secretary of the Interior
Harold L. Ickes with
President Roosevelt, in 1937.

autumn of 1940, shortly before the presidential election, that admitting refugees to the Virgin Islands "might be used effectively against [Roosevelt] in the campaign." Therefore, Wise said, "Cruel as I may seem, as I have said to you before, his re-election is much more important for everything that is worthwhile and that counts than the admission of a few people, however imminent be their peril."[88] Other Jewish leaders likewise steered clear of the issue.

Alaska attracted attention as a possible site of refuge because its settlement and development would coincide closely with America's strategic needs. Aggressive Japan was only 600 miles from the Alaskan shore. Just sixty-five miles away lay the Soviet Union, fresh from its occupation of eastern Poland and the Baltic countries, and not yet an ally of the U.S. against Nazi Germany. An enemy army in Alaska would be within easy bombing range of America's pacific coast. A large labor force made up of European refugees could serve as a bulwark against such an eventuality, by populating and developing the dangerously empty region. The Interior Department and the Labor Department endorsed a 1940 bill proposed by Sen. William King (D-Utah) and Rep. Franck Havenner (D-CA) to promote Alaskan development, in part with refugee workers.[89] Roosevelt told Interior Secretary Ickes he would support only a watered-down version of the plan, in which just 10% of the workers would be Jews, so as "to avoid the undoubted criticism that we would be subjected to if there were an undue proportion of Jews." The State Department and nativist groups strongly opposed allowing any use of Alaska for refugee resettlement, and Roosevelt soon dropped the whole idea.[90]

Mainstream Jewish leaders such as Rabbi Wise did not support the Alaska proposal. "[J]ust because small numbers of Jews might settle there" was not sufficient reason to endorse the scheme, Wise wrote to a colleague. Talk of settling refugees in Alaska "makes a wrong and hurtful impression to have it appear that Jews are taking over some part of the country for settlement."[91] Wise's dismissive response to the mention of Alaska and the Virgin Islands by the rabbinical students' delegation in December 1942 indicated that his thinking regarding the two sites had not changed, despite the dramatic intensification of the persecution of Europe's Jews. Moreover, his assertion to the students that Alaska and the Virgin Islands were impractical as refugee havens because of their climate masked the fact that his own perspective on Alaska and the Virgin Islands was not based merely (if at all) on the weather, but also on his fear that bringing large numbers of Jewish refugees to U.S. territories would provoke antisemitism. The only Jewish organization to endorse the Alaska plan was the tiny Poalei Zion (Labor Zionists of America). Although as a matter of principle the Labor Zionists regarded Palestine as the appropriate destination for European Jewish refugees, they endorsed the Alaska scheme as a matter of life and death which therefore superseded their ideological preferences.[92]

Mobilizing Students Against the Holocaust

The major part of the proposal that the student delegation made to Rabbi Wise – both verbally and in a one-page memo that they handed him[93] – was the building of a broad college campus-based protest movement. They presented a five-part plan to reach out, as college students and clergy-in-training, to fellow-seminarians, fellow-students in general, college faculty, and alumni, and mobilize them to raise public awareness of the Nazi killings and press for U.S. rescue action. They proposed to begin within the world of religious seminaries and "acquaint non-Jewish seminaries with the facts in order to get a joint proclamation of protest and specific demands." They would then "acquaint faculties and student bodies of universities and colleges with the situation in order to get public action." They would also "activate alumni of our institutions to organize Jewish and interfaith meetings for protest and petition to higher churchmen, public officials, Congressmen, etc." Finally, they would "form an emergency general Jewish youth council to consider youth action."[94]

It was a novel idea, ambitious in scope and entirely unprecedented in American Jewish life. It would, for the first time, give Jewish college students a significant role in the shaping of Jewish communal opinion and policy. Perhaps Golinkin and Lipnick thought the proposal might appeal to Wise's own past as a young rebel in the Jewish world. After all, it was Wise who in 1905 had turned down the prestigious pulpit of New York City's Temple Emanul-El because of curbs on the rabbi's sermons, and established the Free Synagogue in order to ensure his freedom to address controversial subjects. It was Wise who, in 1918, established the American Jewish Congress as a challenge to the American Jewish Committee's undemocratic hegemony in organized Jewish life. It was Wise who led a lifelong battle for Zionism within the predominantly anti-Zionist world of Reform Judaism.

By 1942, however, Wise the rebel and dynamo was a figure from the distant past. Two anecdotes involving Wise and Polish Jewry illustrate the change. In his autobiography, Wise described a visit to Warsaw in 1936, when he was widely perceived in the Jewish world as an outspoken activist. "[M]illing thousands were gathered at the railroad station, shouting my name," he wrote. After insisting that "I could not bring myself to put in this record [the] generously meant and exuberantly uttered praises" of his admirers, he proceeded to recount in some detail how he was able to get through the crowds "only with the help of a committee made up of some of the most distinguished leaders of the country." Not only that, but "I could not walk through the Neleveski [central plaza] without being surrounded by friendly, sometimes cheering, throngs."[95] By 1942, however, many Polish Jews saw Wise very differently. In June of that year, Chaim Kaplan, one of the underground chroniclers of the destruction of Warsaw Jewry, wrote in his diary – found twenty years later in a kerosene can buried below the ghetto's rubble – about Rabbi Wise: "A joke is making the rounds: Rabbi Stephen S. Wise is helping. he has ordered the American Jews to say the memorial prayer for the departed souls of Polish Jewry. His foresight is accurate."[96]

The Stephen Wise whom the rabbinical students met in 1942 had become the epitome of an entrenched Jewish organizational leader. Wise now wielded significant control over organized Jewish life, playing a central role in more than a dozen Jewish groups, institutions, and publications. He had cultivated political relationships, from the White House on down, that he was loathe to risk by taking controversial stands. It did not help that he was nearly 69 years old and afflicted by a variety of ailments which were eroding his stamina and hampering his ability to travel. Wise's response to the students' proposal reflected his station in Jewish life. "Wise told us that as a veteran Jewish leader, he knew best what methods of protest should be organized," Golinkin later recalled. "He told us to trust his judgment and be patient." The students who had arrived at Wise's office brimming with passion and angry energy left with their spirits deflated. There was no plan, no agenda, no strategy for protest action.

Certainly organizing a broad student protest movement would not have been an easy task for Golinkin, Lipnick, and Sachs. Even on the campuses of Jewish institutions of higher learning, the persecution of European Jewry was far from the dominant topic of daily conversation, although certainly there were pockets of potential activism. At JTS, only a handful of students actively assisted the European Committee. A similar situation existed at Yeshiva College. An editorial in the student newspaper, *The Commentator*, in early 1943 criticized YC students for their "frightful indifference to the unparalleled plight of their people." It continued: "The Jewish world is crumbling about their eyes and ears, yet their minds and hearts do not seem to be affected... Have the halls of the building resounded to excited discussions of the Jewish tragedy and of ways and means of alleviating it? No!"[97] As for the Jewish Institute of Religion, it is unlikely that students would have engaged in activity that did not have the sanction of Rabbi Wise, its president. Indeed, in late 1943, the JIR Student Organization refused to participate in a petition urging creaton of a U.S. government agency to rescue refugees, because the petition was sponsored by the Bergson Group, a maverick political action committee with which Rabbi Wise was at odds.

Saadia Gelb

On the other hand, in addition to the aforementioned Herbert Weiner, there were a few students at JIR who occasionally made remarks in class urging a more activist response by American Jewry to the killings in Europe. Another JIR student, Saadia Gelb, wrote essays for the Labor Zionist youth magazine *Furrows* strongly criticizing both the Roosevelt administration and the American Jewish leadership.[98]

There were even more formidable obstacles to the possibility of mobilizing college students in general against the Holocaust. By the 1940s, little of the previous decade's spirit of protest remained on America's campuses. Back in the mid and late 1930s, left-wing activists, many backed by the Communist Party or various socialist factions, succeeded in rallying large numbers of college students to the cause of keeping America out of European conflicts.[99] As many as 500,000 students are estimated to have participated in the movement's annual one-hour antiwar strike. That spirit did not endure for very long, however. In the wake of the Nazi-Soviet nonaggression pact of 1939, and the U.S. Communist Party's about-face regarding Germany, disillusioned students left the antiwar movement in droves. The pacifist Fellowship of Reconciliation initiated a non-Communist alternative for college students, the Youth Committee Against War, but once the U.S. entered the war in 1941, the patriotic mood that swept the nation made it impossible for the committee to attract a substantial following. Moreover, student ranks were severely depleted by the draft. It would have been difficult indeed to find the passion or manpower on campuses to establish a protest movement focusing on the plight of Europe's Jews, an issue with which few students closely identified.[100]

Recruiting Jewish students on college campuses would have presented its own set of difficulties. Their ranks, too, were thinned by the draft. In addition, among Jewish students, as among the general student population, there was the problem of apathy. A Jewish activist at the City College of New York in the spring of 1943 reported that the wide range of Zionists attracted to the campus Hillel was "a perfect example of miniature unity – miniature because of the limited numbers."[100a]

Some of the most idealistic Jewish college students were drawn to groups that were not necessarily inclined to take a strong interest in the plight of Europe's Jews. At City College, for example, the Marxist-oriented Jewish college students who clustered around such publications as *Partisan Review* and *Labor Action* regarded the Allies' fight against the Nazis as an "imperialist war" that they could not support. The issue of rescuing Jewish refugees, which they would have regarded as a narrow Jewish concern not suited to their universalist interests, was not on their radar screen.[101]

Even Zionist college students were not automatically prime candidates for a rescue advocacy campaign. The leftwing Hashomer Hatzair movement (which claimed 3,000 members in North America on the eve of the war, although only a portion were college age) was heavily focused on Zionist ideological questions and agricultural training in preparation for immigrating to Palestine. Moreover, the Hashomer Hatzair activists were only a few steps removed from their Marxist classmates in their foreign policy orientation. Thus, even after the U.S. entered the war, one faction of the group continued to regard the war against Hitler as a clash between two camps of unsavory capitalists.[102]

The largest Zionist college campus movement was Avuka, which in its heyday, on the eve of World War II, boasted fifty-five chapters on North American campuses. Officially, Avuka was the student wing of the Zionist Organization of America, although the youngsters' radical-left agenda led to repeated clashes with their adult sponsors. It would not have been easy to convince Avuka activists to set aside other issues in order to focus on the rescue of European Jewry. The aforementioned City College correspondent, for one, complained that Avuka members on campus had remained aloof from Hillel because they were "busy with the solution of the Indian problem." Like other pacifist and Marxist-leaning groups, Avuka denounced England's fight against Nazi Germany as "an imperialist war" that the U.S. should avoid. When America entered the war, some Avuka members declared themselves conscientious objectors rather than fight against Hitler.[103]

Students from several other Zionist groups, however, would likely have taken an interest. Throughout 1942-1944, *Furrows*, the monthly magazine of the Labor Zionist youth movement Habonim, published a steady stream of editorials and articles criticizing the "appalling silence" of the U.S. government in response to the mass murder, and bemoaning the "black record of inactivity of the American Jewish community." The young Labor Zionists accused the established Jewish leadership of, among other things, "lack of imagination," "vacciliations and temporizing," and "wrangling and jockeying for position," and charged that they "bear a heavy guilt for their failure to do enough to stir the conscience of American citizenry..." *Furrows* urged American Jews to undertake "mass expression and political activity," to "shout loud until our pain is heard,"and to "call for help from every quarter."[104]

Similar themes were propounded during the 1940s by *Hamigdal*, the organ of the religious Zionist young adult division, Hashomer Hadati. Its editors lambasted "the indifference of the American people toward our bloody tragedy" and the "utter worthlessness" of Allied statements of sympathy. American Jews must "throw off all fear and raise a mighty outcry against the frightful injustice sanctioned by the democracies," *Hamigdal* declared. "We must storm heaven and earth and compel attention to our tragedy."[105]

In addition to college-age Labor Zionists and religious Zionists, the Revisionist Zionist youth movement Betar would undoubtedly have served as an ample source of recruits for a broad-based student activist movement. There was an active Betar chapter at City College led by Moshe Brodetzky and future Israeli Defense Minister Moshe Arens. During the 1940s, Betar-affiliated college students also frequently took part in rallies, fundraising, and other activities organized by their adult sponsors, the New Zionist Organization of America, to promote rescue and Jewish statehood, focusing on the need to abrogate the British White Paper policy that was keeping most Jewish refugees out of Palestine.[106]

With the JTS activists at its helm, college students from Habonim, Hashomer Hadati, and Betar making up its initial rank and file, and the prospect of additional Jewish and non-Jewish students joining in, the proposal to create a student protest movement was not nearly as far-fetched as Rabbi Wise seemed to think. Perhaps, however, Wise's concern was not so much that it was impossible to build such a movement but that an independent student campaign of this nature would be impossible for him to control. If that was his fear, it was probably well-founded.

The Allies Speak Out

During the second week of December 1942, just before the student delegation met with Rabbi Wise, Allied officials were working behind the scenes to craft a public statement about the Nazi slaughter of the Jews. The British government, trying to deflect criticism by Jewish leaders and members of Parliament over London's cautious response to the mass murders, proposed to the Roosevelt administration that the Allies issue an official statement condemning the killings. The first draft prepared by the British referred to "reports from Europe which leave no room for doubt" that systematic annihilation was underway. The State Department objected to that phrase on the grounds that – as one U.S. official complained – it could "expose [the Allies] to increased pressure from all sides to do something more specific in order to aid these people." The final statement, released on December 17, omitted the phrase "which leave no room for doubt."[107] It also contained no reference to taking any steps to rescue Jews. As one senior State Department official noted to his colleagues during the discussion over the wording, "The plight of the unhappy peoples of Europe, including the Jews, can be alleviated only by winning the war." This sentiment reflected the U.S. policy that would come to be known as "rescue through victory." The final proclamation strongly condemned the Nazis' "bestial policy of cold-blooded extermination" and warned that the perpetrators would face postwar punishment, but went no further. It was signed by the United States, Great Britain, the Soviet Union, and the governments-in-exile of eight German-occupied countries. Pope Pius XII declined to sign because – the papal secretary explained – the Vatican preferred to condemn war crimes in general rather than single out any particular atrocities.[108]

41

The day after their disappointing meeting with Wise, Golinkin and his friends read the newspaper reports of the Allies' joint statement condemning the Nazi genocide. "It was a like a one-two punch to us," according to Golinkin. "First, Rabbi Wise refuses to take our proposals seriously, then the Allied leaders issue a statement promising to punish war criminals after the war but not offering to do anything to save the Jews who were still alive. We realized we would just have to act on our own."[109]

Not only did Rabbi Wise decline the delegation's offer to build a student protest movement, but he did not follow up the December 2 day of fasting and the December 8 meeting at the White House with any program of additional national protests. The mainstream Jewish organizations' efforts in December, January, and February were limited to modest behind-the-scenes steps such as sending telegrams to newspaper editors urging coverage of Nazi atrocities, and financing a newspaper advertisement, signed by German-Americans, denouncing Hitler's slaughter of the Jews. Those steps, while certainly worthwhile, would have been more effective if carried out as part of a broader strategy of influencing public opinion, mobilizing non-Jewish sympathy, and pressing the Roosevelt administration to intervene. At meetings of the American Jewish Congress governing council during this period, participants raised a variety of interesting proposals, from holding "processions of hundreds of thousands of Jewish men, women and children in the streets of New York and, if possible, other cities," to mobilizing prominent Catholic laymen such as former Republican presidential candidate Alfred E. Smith to help convince "the Catholic Church [to] invoke the power of excommunication" against Nazi leaders.[110] But most such proposals never left the drawing board. Few Jewish leaders were possessed of the sense of urgency needed to undertake such unorthodox protest actions.

Instead of focusing exclusively or even primarily on the plight of Europe's Jews, major American Jewish groups continued to devote a substantial portion of their resources to a variety of domestic and foreign issues, as well as to mundane inter-organizational matters. Hayim Greenberg, editor of the Labor Zionist publications *Jewish Frontier* and *Der Yiddisher Kemfer*, sarcastically proposed that "a day of prayer and of fasting should be proclaimed for the five million Jews now living in the United States [because of] the hardness and the dullness that has come over them... a kind of epidemic inability to suffer or feel compassion" for European Jewry. "American Jewry has not done – and has made no effort to do – its elementary duty toward the millions of Jews who are captive and doomed to die in Europe!"[111]

The inability of many Jewish leaders to appreciate the urgency of European Jewry's plight was evident in their adherence to regular vacation schedules even at critical times. Palestine Labor Zionist leader David Ben-Gurion, visiting New York in the summer of 1942, found it impossible to arrange a meeting of Zionist leaders on a Friday afternoon because "even with Rommel nearing Alexandria, everybody left for the country for the week-end."[112] The following summer, Dr. Nahum Goldmann, co-chairman with Rabbi Wise of the World Jewish Congress, discussing with a State Department official a plan to rescue Jewish refugees from Rumania and France, remarked at the end of the meeting that he "was leaving on his vacation at the end of the week," so any further discussion of this critical rescue plan would be left to one of his deputies.[113] Wise's rival for the leadership of American Zionism, Abba Hillel Silver, complained bitterly when a meeting between Zionist officials and the U.S. Secretary of State was delayed because Wise was vacationing at Lake Placid: "The Zionist Movement in these critical war times must conform with the lecture schedule and the vacation schedule of Dr. Wise," he groused. But Silver was not immune from such criticism, either. Zionist activist Emanuel Neumann, who was assigned to broker a crucial power-sharing arrangement between Silver and Wise in 1944, recalled in his memoirs how "Silver went to Maine with his family for their summer vacation, while I was left in New York, entrusted with the delicate and difficult task of working out the tricky details of the future management of the Council between these two formidable principles, Wise and Silver."[114] That council was the American Zionist Emergency Council, the name of which ironically conveyed a greater sense of urgency than that displayed by those who coveted its helm.

Union Theological Seminary, as seen from the main entrance of the Jewish Theological Seminary.

No More Business as Usual

The JTS students were determined to shatter this "business as usual" atmosphere. Unable to secure Rabbi Wise's cooperation, they decided to go their own way. They began by setting their sights on their neighbors, the students of the Union Theological Seminary, located directly across the street from the Jewish Theological Seminary. Established by the Presbyterian Church in 1836, UTS soon emerged as one of the premier liberal Protestant theological seminaries in the United States. During the 1940s, its faculty included such prominent theologians as Paul Tillich and Reinhold Niebuhr.

J. Herbert Brautigam, Jr., student leader at the Union Theological Seminary, in 1940.

In late December 1942, Golinkin, Lipnick, and Sachs met with UTS student president J. Herbert Brautigam, Jr. and proposed holding an inter-seminary conference on the plight of European Jewry, with sessions alternating between the two campuses. Brautigam immediately assented. The JTS students handled the logistics for the event and recruited Jewish speakers, while Brautigam and his friends con-

44

tacted Christian speakers and solicited the participation of other Christian seminaries. Golinkin reluctantly agreed to the UTS students' request to balance the participation of a pro-Zionist speaker from the JTS faculty by also inviting a representative of the American Council for Judaism, a group recently established, primarily by Reform rabbis, for the purpose of opposing Zionism.

The JTS administration readily accepted the students' request that it serve as co-host of the event. In addition, both Seminary president Rabbi Dr. Louis Finkelstein and Rabbi Dr. Robert Gordis, professor of Bible, agreed to be speakers. Golinkin, Lipnick and Sachs found the Seminary leadership to be generally sympathetic to their committee's activities, although the administration did not take any steps to encourage their work or offer to provide any specific assistance to the committee beyond hosting the Inter-Seminary conference.

JTS leaders had taken a strong interest in the plight of German Jewry from early on. During the 1930s, Seminary president Cyrus Adler and then-provost Finkelstein undertook numerous efforts to help German Jewish scholars escape Hitler by bringing them to the United States to serve on the faculty of JTS or other institutions.[115] The administration did not, however, ease its rigorous employment criteria such as perfect fluency in English, which made it hard for some German Jewish scholars to qualify for positions on the Seminary's faculty. Similarly, the Seminary declined to relax its admissions standards for Jewish students from Germany, and thus only a small number of them were able to use admission to the Seminary as a means of escaping the Nazis.[116] Dr. Finkelstein, who succeeded Adler as president in 1940, believed the best response to Nazism was for the Seminary to focus on its traditional mission of preparing rabbis and Judaic scholars to build up American Judaism. Former students recall little in the classrooms, publications, or daily life at JTS in the 1940s that reflected a specific concern for Europe's Jews.[117]

In retrospect, some students regretted that to a large extent, life on campus carried on as usual, despite the slaughter in Europe. Baruch Silverstein ('40), for example, later wondered "why Seminary students did not arrange hunger strikes, chain themselves to the White House, or at least stand sobbing at street corners and subway entrances." Saul Teplitz ('45), whose wedding celebration was held on campus in June 1944, at the height of the deportation of Hungarian Jews to Auschwitz, subsequently noted with "deep regret" that "we didn't give a second thought to the appropriateness of a celebration on the day when thousands of Jews were being murdered."[118] The reality was that at JTS, as in much of the American Jewish community, the events in Europe, even when fully known, often did not intrude on daily life. The Golinkin-Lipnick-Sachs committee thus represented a significant innovation at the Seminary.[119]

The "Inter-Seminary Conference of the Plight of European Jewry Today," timed to coincide with National Brotherhood Week, convened on Monday, February 22, 1943. Despite the New York winter weather, 167 Christian and Jewish students took part,[120] as did a number of faculty members. It appears that thirteen metropolitan-area Christian and Jewish seminaries were represented: Berkeley Theological Seminary, Biblical Seminary, Drew Seminary, General Theological Seminary, Jewish Institute of Religion, Jewish Theological Seminary, Moravian Theological Seminary, New Brunswick Theological Seminary, Princeton Theological Seminary, St. Vladimir's Theological Seminary, Union Theological Seminary, Yale Divinity School and Yeshiva College.[121]

The morning session, held at JTS, opened with a speech by Brautigam, as conference chair. No transcript of his remarks, or those of the other speakers, is extant, but summaries that subsequently appeared in the European Committee's newsletter *The Challenge* offer a glimpse of the speakers' presentations.

Brautigam charged the Allies with having responded to the mass murder "with a kind of moral paralysis." He was also sharply critical of the church, charging that it had so far spoken only in "hollow tones of moral generalities." The time had come, he said, to start making "demands on the conscience and opinion of America" for action to save Jews from Hitler.

Rabbi Philip Bernstein (left) with Rabbi Stephen Wise, in the 1940s.

Brautigam was followed by Rabbi Philip Bernstein of the Jewish Welfare Board, who emphasized the importance not only of "immediate steps to save

Three of the
speakers at the
Inter-Seminary Conference.

Dr. Henry Smith Leiper   George Warren   Varian Fry

lives," but also "a more permanent solution to the problem of European Jewry." The permanent solution, he said, was Palestine.[122]

The final speaker in the JTS portion of the program was Varian Fry, literary editor of *The New Republic*, a man who, more than any other American, had directly participated in the rescue of Jews from the Nazis, although his efforts were not widely known at the time. In late 1940, Fry had traveled to Vichy France at the behest of the New York-based Emergency Rescue Committee to arrange the escape of refugee artists and intellectuals, mostly Jews, who were targeted by the Nazis. Fry created an underground network that smuggled some 2,000 refugees out of France, mostly by foot across the Pyrenees. The rescued included such luminaries as the painter Marc Chagall, the Nobel Prize-winning scientist Otto Meyerhof, the poet Franz Werfel, and the philosopher Hannah Arendt. In response to complaints by the Nazis and the Vichy authorities, the State Department in late 1941 canceled Fry's passport, ending his rescue mission.[123]

In his remarks at the interfaith conference, Fry suggested three practical steps to aid the Jews of Europe: an Allied declaration to the German people defining war criminals and threatening to punish them; modification of the Allied blockade of Axis countries in order to provide food to the Jews there; and an offer of asylum in the United States for any Jews able to escape Hitler.[124]

The afternoon session, held at UTS, featured speeches by several experts in refugee relief, followed by church leaders and then two Jewish spokesmen. George Warren, secretary of the well-meaning

47

but ineffectual President's Advisory Committee on Political Refugees, surveyed the status of Jewish refugees in various countries and possibilities for rescue. Howard Kershner of the American Friends Service Committee, expanding on one of Varian Fry's recommendations, emphasized the need to send food to starving refugees in Europe, despite the blockade. Dr. Henry Smith Leiper, foreign secretary of the Federal Council of Churches, called on the church leadership in the United States and Europe "to abandon its complacency and urge that aid be granted European Jewry now, and mold public opinion in that direction." The most disappointing speaker probably was Dr. Willard Johnson, assistant to the president of the National Conference of Christians and Jews, who spoke generally of the need for "good will among religious groups."

The final session of the afternoon concluded with two rabbinical speakers, the pro-Zionist JTS Prof. Robert Gordis, and Rabbi Hyman Schachtel of the anti-Zionist American Council for Judaism. The JTS student activists had hoped to keep Jewish differences over Zionism out of the conference, lest they distract from the focus on rescue. They therefore requested, and received, from Rabbi Schachtel a commitment in advance to refrain from mentioning the Council in his remarks. When Schachtel stepped to the podium, however, he identified himself as a member of the Council. That prompted Gordis to interrupt and declare that just as the Holy Roman Empire was neither holy, nor Roman, nor an empire, the American Council for Judaism was "neither American nor representative of Judaism."[125]

Left: Robert Gordis presenting prayer book to unidentified man in the 1940s.
Right: Rabbi Hyman Schachtel, in the 1940s.

The only known photograph of the Inter-Seminary conference, taken at the dinner session.

In their remarks, both rabbis emphasized the importance of Palestine as a haven for Jews fleeing Hitler. "There is no difference of opinion among Jews on the subject of Palestine as a place of refuge," Schachtel emphasized. "There is a divergence of opinion over the type of government which Palestine should have." During the question period, JIR student Usher Kirshblum reignited the controversy with a heated critique of Schachtel's anti-Zionism, but Jerry Lipnick managed to cut him short in order to preserve the peace. Moshe Goldblum, who was active in the European Committee, worried afterwards that Schachtel's "pleasant manner" and emphasis on "Jewish-Christian brotherhood" might have resonated more strongly among the Christian delegates than did Gordis's remarks about the persistence of antisemitism through the ages. Indeed, one of the Christian students remarked that while Gordis "spoke like Isaiah," Schachtel "spoke like Jesus."[126]

The delegates returned to JTS for a dinner session to conclude the conference. The only known photograph of the conference, taken

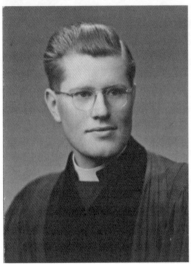

Four of the Christian seminary students who attended the Inter-Seminary conference. Clockwise from top left: Douglas MacDonald, of the New Brunswick Theological Seminary; Ivol Godby, of the Yale Divinity School; Earl R. Shay, of the Moravian Theological Seminary; and Richard Beving, of the New Brunswick Theological Seminary.

during the dinner, shows row after row of young men in jackets and ties, and a handful of young women, filling the dining area from wall to wall. A few are smiling, but most of the expressions reflect the somber mood of the day's proceedings. JTS president Dr. Louis Finkelstein was the only speaker at the concluding session. "All of us have had a share" in creating the dismal situation in which the world found itself, he told the conferees. "[F]or those past ten years we failed to recognize the real menace of Hitler, and we did nothing at all to combat him. For this failure we should all feel a deep sense of guilt."

Dr. Louis Finkelstein, President of the Jewish Theological Seminary.

"Isolationism," he said, was "responsible for so much of our woe – and so much of the Jewish woe." He was referring not to the prewar isolationism of Americans seeking to avoid international conflicts, but rather the tendency of members of one racial or religious group to isolate themselves from people of different backgrounds. It was this "unwillingness to accept all men as our brothers" which was the root of the problem, according to Dr. Finkelstein. He noted that "even the immigration quotas of this country are based upon the myth of Nordic superiority over the Mediterranean peoples." The only hope for mankind, he said, was to "break down this isolationism," and he saw the inter-seminary conference as a step in that direction:

> This meeting tonight indicates that it is within our power to break down this isolationism. Many faiths are represented here, and there is a desire on our part to work together. That is the way it should be, for in order to end both political and religious isolationism, it is necessary for us to concern ourselves more and more with the world problems and try to solve them by thinking and acting together.[127]

Finkelstein's broad philosophical approach contrasted with the student activists' emphasis on specific, practical steps to rescue Jewish refugees. While there was nothing in the JTS president's address with which Golinkin, Lipnick or Sachs disagreed, their purpose in convening the conference was not to take comfort in generalities about world brotherhood, but rather to focus attention on concrete steps to alleviate the plight of European Jewry. For the student activists, Dr. Finkelstein's orientation underlined a generation gap of which they were becoming painfully aware: too many of their elders seemed content with generalities and unable to comprehend the urgency of the situation.

Before dispersing, the conference attendees held an interfaith worship service consisting of the responsive recitation of selections from the book of Psalms, as well as English translations of the *El Maleh* and *Hashkivenu* prayers. It was composed by Yeshiva College student Irwin Gordon.[128]

The students also adopted a series of resolutions which not only challenged the Allies' policy toward the Holocaust but also, in some respects, went further than the positions taken by mainstream Jewish organizations.[129] They began with an affirmation of religious obligation: "[It] is the duty of the Church and the Synagogue, and their leaders, to try to mold the opinion of America so that all may realize the religious importance" of promoting rescue.

The second resolution declared it "the duty of the American people to demand that the governments of the United States, Great Britain, and the other United Nations proclaim that, at least for the duration of the emergency, the lands of the United Nations will be opened to all the refugees who can be saved from Europe." The resolution emphasized that "America especially should show an example to the rest of the world by its willingness to accept refugees immediately."

Another resolution asserted that Palestine "should be opened for all those refugees who can be brought to the Holy Land," and that the Roosevelt administration "should exert its influence on the British government" to that end.

In contrast with the Allied policy of refusing to negotiate with the Nazis over the fate of the Jews, one conference resolution urged the U.S. to enter into talks, via intermediaries, with the Hitler regime and the governments of German satellite countries, to bring about the release and emigration of their Jewish populations, particularly children.

The delegates also called for providing "food for the relief of the starving peoples of Europe, especially the children," which contravened the Allies' blockade preventing food and other goods from reaching Axis territory.

In addition, a "Post-Conference Committee" was appointed to publicize the conference resolutions, establish contacts with Jewish and Christian leaders, and initiate other means of promoting rescue in the religious world and beyond.[130]

One week after the conference, on March 1, 1943, the established Jewish organizations held their first major public protest since the December 2 day of prayer and fasting. The "Stop Hitler Now" rally, held at Madison Square Garden, was organized by the AJCongress and cosponsored by all of the other major groups except the AJCommittee, which, as a matter of principle, refused to endorse public demonstrations.

The resolutions adopted at the March 1 rally represented the first policy platform adopted by the Jewish establishment groups since the confirmation of the Nazi genocide more than three months earlier. Like the positions taken by the Inter-Seminary Conference, the March 1 resolutions urged contacts with the Axis to secure the release of Jews, as well as the feeding of Jews in Axis-occupied areas regardless of the Allied blockade. The March 1 attendees called on Great Britain to open Palestine, although they did not urge the Roosevelt administration to pressure the British, as the students had. The establishment groups also urged the creation of refugee havens in Allied countries, including America. They specified that sanctuaries in the United States should be designed in accordance with the existing quota laws, which was not as bold as the students' call for havens for "all" refugees for the duration of the war.[131]

Still, even within the existing quotas, a substantial number of Jews could have been rescued. During the previous year (1942), the German-Austrian quota was only about 18% filled; the Polish quota was 14% filled; the French quota was 35% filled. Between 1933 and 1945, a total of about 190,000 quota places from Germany and Axis countries were left unused. There were so many empty spaces because the State Department continued to instruct consuls abroad to look for every opportunity to reject visa applications. An additional regulation imposed by the State Department in 1941 barred admission to anyone who had "close relatives" in Axis territory, on the theory that the Gestapo might blackmail them into becoming Nazi spies by threatening their kin.

The fact that many quota places were unfilled was known to Jewish organizations at the time and surfaced occasionally in the press. In fact, it was the occasion for one of the most critical editorials ever to appear in a mainstream Jewish newspaper regarding the Roosevelt administration's policies. The March 12, 1943 editorial in the *Philadelphia Jewish Exponent* pointed out that "even within the limit of the immigration laws, refugees have not been admitted to this country because they have been strangled by the red-tape which the State Department has manufactured to make entry into the United States supremely difficult." The editorial went so far as to charge that there existed an "anti-Jewish spirit either in Washington itself or among American consuls abroad who have departed far from the very spirit, if not the letter, of the immigration laws in order to obstruct the admission of Jewish refugees." To publicly suggest that antisemitism was shaping the Roosevelt administration's refuge policy was virtually unheard of in the American Jewish community at that time.[132]

The JTS students, too, were aware of the phenomenon of the unfilled quotas. In an unpublished analysis of U.S. refugee policy that the students prepared later that year, they wrote, citing reports from the World Jewish Congress: "In no year since 1933 has the American quota been filled (18.3% was the maximum used). In 1942-43 only 5.9% of quota was used... No attempt has ever been made to merge national quotas in order to utilize unused visas."[133] The numbers were imprecise, but the overall point was correct.

The Rise of the Bergson Group

At the same time the JTS students were making preparations for their conference, another, and even more ambitious, effort was underway to raise public awareness of the Holocaust. It was spearheaded by 27 year-old Hillel Kook, an activist in the Irgun Zvai Leumi, the Palestine Jewish underground militia aligned with the Jabotinsky movement. During the late 1930s, Kook was a leader in the Irgun's effort to smuggle European Jews to Palestine in defiance of British immigration restrictions. In 1940, Kook, together with other Irgun emissaries and Jabotinsky followers, was sent to the United States,

Peter Bergson (Hillel Kook)   Ben Hecht

where his work focused on promoting the creation of a Jewish army to fight alongside the Allies against the Nazis. Upon his arrival in the U.S., Kook – whose uncle was Abraham Isaac Kook, the Chief Rabbi of Mandatory Palestine – began using the name Peter Bergson to shield his famous family from unwanted publicity. Like Noah Golinkin, Bergson read the news of Stephen Wise's November 1942 press conference and immediately threw himself into the struggle for the rescue of Europe's Jews. With a tiny office in midtown Manhattan and a skeleton secretarial staff, Bergson and his colleagues began devising a strategy to publicize the Holocaust and promote rescue.

Their first major project was "We Will Never Die," a theatrical production created for the Bergson Group by screenwriter Ben Hecht (famous for such Hollywood blockbusters as *Gone with the Wind* and *Scarface*). Hecht, who had been active in Bergson's Jewish army campaign, hoped to have the production co-sponsored by a broad coalition of Jewish organizations. But his January 1943 meeting in New York City of Jewish organizational representatives – "from the powerful B'nai B'rith to a society of Brooklyn rabbis," as Hecht later recalled – dissolved into chaos:

> The representative of the American Jewish Congress stood up, pointed a finger and cried out, "As an organization, we refuse to work with Morris Goldfarb! Never will the American

Jewish Congress join up with anything in which the Arbeiterring [the socialist Workmen's Circle group] is involved!" A man, possibly Morris Goldfarb, was on his feet yelling back, "And we will never work with the American Jewish Congress in 1,000 years!" Other voices arose. English and Yiddish outcries filled the room. Within five minutes, a free-for-all, bitter as a Kentucky feud, was in full swing. The 32 Jewish organizations were denouncing each other as socialists, as Fascists, as Christians, as undesirables of every stripe.

The door opened and the 33rd representative entered. He understood instantly what was going on and began yelling without taking his hat off. I retreated to the bedroom. The spectacle of Jews comically belaboring each other in the worst hour of their history sickened me.[134]

Jewish Disunity

It sickened the JTS students, too. As Golinkin, Lipnick, and Sachs pondered their next step after the Inter-Seminary Conference, they looked out across the vast landscape of the Jewish organizational world and saw a panoply of groups mired in conflict and competition. For all the worthwhile purposes these organizations served, they were, as Ben Hecht's experience illustrated, too often consumed by disagreements rooted in theology, politics, or competition for supporters. These rivalries generated endless intra-organizational turf wars and an atmosphere of mistrust that was not substantially dissipated by the disaster engulfing Europe's Jews. Defense groups, such as the American Jewish Congress and American Jewish Committee, were sharply at odds over the appropriate strategies for protecting Jewish rights in the public sphere and representing Jewish interests in dealings with the U.S. and other governments. American Zionists, non-Zionists, and anti-Zionists quarreled over Palestine's future. Among the Zionists, factions divided along political, religious, and even gender lines promoted competing visions of the future Jewish homeland. Each of Judaism's religious denominations boasted its own association of synagogues, organization of rabbis, and theological institutes. There were also umbrella groups galore – the Synagogue Council of America tried to present a unified voice for the religious factions; the Emergency Committee for Zionist Affairs sought to do likewise for American Zionists; and the United Palestine Appeal aimed to unify fundraising campaigns for Palestine projects.

A series of councils and committees tried to bridge the gaps between the defense organizations so as to present a united Jewish voice in Washington and elsewhere in the public arena. But these efforts were fitful and short-lived. The Joint Consultative Council, created in 1933 to represent the American Jewish Congress, American Jewish Committee, and B'nai B'rith, collapsed three years later when the AJCongress and AJCommittee could not agree on which group should submit a particular petition to the League of Nations.[135] A General Jewish Council, established in 1938 and encompassing the AJCongress, AJCommittee, B'nai B'rith, and Jewish Labor Committee, was soon rendered ineffective by constant power struggles between the organizations. As a result, its historian has noted, "rigor mortis set in before its actual death" in 1941.[136] As will become evident, subsequent efforts at Jewish unity fared no better.

Shattering the Silence

Not only were the major Jewish organizations reluctant to cooperate with each other; they also refused to work with the Bergson Group. An official of the AJCommittee who attended the January 1943 meeting concerning "We Will Never Die" wrote afterwards to a colleague: "They may in fact produce a pageant. It may even have literary merit. Obviously we as a Committee should have nothing to do with this venture."[137] Some Jewish leaders feared that Bergson's vocal activism would usurp their own role in the Jewish community. Others worried that dramatic public activities such as Hecht's pageant might provoke anti-Semitism. Some would not work with Bergson because their particular factions in the Zionist movement regarded him as their political rival due to his association with Jabotinsky.

The Allied governments, too, looked askance at "We Will Never Die." The White House declined to send a message to be read aloud at the premiere, fearing the publicity surrounding the show would increase pressure to admit Jewish refugees to the United States. The British, for their part, regarded the pageant as "implicitly anti-British," because its appeal to the Allies to find havens for Jewish refugees could include letting them enter Palestine – something London vehemently opposed, for fear of angering Arab opinion.

Despite the lack of cooperation, Bergson and Hecht went ahead with "We Will Never Die" on their own. Starring Edward G. Robinson, Paul Muni, Sylvia Sidney, and Stella Adler, and directed by Moss Hart with an original score by Kurt Weill, it played to audiences of more than 40,000 in two shows at Madison Square Garden on March 9, 1943. In the months to follow, it was staged in Philadelphia, Boston, Chicago, the Hollywood Bowl in Los Angeles, and Washington D.C., where the audience included First Lady Eleanor Roosevelt, six Supreme Court justices, numerous members of the international diplomatic corps, and an estimated 300 members of Congress. In addition to the more than 100,000 people who viewed the shows, the performances received substantial media coverage. Mrs. Roosevelt was so moved that she devoted part of her next syndicated column to the pageant. For millions of American newspaper readers, the news about "We Will Never Die" may have been the first time they had heard about the Nazi mass murders. For the JTS students who read the extensive coverage that "We Will Never Die" received in New York's newspapers in March, the pageant was an inspiring example of grassroots activists organizing independent action to fill the vacuum left by the established leadership.

"The Conference is Not Over"

During the weeks following the Inter-Seminary Conference, the JTS students strove to maintain the momentum that the gathering had generated. "The Conference is Not Over," declared the headline of a four-page mimeographed newsletter that they distributed at JTS and UTS. It pleaded with students to guard against "allow[ing] the matter which called us together to slip from our minds." Anyone who believed "that the danger which faced European Jewry would disappear because of the impact of our deliberations" needed to face the cold reality that "since our conference, the United States and its allies have not taken any action whatever to save the five million

Jews of Europe who can be saved." The newsletter urged its readers, "[W]e must not cease from our God given task until there is sent abroad in this land an ever swelling chorus of 'We are our brother's keeper.' "[138]

A similar *J'Accuse*, but aimed at America's churches, appeared in the UTS student publication, *The Union Review*, in March 1943. It was authored by student president J. Herbert Brautigam, Jr., co-organizer of the Inter-Seminary conference. "Having emoted [at the conference] we have returned to our normal routines," he charged. "In the three weeks since, *what have we done*? In the three months since the United Nations published its documentation of Hitler's campaign for the systematic extermination of the Jews in Europe, what have the United Nations done? Two million Jews have died, deliberately murdered; five million more face the same fate. And we confront the situation with a kind of moral paralysis."

While it was true that most of the public opposed increased immigration, the duty of religious leaders is "to try to mold [public] opinion," Brautigam contended. "This is a matter of life and death. It is literally a matter of hours and days. Can the Church speak forth in any but hollow tones of moral generalities, or can it make demands on the conscience and opinion of America that will make it possible to help those of our spiritual community who suffer?"[139]

The Inter-Seminary conference had an even greater impact at Yeshiva College, where it generated not only articles in the student press but at least two rallies. Two days after the conference, YC senior Irwin Gordon, who had participated in both the December 1942 students' meeting with Rabbi Wise and the JTS-UTS conference, organized an assembly of more than 300 students at Yeshiva College's high school, the Talmudical Academy. The speakers echoed the JTS European Committee's emphasis on practical action rather than general statements of outrage. Gordon, the main speaker, urged the students to help bring public opinion "to bear on our government in order to insure effective action." TA student president Sam Okun "told the students of concrete ways and means in which American public opinion could be aroused," *The Commentator*, YC's student newspaper, reported. Gordon also helped organize a second assembly on campus that same week, attended by YC students, faculty, and alumni. At that gathering, YC student council president Jacob Walker issued "a spirited plea" to

Sam Okun   Jacob Walker   Abraham Zuroff

the attendees "to send letters to [their] representatives in Congress, protesting America's indifference to the plight of the Jews." Another speaker, YC Student Organization president Abraham Zuroff, called for "action, not pity," echoing the headline of a Bergson Group advertisement in the *New York Times* earlier that month. The YC Student Organization subsequently prepared a seven point program for promoting rescue action, patterned on the recommendations of the Inter-Seminary conference, and sent it to student leaders at 300 colleges around the country as well as to numerous Anglo-Jewish newspapers. An editorial in *The Commentator* expressed hope that "the recent student meetings and the excitement they have aroused indicate, perhaps, the genesis of a new attitude on the part of the students" with regard to the plight of European Jewry.[140]

To drum up continued interest in the issue, the JTS students sent copies of the conference resolutions to Jewish and Christian leaders. Additional meetings were held between the JTS students and their new friends at UTS. Lipnick authored a report about the conference, which was distributed by the Religious News Service. Golinkin, Lipnick and Sachs held meetings with a number of Jewish organizational leaders, including Zionist author Maurice Samuel, U.S. Labor Zionist leader Hayim Greenberg, and A. Leon Kubowitzki, chairman of the rescue committee of the World Jewish Congress. The students wrote letters to a number of other Jewish leaders, urging the mainstream Jewish organizations to take a greater interest in the rescue issue. Most of the replies they received were little more than perfunctory acknowledgments. An exception came from Carl Alpert, editor of the American Zionist journal *New*

Palestine, who responded that in view of "the progressiveness, the imagination and the energetic spirit" of the students, "perhaps it would not be such a bad idea if all leaders of American Jewry were to abdicate and a committee of students from the respective Rabbinical seminaries were to take over for a period of six months."[141]

A Midrash on the Holocaust

Additional insight into the students' thought process may be gleaned from a sermon-in-progress that Jerry Lipnick wrote on March 7, 1943 for his Homiletics Class at JTS. It was shortly before Purim, when synagogue services include a reading of Torah verses pertaining to the Amalekites, a tribe that launched an unprovoked assault on the Jews shortly after the exodus from Egypt. Lipnick's assignment was to prepare a sermon based on a Midrash (*Sifrei Devarim* parag. 67 and parallels) concerning the Amalekites. Because of the attack, the Midrash states, God commanded the Jews to undertake three specific tasks when they entered the Land of Israel: appoint a king, build a temple, and blot out the remembrance of Amalek. Why those three? According to Lipnick, the appointment of a king represented Jewish national survival and construction of the temple represented Jewish religious survival, while blotting out Amalek – the symbol of eternal antisemitism – was "the guarantee for group survival."

From there, Lipnick proceeded into an extended analogy between Jewish survival in ancient times and in his own era. In the 1940s, the Allies "are supposedly fighting a war against a modern Amalek who threatens their survival and the survival of all of the peoples of the earth," he wrote. He quoted President Roosevelt saying the Allies were "fighting today for security and progress and for peace not only for ourselves but for all men, not only for our generation, but all generations" and "fighting... to uphold the doctrine that all men are equal in the sight of God." If the war is indeed a war "for the freedom of all peoples, a war for democracy," Lipnick asserted, "then [the Allies] should certainly grant the Jewish people the right to continue as a nation and as a religious community."

The Jews have been "ground into the dust in Hitler-dominated Europe," Lipnick wrote. "About half the Jewish people in the world today have either been killed or are threatened with death." The Allies have the ability to rescue many of them, and since such intervention would be consistent with their declared war aims, there is no reason to hesitate. "If the United Nations are fighting for freedom, then certainly they should be fighting to save the lives of those to whom they are willing to give that freedom," Lipnick explained. "The saving of the 5,000,000 Jews of Europe should not be a postwar aim; it should be engaged in immediately." Thus rescue becomes a test of the Allies' sincerity.

He then outlined a series of specific steps for the Allies to take: rescuing Jews from Nazi satellite countries; providing food to starving Jewish communities; publicizing atrocities; pledging to undertake reprisals; opening Palestine to unlimited Jewish immigration; and, after the war, facilitating the establishment of a Jewish state. Although the Jews are presently weak and stateless, the Allies should be guided by the ancient Hebraic principle of treating the strong and the weak according to the same law. "The United Nations, if they are sincere, must recognize the justice of the Jewish claim to be a nation and a religious community, even though we are small in the eyes of the world."[142] The intertwining of ancient texts with the fight for justice would be a theme of Lipnick's sermons throughout his subsequent rabbinical career, as it would be for Golinkin and Sachs as well.

"Retribution is Not Enough" – A Manifesto for Rescue

During the days following the February 1943 Inter-Seminary conference, the activist trio also composed a manifesto, which was published in *The Reconstructionist* on March 5. Readers were alerted from the start that the article would touch some nerves – it began with a message from the editors: "The following statement by a committee of students of the Jewish Theological Seminary presents a serious challenge to American Jewry and particularly to the American Synagogue," it explained. "There may be disagreement as to some of the methods proposed by this committee, but its recommendations certainly merit public discussion that may lead to action."

The three students entitled their essay "Retribution is Not Enough," a reference to the Allied leaders' promise to exact retribution against Nazi war criminals – a promise that represented the sum total of their response to the genocide. "We do not want retribution for Jews who have already died," the JTS activists wrote. "We prefer help for those Jews who yet live." The Allies had failed to take "any steps beyond protest to indicate that they are really concerned" about stopping the killings, and "in failing to act speedily, they have become partners in these horrible crimes."

The bulk of the students' criticism, however, was aimed at American Jewry. "We Jews who live in the staid serenity of America have failed to grasp the immensity of the tragedy," they wrote. To convey the dimensions of the slaughter, they pointed out that "Were the entire Jewish populations of Boston, Cincinnati, Baltimore, Philadelphia, Chicago, San Francisco, Cleveland, St. Louis, Los Angeles, and Detroit slain, it would be little over half the number of those who have already been annihilated in Europe." In the face of this catastrophe, they asked bitterly:

> What have the rabbis and leaders of these cities, or of New York, done to arouse themselves and their communities to the demands of the hour? What have the rabbinical bodies representing the Orthodox, Conservative, and Reform groups attempted in order to impress upon their congregations the necessity for action now? What have they, or any other responsible organizations within American Jewish life, undertaken to awaken the conscience of the American people?

The students decried what they saw as the defeatist mood permeating the Jewish community. "Most of us, it appears, have already given up on European Jewry in our hearts," they charged. "[O]thers have acquiesced in their helplessness... [I]n order to save five million human beings who have been doomed to die, we must take bold and ambitious measures... [W]e need mass action on a nation-wide scale, mass action that involves bucking the people and the American government. But bucking injustice is our religious duty!"

The JTS students then outlined a far-reaching campaign of political action, in two phases. One phase would be spearheaded by America's rabbis. "Since the synagogue is the one institution in American Jewish life which can reach the greatest number of Jews, the synagogue should take the lead in this all-out effort to ameliorate the condition of European Jewry." The campaign would begin with the proclamation of "Aid European Jewry Now" Week, during which there would be "special services and programs" focusing on ways to pressure the Allies to rescue Europe's Jews. One day during the week would be declared "Shivah Day," a reference to the mourning rituals traditionally observed following the death of a spouse or close relative. Unlike the fasting and mourning of the previous December 2, "this time we should pray and mourn for a purpose – to call for concrete assistance from the United Nations and from our own country in particular."

Even after the conclusion of the week, certain practices would be instituted in Jewish religious life to help maintain communal awareness: "a uniform prayer followed by a minute of silence should be recited wherever Jews gather in numbers of ten or more – at parties, weddings, meetings, etc.," and "a uniform prayer, such as an extra Kaddish [the prayer recited by mourners] should be recited by the entire congregation in all synagogue services... In this way we would mourn those Jews who have no one left to mourn for them, and we would always remind ourselves of our obligations to those Jews in Europe who still live."

The students' program of action included two points aimed specifically at mobilizing the support of non-Jews. As they had demonstrated in organizing the Inter-Seminary Conference, the JTS activists recognized that winning the support of the general public was crucial to prove to the Roosevelt administration that rescue was an issue of concern not just to American Jews but to the broader public as well. "Large interfaith meetings should be held simultaneously throughout the country," the students proposed. "There should be one meeting in each city, and in the large cities one in each section, where uniform demands for action should be made to the United Nations and our own government." At the same time, an "Emergency Committee for European Jewry," with subcommittees in each city, should be created for the purpose of utilizing "radio, press, film advertisements, etc." to reach "every type of Gentile and nonsectarian organization."

All these efforts would be channeled towards asking the Roosevelt administration and its allies to take a series of rescue actions: create temporary havens where refugees could stay until war's end (the article specified the Virgin Islands as one feasible destination); pressure the British to open Palestine; evacuate Jews from countries likely to be invaded by the Nazis; and provide food to

Jews in Axis countries. They also added two steps that had not been included in the Inter-Seminary conference resolutions: encourage local populations in Europe, through leaflets and radio broadcasts, to oppose the killings; and create "a Jewish army to be composed of Palestinian and stateless Jews." The latter proposal directly echoed the language of the Bergson Group's campaign for a Jewish army in 1941-1942, an initiative of which the JTS students were well aware.

The "Retribution" article concluded with a heartfelt plea:

> The lives of five million Jews hang in the balance. It is up to us to do everything possible to save them *now*. Each day's delay means thousands of lives lost. When the final tabulation of those murdered has been published, will American Jewry be able to say: "*Yadenu lo shafku et hadam hazeh*" (Our hands have not shed the blood") ?[143]

Chapter 3

THE SEFIRA CAMPAIGN

In attempting to measure the impact of the students' article in *The Reconstructionist*, one must keep in mind that the influence wielded by the magazine stemmed not from how many people read it, but which people read it. Although its circulation was modest, *The Reconstructionist* was read by Jewish leaders, rabbis, and other intellectuals – those who played a major role in shaping Jewish organizational policy and Jewish public opinion. They were, in other words, precisely the people the JTS activists wanted to reach. Moreover, an editorial in the same issue began, "We heartily endorse the demand for immediate practical action voiced by the Seminary students in the article 'Retribution Is Not Enough', printed elsewhere in this issue..."[144] This blunted any danger that the article would be seen as a well-intentioned but irresponsible rant of a few hotheads.

Among those who read the students' essay were senior leaders of the Synagogue Council of America (SCA), the umbrella group for Conservative, Reform, and Orthodox synagogues.[145] At about the same time, the SCA leadership also received a private memorandum from Golinkin, Lipnick, and Sachs, summarizing the proposals made at the Inter-Seminary Conference. Five days after the article

Dr. Israel Goldstein

appeared in *The Reconstructionist,* the Council established a Committee for Emergency Intercession in order to "stimulate public opinion" in support of Allied rescue action. On March 26, 1943, SCA chairman and JTS alumnus Dr. Israel Goldstein invited Lipnick and Golinkin to attend a small meeting of Jewish leaders to plan the agenda of the Intercession Committee. (In a subsequent letter to the JTS activists, Goldstein said it was "a source of great inspiration to the older colleagues to see the [JTS] student body so deeply concerned with the tragic plight of our people.") The council's decision to assign a role of such policy-making significance to two students testified to the activists' seminal role in bringing about the establishment of the new committee.[146]

The Synagogue Council planning meeting was unquestionably a triumph for the JTS trio. At the students' suggestion, the attendees developed a plan not for just one Aid European Jewry Week, but for a six-week long nationwide campaign organized in conjunction with the weeks of semi-mourning following Passover, known as Sefira. Instead of a single "Shivah Day," there would be an entire week of mourning rites at the conclusion of the six weeks, to be called a "Period of Mourning and Intercession." The SCA would urge its member-synagogues to implement a series of steps to raise communal awareness of European Jewry's plight and inspire political action for rescue. "Special memorial services" would be held throughout the six weeks. Mondays and Thursdays would be declared "partial fast days." "Occasions of amusement" would be limited. Extra monetary contributions would be made to refugee relief agencies. "Special prayers" would be recited and "moments of silence" observed, both "at home and in public meetings." "Frequent religious gatherings" would be organized "by the leading rabbis" to draw attention to the Jewish situation in Europe. Lipnick and Golinkin were assigned to work with Intercession Committee director Rabbi Ahron Opher in designing the packet of materials that the council would distribute.[147]

The packet led each synagogue through the process of creating an environment of awareness, mourning, and constructive action. It included a step-by-step outline for holding a memorial service for Hitler's Jewish victims; a sample letter to fellow-rabbis, urging them to take part in the campaign; a sample protest letter that both rabbis and their congregants could send to political and religious leaders;

sample press releases to publicize their activities; and sample resolutions to be adopted at public gatherings. The packet also included another Golinkin innovation: a black ribbon, designated as a *siman avelus*, or mourning symbol, to be worn on one's lapel throughout the six weeks.[148]

Three original prayers in Hebrew and English were included in the packet.[149] The first two were authored by Golinkin.[150] One was intended to be recited at all public meetings held during the Sefira period. It began with the opening lines of Psalm 22, "My God, my God, why hast Thou forsaken me?" Continuing along this theme and utilizing familiar phrases from the liturgy and biblical texts, the nine-stanza prayer expressed anguish that God was hiding Himself, so to speak, from the suffering of the Jewish people. It appealed to Him to "turn from Thy wrath" and "deliver us not into the power of the tyrants."

The second prayer, four stanzas in length, was meant to be added at the end of the traditional *Birkat ha-Mazon* which is recited after every meal. "How can we enjoy our food while we know that our brothers perish by famine and sword?," the text asked. In addition to appealing for mercy for the Jews in Europe, this prayer also included a request for divine assistance in facilitating greater compassion and activism by American Jews:

> Create in us, O God, a new heart responsive to the agony of our people, the suffering remnants of Israel: May we know of no rest 'til we have stretched out our hands to them in help.
> Father of mercy, create in us a spirit of compassion and loving kindness, to share our bread with the starving and to seek rescue for those who can be saved, that they may live because of us.

The packet also included a new version of the ancient *Yizkor* prayer.[151] *Yizkor*, in which relatives who have passed away are remembered, is recited aloud in every synagogue on the final day of each major Jewish religious holiday, and one such occasion would arise during the Sefira weeks – on the last day of Passover. The Synagogue Council version began with a remembrance of fallen Allied soldiers and then proceeded into a vivid description of ways in which Europe's Jews had been persecuted:

Age-old communities have been devastated, their guardians slain and scattered, their sanctuaries desecrated, their houses of learning razed and their treasures burned and looted... May the Lord remember the souls of the sons and daughters of Israel who have fallen prey to men of violence. Countless numbers of them have been tortured, slaughtered and buried alive, in daylight and in darkness, in forest and in field, taken from the pursuit of their labors, from the study of Thy law, from their homes, while fleeing from the pursuing sword.

It concluded, not surprisingly, with not-so-veiled references to the need for American Jewish awareness of the slaughter and action for rescue: "[W]e pray Thee, O God, that the memory of these, the dear and beloved, shall never vanish from our thoughts. May they live in our hearts, and in our will and in our actions."[152]

In early April 1943, the packets were mailed to some 3,000 rabbis, lay leaders, and principals of Jewish schools. Announcements that the SCA project was underway appeared widely in the Jewish press, thereby drawing attention to the situation in Europe as well as encouraging local activity based on the Synagogue Council's suggestions.[153]

Changing the American Jewish Mood

The students' emphasis on rites associated with mourning boldly attempted to transform the mood in the American Jewish community by profoundly altering everyday life. The dances and social gatherings that were a mainstay of communal leisure time would become few and far between. In every synagogue, the ark would be draped in black, worshippers would wear black ribbons, and extra prayers for the deceased would be recited. At home, the *birkat ha-mazon* recited after each meal would include an extra prayer referring to the plight of the Jews in Europe. The entire atmosphere in the community would change to reflect the urgency and enormity of the European catastrophe. The "staid serenity" enveloping American Jewry, which the students had decried in the pages of *The Reconstructionist*, would be shattered. Now everyone would constantly have before them ways to "remind ourselves of our obligations to those Jews in Europe who still live."

The students' strategy took direct aim at the troubling phenomenon of business-as-usual in the American Jewish community. Other
observers also noticed this problem. A January 1943 editorial in the
Jewish Spectator, for example, found it "shocking and – why mince
words? – revolting that at a time like this our organizations, large
and small, national and local, continue 'business as usual' and
sponsor gala affairs, such as sumptuous banquets, luncheons,
fashion teas, and what not[.]"[154] Advertisements appearing in the
leading American Jewish periodicals during the Holocaust years
showcased the array of leisure activities one would expect the public
to patronize in ordinary times: Jewish-oriented resort hotels,
concerts, dances, bazaars and carnivals, sea water baths near the
Atlantic City boardwalk, sulphur baths in the Catskills. One Zionist
youth movement did announce a "No-Luxury Week" for its
members after 1943; it was not, however, in response to events in
Europe, but rather was intended for the purpose of familiarizing
them with the rigors of life in Eretz Yisrael.[155]

Anecdotal evidence indicates that some individuals and small
groups of Jews did visibly alter their daily behavior in response to
news of the slaughter in Europe. For example, Rabbi Baruch David
Weitzmann, spiritual leader of a synagogue in the Brownsville
section of Brooklyn, issued a ruling for his congregation that
"because we have to feel the *tsa'ar* [pain] of the Jews who are being
killed in Europe, there can be no festivities, no parties, no music."
The rabbi's daughter later recalled:

> If somebody wanted to get married, they came to our house,
> there was a little *chuppah* [wedding ceremony], some cake and
> soda, nothing more. No celebrations, no dancing, just the
> *chuppah* and that's all. He explained to us, "You cannot
> celebrate at a time when other Jews are dying."[156]

In a similar spirit, the Yeshiva College administration during the
1940s suspended public festivities such as the Chag Hasemicha, the
celebration of the ordination of the graduating rabbinical class. On
the other hand, YC student-run public parties on the holidays of
Chanukah and Purim continued without interruption.[157] This
tendency to carry on life as normal was precisely what the JTS
students aimed to disrupt.

Stirrings in the Jewish Establishment

Meanwhile, on the political front, there were stirrings of activity within the Jewish establishment. The continued flow of atrocity reports from Europe and the Allies' failure to aid the Jews galvanized eight major Jewish organizations in March 1943 to create a Joint Emergency Committee on European Jewish Affairs (JEC). It was the first serious attempt at intra-organizational cooperation in response to the Nazi genocide. The members were the AJCommittee, AJCongress, B'nai B'rith, the socialist Jewish Labor Committee, the American Emergency Committee for Zionist Affairs,[158] the Synagogue Council of America, and two Orthodox groups that were not part of the SCA, Agudath Israel and the Union of Orthodox Rabbis. The Bergson Group was not invited to join.[159]

The Joint Emergency Committee got off to a promising start, organizing well-attended protest meetings in forty cities around the country in the spring of 1943. To the JTS students, the creation of the JEC and its initial burst of activity appeared to augur a new spirit among the mainstream Jewish organizations. For the first time, the established leaders seemed to recognize the need for unity and urgency. But would they sustain an activist approach in the months to follow? The question was critical because many of the JEC's behind-the-scenes political contacts met with frustration, thus resurrecting the painful dilemma over whether to publicly take issue with the administration. Rabbi Wise and AJCommittee president Joseph Proskauer held meetings with Undersecretary of State Sumner Welles and British Foreign Minister Anthony Eden in late March 1943, but found them completely unreceptive to any suggestions for Allied intervention on behalf of the Jews. Wise's attempts to arrange a meeting with President Roosevelt in April were rebuffed as the president's advisers sought to deflect pressure on the refugee issue.

Meanwhile, a rising tide of calls in the British parliament, media, and churches for Allied assistance to Jewish refugees in the spring of 1943 prodded the British Foreign Office and the State Department to discuss holding an Anglo-American conference on the refugee problem. The island of Bermuda, far from the prying eyes of protesters and the news media, was chosen as the locale. Like the abysmal Evian conference five years earlier, Bermuda was born of the Allies' desire to appear to be concerned about the refugees without taking concrete steps to alleviate the Jews' plight. The Joint Emergency Committee requested permission to send a delegation to the conference. The request was rejected. The JEC then presented Undersecretary Welles with a list of proposals for rescue action. The proposals were ignored.

The Bermuda conference opened on April 19, 1943, ironically on the very same day the Nazis prepared to annihilate the remaining Jews of Warsaw and Jewish fighters launched a desperate armed revolt. Throughout the twelve days of deliberations, the U.S. delegates reiterated America's refusal to take in more refugees and the British representatives refused even to discuss Palestine. In a May 4 letter to Assistant Secretary Long, Jerry Lipnick, writing on behalf of the European Committee, challenged the failure of the conference to develop serious rescue plans. Long replied that the conference's decisions had to remain secret because of "military necessity" and "the desire not to prejudice the interests of the refugees."[160] Bermuda produced no meaningful change in Allied policy toward Jewish refugees. Clinging firmly to the "rescue through victory" policy, Assistant Secretary of State Adolph Berle asserted in a message to a Jewish rally in Boston two days after Bermuda's conclusion that "nothing can be done to save these helpless unfortunates" except to win the war.[161]

The failure of the Bermuda conference provoked the first serious public criticism of the administration's refugee policy. Congressman Samuel Dickstein (D-NY), chairman of the House Immigration Committee, declared: "Not even the pessimists among us expected such sterility." Rep. Emanuel Celler (D-NY) accused the delegates in Bermuda of engaging in "more diplomatic tight-rope walking," at a time when "thousands of Jews are being killed daily." Celler pointedly characterized Bermuda as "a bloomin' fiasco" – a shot at another Jewish Congressman, Sol Bloom (D-NY), who supported the State Department and served on the U.S. delegation to Bermuda.

The Bergson Group responded to the conference with a large newspaper advertisement headlined "To 5,000,000 Jews in the Nazi Death-Trap, Bermuda was a Cruel Mockery." Some mainstream Jewish leaders spoke similarly. Dr. Israel Goldstein of the Synagogue Council of America blasted the conference as "not only a failure, but a mockery," and bluntly added that "the victims are not being rescued because the democracies do not want them, and the job of the Bermuda conference apparently was not to rescue victims of Nazi terror but to rescue our State Department and the British Foreign Office from possible embarrassment." The Labor Zionist magazine *Jewish Frontier* charged that the delegates to Bermuda had acted "in the spirit of undertakers." Even Stephen Wise characterized the Bermuda parley as "a woeful failure."[162] The Joint Emergency Committee was slow to respond – it took more than a month to compose its response – but when it did, it went further than any of its member-organizations had previously gone in challenging U.S. policy. Directly challenging the administration's "rescue through victory" philosophy, the JEC wrote: "To relegate the rescue of the Jews of Europe, the only people marked for total extermination, to the day of victory is... virtually to doom them to the fate which Hitler has marked out for them."[163]

Reaching the Grassroots

Fortuitously, the first of the Synagogue Council of America's three mass mailings for the Sefira campaign reached its recipients during the third week of April. Rabbis and synagogue board members were discussing participation in the SCA campaign the same week they were reading news accounts of the Bermuda conference and the Jewish armed revolt against the Nazis in the Warsaw Ghetto, both of which began on April 19.

The Sefira project touched a responsive chord at the grassroots level. It enabled ordinary Jews, even in far-flung communities, to participate in concrete protests against the Nazi atrocities. It provided a way for individual Jews to feel they could do something meaningful in response to the awful news from Europe. A Jew in Tulsa or Charlotte could – as one Jewish weekly editorialized – take part in this "spiritual response," as a complement to the "mass rallies of protest, huge pageants, [and] full page advertisements" that some larger Jewish communities had sponsored.[164]

Measuring the level of Jewish participation in the Sefira campaign is difficult. According to Rabbi Opher of the Synagogue Council, the Intercession Committee received "hundreds of letters and tele-grams" from synagogues pledging full participation.[165] There is, however, no way to know how many individuals in a given community observed partial fast days or limited their party-going.

By contrast, public activities, such as the recommended prayer-and-mourning rallies, typically attracted news media coverage. Thus it is known that during April and May 1943, there were many such rallies, sometimes led jointly by Reform, Conservative, and Orthodox rabbis in an uncommon display of unity. They were held from New York City, Boston, Hartford, and Newport in the East, to Richmond, Charleston, Memphis, and Galveston in the South; Oakland, San Francisco, and Los Angeles in the West, and many points in between, including not merely large metropolitan areas such as Chicago, Detroit, and Denver, but also Tulsa, Omaha, Youngstown, St. Paul, and numerous communities across Pennsylvania. Even "Resort Jewry," in and around the resort hotels of Atlantic City, held memorial rallies.[166]

At the conclusion of the Sefira period, 500 Orthodox, Conservative, and Reform rabbis held a dramatic convocation in New York City. Intra-Jewish conflicts nearly derailed the event, however. The SCA's plan to hold the rally at the West Side Institutional Synagogue was stymied by board members' objections to having non-Orthodox rabbis speak. An attempt to secure another modern Orthodox synagogue, Shearith Israel (the Spanish & Portugese Synagogue) failed for the same reason. Rabbi Joseph Lookstein, known for his broadminded approach on such issues, stepped in and offered to host the rally at his synagogue, Kehilath Jeshurun, on the Upper East Side.[167]

A typical memorial assembly featured speeches by the mayor or other local dignitaries as well as rabbis, followed by recitation of the prayers circulated by the Synagogue Council. Many of the rallies had their own distinctive features. In Denver, for example, the rally began with a procession of Boy Scouts to a podium with

Rabbi Joseph Lookstein in the 1940s.

flags of the Allied nations. In Des Moines, Catholic, Protestant, and Jewish clergymen took to the airwaves with a special radio broadcast about the plight of European Jewry. Following the Memphis assembly, residents listened to a radio broadcast about a German Jewish refugee who had settled in their community with relatives in the 1930s, then enlisted in the U.S. Army and lost his life fighting the Nazis.[168]

Some communities took extra steps to underline the solemnity of the rallies. A Hebrew Sunday school in the Bronx, for example, canceled the traditional entertainment at its graduation exercises as a gesture of solidarity with that day's memorial rally. A Junior Hadassah chapter in Freeport, Long Island, and a Hebrew Sunday school in nearby Hempstead both canceled their scheduled dances so their members could attend a memorial event. The sponsors of the Richmond, VA, rally announced there would be no speeches at the event, so that nothing would interfere with the mood of "solemn worship." In Newport, RI, and Albany, NY, Jewish children held separate memorial services "for oppressed children in the conquered nations" (another idea taken from the Synagogue Council packet).[169]

Christian Participation in the Protests

The SCA's simultaneous effort to raise Christian awareness of the Holocaust met with less success. In some communities, such as Chattanooga, Norwalk, Denver, and Raleigh, local Christian clergymen made guest speeches at Jewish community gatherings on the designated "Day of Compassion." In addition, churches held their own prayer services for European Jewry in some other cities, such as Indianapolis, Detroit, St. Paul, Milwaukee, and a number of towns in New York, Alabama, and Pennsylvania.[170] In many larger cities, however, the response was meager. In Boston, for example, despite a heavy publicity campaign, including mailings, subway posters, newspaper advertisements, and a sponsoring committee featuring an array of governors, mayors, and congress members, only eight area clergymen organized memorial services. In New York City, too, there were only a few participants. In Pittsburgh, a Jewish organization hoping to prepare an article for the local press about the Day of Compassion events could not find a single church that intended to take part. Overall, only a small handful of America's many thousands of churches sponsored special services or otherwise took part in the memorial activities.[171]

The failure of most churches to take part in the Day of Compassion is consistent with the response of U.S. Christian religious leaders and institutions to the plight of European Jewry throughout the Hitler years. The Federal Council of Churches, the national umbrella organization for twenty-five American Protestant denominations, did little beyond occasionally expressing its sympathy for the Jews and its support for rescue. During the prewar period, the FCC endorsed legislative measures to aid Jewish refugees, such as the 1939 Wagner-Rogers bill to admit 20,000 German refugee children and the 1940 King-Havenner bill to open Alaska to some Jewish refugees. But it did not take the lead on such projects, nor did it make the refugee issue an item of significance on its agenda. In the wake of the Allied confirmation of the Nazi genocide in December 1942, FCC leaders pledged to cooperate with Jewish organizations in mobilizing Christian involvement in protests. But the only major Holocaust-related project on which the FCC collaborated, the Day of Compassion, did not materialize until nearly five months later. Despite the fact that the FCC provided church leaders with a packet of materials to guide the proposed memorial services, and undertook a mailing to 70,000 Protestant ministers of an issue of the FCC Information Service newsletter devoted entirely to the mass murder of the Jews, relatively few churches participated in Day of Compassion events.[172]

Most of the American Protestant press likewise showed little interest in the persecution of Europe's Jews. The only Protestant periodicals that reported the issue with some frequency were two small-circulation newspapers devoted to converting Jews to Christianity.[173] Even the Union Theological Seminary's *Union Review* published only one article concerning the plight of the Jews in Europe, student president J. Herbert Brautigam's aforementioned March 1943 broadside blasting American Christian indifference toward the Holocaust.[174]

The most influential American Protestant publication, the weekly *Christian Century*, spoke of the Jewish plight on only a handful of occasions, and not always helpfully. In the wake of the 1938 Kristallnacht pogrom, for example, *Christian Century* responded to talk of increasing Jewish immigration by publishing an editorial urging that U.S. immigration laws be "maintained or even further tightened." (By contrast, during the German blitz of London, the editors urged that English children be brought to the United States since, as minors, they would "place no strain on this country.")[175] A *Christian Century* editorial on Rabbi Wise's November 1942 press conference confirming the mass killings accused Wise of exaggerating the casualty figures. The editors wondered if "any good purpose is served by the publication of such charges." Confronted the following month by the Allies' verification of the genocide, a *Christian Century* editorial conceded that "extermination of a race" was underway but added: "The right response to the Polish horror is a few straight words to say that it has been entered in the books, and then redoubled action on the Tunisian, Russian, Italian and German fronts and on the production lines."[176]

In actual refugee work, too, only the very smallest of Protestant denominations became involved. The Quakers' American Friends Service Committee played an active role in refugee work, with AFSC agents in Europe directly organizing rescue and relief activities.[177] Likewise the Unitarian Church, through its Unitarian Service Committee, undertook numerous rescue projects in Europe. Among its notable activists were the Massachusetts pastor Rev. Waitstill Sharp and his wife Martha, who worked with Varian Fry's network smuggling refugees out of Vichy France.[178] The tiny Church Peace Union, headed by Dr. Henry Atkinson, sought unsuccessfully to persuade the major church bodies to take a greater interest in the Jewish issue. Unfortunately, these were the exceptions, not the rule, in American Protestant responses to the Holocaust.

The American Catholic response to the Holocaust was similarly characterized by disinterest, and sometimes worse.[179] The Catholic magazines *Commonweal* and *America* did periodically report on the persecution of Europe's Jews and urge rescue measures. But the rest of the American Catholic press printed very little about the raging Holocaust.[180] The Catholic Committee for Refugees (est. 1937) helped only a small number of people (many of them not Jews) and the financial support it received from the church was so meager that the CCR had to be funded in part by the American Jewish Joint Distribution Committee. Two relief agencies established by the National Catholic Welfare Conference, the Bureau of Immigration and the War Relief Services, focused their attention entirely on Catholic refugees.[181]

American Catholic leaders paid only brief lip service to the plight of the Jews. Between 1941 and 1945, the National Catholic Welfare Conference, which spoke for U.S. bishops, issued just two brief statements pertaining to the Nazi persecution of European Jewry. One, in 1941, condemned "the inhuman treatment" to which Jews had been subjected. The other, in 1942, acknowledged the "cruel indignities heaped upon Jews," but referred at greater length to the suffering of bishops around the world and the "extermination of the people of [Poland]."[182] Both resolutions were issued prior to the public confirmation by the Allies of the Nazi genocide; during the two-and-a-half years from the Allied confirmation until the end of the war, the NCWC did not adopt any resolutions about the slaughter of the Jews.

On the positive side, a small but influential group of Protestant religious leaders lent their names, and sometimes more, to the Bergson Group's rescue campaign. For example, Union Theological Seminary president Henry Sloane Coffin, together with the Episcopal bishops of New York and Harrisburg, the dean of the Protestant Theological College, and other Christian clergymen, publicly called for passage of a Bergson-initiated congressional resolution on rescue; and the Methodist Resident Bishop, William J. McConnell, testified before Congress in support of the resolution.[183] The Episcopal bishop of Los Angeles, Rt. Rev. W. Bertrand Stevens, served on the sponsoring committee of the Hollywood Bowl performance of "We Will Never Die." Rev. Stevens, together with the Episcopal bishops of Lexington (KY) and Iowa, General Theological Seminary president Howard Chandler Robbins, and Guy Emery Shipler, editor of *The Churchman*, co-sponsored the Bergson group's 1943 emergency conference on rescue (see below).[184] The Methodist bishop of Virginia, James Cannon, Jr., was a speaker at that conference as well as a signatory on many Bergson newspaper ads. The presiding bishop of the Episcopal Church, Henry St. George Tucker, also spoke at the 1943 conference, despite a personal plea by Rabbi Stephen Wise to cancel his association with the Bergsonites.[185]

Other prominent Protestant clergy involved with the Bergson Group included the Rev. Duncan Browne, who was active in its Chicago chapter; the Methodist bishop of Boston, Rt. Rev. Lewis O.

Hartman, Unitarian church leader Dr. Albert C. Dieffenbach, Rev. Dr. C. Gordon Brownville (Baptist), and Rev. Dr. Fred Winslow Adams (Methodist), who were active in the Boston branch; and Methodist bishop G. Bromley Oxnam, of New York, who served as honorary chair of Bergson's second emergency conference, in 1944.[186]

The Bergson Group utilized unorthodox tactics to draw attention to the rescue issue. At a time when mainstream Jewish organizations seldom used the medium of newspaper advertisements to advance their causes, the Bergsonites placed more than 200 large, sharply worded ads in newspapers around the country during 1941-45. They featured provocative headlines such as "How Well Are You Sleeping? Is There Something You Could Have Done to Save Millions of Innocent People – Men, Women, and Children – from Torture and Death?" and "Time Races Death: What Are We Waiting For?" Many of the ads featured long lists of prominent authors, actors, musicians, artists, and political figures who endorsed the Bergson rescue campaign.[187]

Another critical component of the Bergson committee's efforts was its week-long Emergency Conference to Save the Jewish People of Europe, which attracted more than 1,500 delegates to the Hotel Commodore in New York City in July 1943. Determined to disprove the administration's "rescue through victory" approach, the conference featured panels of experts outlining specific, practical ways to save Jews from Hitler. In addition to challenging the centerpiece of U.S. policy toward European Jewry, the conference demonstrated vividly that the cause of rescue enjoyed support across the political spectrum.

Its nineteen co-chairmen included conservatives such as former president Herbert Hoover (who addressed the delegates by radio) as well as liberals such as American Labor Party leader Dean Alfange; Republican senator Arthur Capper as well as Democratic senator Elbert Thomas, Roosevelt cabinet member Harold Ickes as well as FDR's arch-critic William Randolph Hearst. The speakers on the panels included a broad cross-section of prominent journalists, labor leaders, military personnel, members of Congress, and the executive secretary of the NAACP. A coalition of such diversity also posed an implicit political challenge, since it demonstrated to the White House, on the eve of an election year, that rescue was an issue that mattered to a significant number of voters beyond the Jewish community.[188]

Galvanizing the Jewish Establishment

The Bergson Group and the JTS students were not the only ones dissatisfied with the mainstream Jewish leadership's response to the Holocaust. Within the ranks of the established Jewish groups, too, there were serious signs of frustration over the established leaders' cautious approach. In meetings of the Joint Emergency Committee for European Jewish Affairs during the spring and summer of 1943, Rabbi Wise struggled to control his increasingly restless colleagues. The Jewish Labor Committee in particular repeatedly pressed Wise and Proskauer for more action. When the Labor Committee's Jacob Pat complained to AJCommittee president Joseph Proskauer about the Joint Emergency Committee's inactivity, Proskauer, on his way to a vacation in Lake Placid, wrote in exasperation:

> Will you let me know specifically what you think the Emergency Committee ought to do? Of course it is inactive now. It is inactive because there isn't a single thing that I can think of it should do, and to keep on just threshing around is harmful and not helpful in my judgment.[189]

Joseph Proskauer

81

There was, in fact, no shortage of ideas. In fact, at meetings of the Joint Emergency Committee throughout the spring and summer of 1943, delegates proposed an array of interesting and innovative project proposals. Undoubtedly much to Rabbi Wise's chagrin, some of the most militant suggestions came from his own closest associates. AJCongress delegate Carl Sherman suggested undertaking a "forceful public campaign" to convince the administration to adopt the JEC's rescue program. Another AJCongress delegate, Lillie Shultz, said the State Department's attitude toward rescue "is still very cold....The President must be shown that the country is aroused."[190] Nahum Goldmann, co-chairman along with Rabbi Wise of the World Jewish Congress, asserted that "the time ha[s] come to change our policy. We have to oppose the American and British government's attitude and act accordingly in our mass meetings and elsewhere." Goldmann proposed a public mass meeting of "1,000 to 2,000 representatives of all Jewish organizations, to publicize the refusal of the Allies to have our large program discussed at the Bermuda Conference." Wise sidetracked Goldmann's suggestion by assigning it to a newly-created subcommittee of five, led by himself and Proskauer.[191] Roosevelt "is still our friend, even though he does not move as expeditiously as we would wish," Wise wrote in a note to Goldmann afterwards. Moreover, he warned, for Jews to say "that the President and our government will not do anything for the refugees is morally and perhaps even physically suicidal."[192]

There were numerous additional suggestions for stronger action. Isaiah Minkoff, representing the General Jewish Council, urged the five co-chairs of the Joint Emergency Committee to hold a press conference in Washington at which they would "inform the press about our feelings." Henry Montor, vice president of the United Palestine Appeal, "proposed that throughout the country groups of Jews should be asked to go to Washington at a certain date and call on their representatives and Senators."[193] Dr. Israel Goldstein, president of the Synagogue Council of America, urged that Congressman Sol Bloom be "publicly disavowed" because of his defense of the Bermuda Conference. Dr. Isaac Lewin, representing Agudath Israel, suggested approaching the U.S. envoy to the Vatican, Myron Taylor, to seek papal intervention on behalf of the Jews. Jacob Pat of the Jewish Labor Committee called for a public protest meeting. Rabbi Avraham Kalmanowitz, of the Union of

Orthodox Rabbis, urged the JEC to establish a permanent office in Washington in order to lobby Members of Congress on the rescue issue.[194]

That was not all. While Proskauer was claiming, in June 1943, that there "isn't a single thing" he could think of for the JEC to do, the JTS students had, back on April 25th, sent a three-page "Program of Action" to Proskauer, Wise, and each of the JEC's member-organizations. The memorandum opened with a quote in Hebrew and English: "When one delays even a moment in redeeming captives – wherever it is possible to hasten – he is considered as one who spills blood."[195] Writing six days after the opening of the Bermuda conference, the students charged that the meager results from the conference were "sad proof that our State Department is not yet ready to do everything possible to save European Jewry." Therefore "only a program of public enlightenment, unprecedented in Jewish history, can force the hand of our government." A willingness to spend "hundreds of thousands of dollars" and "the utilizing of the full-time energy of thousands of communal leaders and workers" is "the only answer worthy of American Jewry," they contended.

The students' memo argued that while the Jewish delegations to Washington, the rallies in various cities in the spring of 1943, the Sefira campaign, and the upcoming Day of Compassion were a good start, much more was needed. "There is still lacking, however, a comprehensive program designed to place the full weight of the American Jewish community and the humanitarian forces within this country squarely behind" an all-out campaign for rescue. The students then proceeded to outline exactly the sort of comprehensive program they had in mind.

First, "an Emergency Office with full-time staff must be set up immediately." Although it might seem obvious that, given the magnitude of the crisis, such an office should have been opened immediately upon the founding of the JEC, in fact, the JEC had been operating throughout its four-month existence on an ad hoc basis. Its meetings were held in the offices of the American Jewish Congress, and its activities were conducted piecemeal by volunteers or clerical staff on temporary loan from other groups.

The new JEC national headquarters would carry out a multi-pronged campaign. It would mobilize various organizations –

"political, religious, labor and fraternal" – to promote rescue through resolutions, publications, and directives to their local affiliates. It would sponsor national radio broadcasts several times weekly ("Prominent Hollywood names should be enlisted since they carry an audience") as well as full-page newspaper ads. "Remember," the students admonished, "cigarettes are no more important than human lives."

The proposed new national JEC office would also organize three major events. The first would be what the students called "a March on Washington," although, like several of the aforementioned proposals made by delegates at JEC meetings, it would actually consist more of lobbying than marching: "prominent Jewish and Christian citizens from each of the states of the Union should converge on Washington simultaneously in order to see their Senators and Congressmen and to urge them to advocate rescue activities." Second, the JEC should organize "a dramatic emergency conference" of all New York-area Jewish organizations. Third, there should be "an emergency conference of Orthodox, Conservative, and Reform rabbis," which would be "unprecedented in synagogue history."

The JTS students were also concerned at indications that the forthcoming American Jewish Conference, a national gathering of major Jewish organizations to discuss various issues, would not give sufficient attention to rescue. The students' memo therefore urged the JEC to help ensure that the American Jewish Conference would "place this problem at the top of its agenda."

The second part of the students' memo offered specific suggestions for promoting rescue on the local level, such as developing a form letter to send to newspapers, creating telephone squads, training canvassers, mobilizing local Christian groups and VIPs, distributing leaflets on street corners, sponsoring local radio spots, introducing rescue resolutions in local city councils and state legislatures, and encouraging the wearing of "black ribbons symbolizing mourning and protest... until the holiday of Shavuoth."

"By day and by night, even on holidays, the Jewish community of America should be working," the JTS students concluded their appeal. "All other communal activity should be geared so that this problem takes precedence. Thousands of Jewish lives are being destroyed daily, and American Jewry has not yet found its soul."[196]

Proskauer replied to the JTS students with a one-sentence note acknowledging receipt of their long list of ideas.[197] Yet despite having before him both the JTS students' proposals and the many ideas suggested at recent JEC meetings, Proskauer told Jacob Pat of the Jewish Labor Committee in June 1943 that "there isn't a single thing that I can think of [that the JEC] should do."[198] In a sense, Proskauer was merely being frank. He really could not think of anything the JEC should do, because he was temperamentally unsuited to conceiving new or unusual ways to address Jewish concerns. Part of the problem, however, was deeper than a failure of imagination. All the proposals put forth both by the JTS students and the various JEC delegates involved American Jews publicly criticizing the policies of the president of the United States. This was something that Proskauer – and Stephen Wise as well – simply could not countenance. They were convinced that a public Jewish challenge to the highest authority in the land would ignite a wave of antisemitism, and they were not willing to risk such an eruption.

More Pressure on Wise

Two emissaries from Palestine added to the pressure on Wise and Proskauer in the summer of 1943. Leib Jaffe, visiting New York on behalf of the *Keren ha-Yesod* (Palestine Foundation Fund), wrote Wise on June 2 to complain that American Jewry "is silent... Life goes on normally and quietly as if nothing were happening... We cannot be silent. Jewish history will never forgive it. The blood of our brethren cries out to us." Jaffe urged the JEC to "proclaim a day of mourning and protest for all American Jews" and bring "hundreds of thousands of Jews into the streets to express their grief and indignation." Jaffe acknowledged there had been "demonstrations in

Leib Jaffe

85

halls and in synagogues" – probably a reference to the Day of Compassion memorial rallies in May – but believed more dramatic steps were needed.[199] Six days after Jaffe sent his letter, participants in an AJCongress executive committee meeting proposed "holding a mass street demonstration with respect to the atrocities." Wise vetoed the suggestion.[200]

The JEC did not meet again until July 15, nearly two months after its previous session. That long gap is itself testimony to the seeming lack of urgency on the part of the establishment that activists such as the Bergson Group and the JTS students criticized. Leib Jaffe arranged for himself and Rabbi Meyer Berlin, the leader of Palestine's religious Zionist movement, who was also visiting New York City, to attend the July 15 meeting. There Berlin "complained bitterly about the indifference, inadequate action, and lack of feeling on the part of the American Jews" with regard to European Jewry. Jaffe, who also spoke at the meeting, urged the JEC leaders to organize "mass demonstrations" and "get hundreds of rabbis out of their houses so that they march in the demonstration[s] with Torah scrolls in their hands." Jaffe also cited a message from the Jewish underground in the Warsaw Ghetto which pleaded: "If you feel our pain, leaders of Israel, rise and go to the American representatives, and to the [British] Foreign Ministry offices, and stay there until they put you in jail, and if they arrest you, go on a hunger strike until you die!" In view of the gravity of the situation, he said, "We have to do something that goes beyond the norm, an event as great as the tragedy that has befallen us, an event that will waken the spirit of the quiet Jews and will shock the cold and cruel world." Rabbi Wise replied to Berlin that the JEC was already doing "everything that was practically possible" to promote rescue. According to Jaffe, Wise "reacted [to Jaffe] emotionally to the extent of being frightened." Wise "viewed the speeches as a rebuke directed towards him" and reportedly told Jaffe that he could not sleep for two nights afterwards.[201]

The next meeting of the JEC, on August 10, 1943, "devoted considerable time to a discussion of more forceful action which might be taken," the minutes reported. Meyer Weisgal of the Jewish Agency proposed "a demonstration in the streets of New York." David Wertheim of the U.S. Labor Zionists called for a "march on Washington by leaders of various Jewish communities" to dramatize their demand for rescue. The boldest proposal came from the least expected source. Lillie Shultz of the AJCongress suggested using the "Jewish vote" as a weapon of political pressure against Roosevelt.

The time has come, she said, to be critical of lack of action and in view of the fact that this is the eve of a presidential election year, ways can be found to indicate to the administration, and possibly through the political parties that the large and influential Jewish communit[y] will find a way of registering its dissatisfaction over the failure of the administration to take any effective steps to save the Jews of Europe.[202]

Shultz's proposal was remarkable both for its unprecedented nature and its surprising source. More than 90% of Jewish voters had supported FDR's re-election bids in 1936 and 1940, and public Jewish criticism of any administration policies was virtually unheard of. A threat to turn Jewish votes against the president or the Democratic Party would have represented an astounding step for the Jewish leadership. Moreover, Rabbi Wise, the founder and longtime leader of Shultz's American Jewish Congress, had on numerous occasions vigorously denied the notion that there was such a thing as a 'Jewish vote' and periodically issued appeals to the Jewish community to vote as Americans, not Jews. Wise feared that a public perception of the existence of a monolithic Jewish voting bloc would provoke antisemitic resentment.[203] That an official of the AJCongress would suggest threatening to vote against Roosevelt – an idea that was seconded, in the meeting, by Judge Morris Rothenberg of the United Palestine Appeal – is a further indication of the depth of dissatisfaction in the Jewish community over the administration's failure to aid Europe's Jews.

Ultimately, however, JEC co-chairs Wise and Proskauer made sure that none of these calls for marches on Washington, electoral pressure on the Democrats, or other public protests against the administration, ever advanced to the point of realization. For Proskauer and his AJCommittee colleagues, the very idea of mass Jewish protests was anathema. For Wise, the notion of Jews publicly challenging President Roosevelt's policies was equally abhorrent. Proskauer and Wise blocked "proposals for more forceful action" by referring them to a subcommittee which they controlled, and which never acted on them.

Showdown at the American Jewish Conference

Against this backdrop of escalating tensions within the Jewish leadership and the growing frustration in the American Jewish community over the Roosevelt administration's refugee policy, Stephen Wise and the AJCongress ignited another major communal controversy. Beginning in early 1943, Wise actively promoted the idea of holding elections to a national Jewish conference that would speak for the entire Jewish community on major issues. Given the increasingly pro-Zionist mood in the community, Wise believed that Zionist groups, such as those he headed, would sweep to victory and dominate the event. The initial planning summit, held in Pittsburgh in January 1943, envisioned that the main issues before the conference would be the postwar status of world Jewry and the future of Palestine. Dr. Isaac Lewin, an Agudath Israel delegate to the meeting, urged inclusion of rescue in the agenda, but was rebuffed by chairman Henry Monsky, president of B'nai B'rith, who said the gathering "was called for a different purpose."[204]

When the formal call for the conference was issued in April, it likewise omitted rescue. When the AJCongress, in June, announced a ten-point program that it hoped the conference would adopt, the list included compensation for Jewish victims of the Nazis, postwar punishment of war criminals, and the right of European Jews to return to their homes – but rescue was not included.[205] Likewise, Rabbi Wise's pre-conference "Forecast," in the pages of his monthly journal *Opinion*, made no mention of rescue.[206]

As the August 29 opening of the American Jewish Conference approached, a groundswell of pressure on the rescue issue began to build. Two Orthodox groups, Agudath Israel and the Union of Orthodox Rabbis, repeatedly pressed for rescue to be included on the conference agenda. At the July 14 AJConference planning session, delegates from the Jewish Labor Committee proposed, unsuccessfully, that rescue be made the main theme of the conference.[207] Some elements within the conference's own organizing leadership pressed for more attention to rescue. Synagogue Council of America president Dr. Israel Goldstein, a close colleague of Rabbi Wise, argued as early as May that the second item on the AJConference agenda, after Palestine, should be the need to "stir our own government and its allies to rescue speedily, not leisurely, the remnants of Jewry in the Nazi satellite lands..."[208] Goldstein and other Jewish leaders involved in the conference preparations were among the recipients of an ongoing stream of letters from the JTS student activists, stressing the need to focus on rescue above all other issues.[209]

There was criticism in the Jewish press as well. "Is the Conference to take no measures to save from extermination now what is left of European Jewry?," a columnist for the *National Jewish Ledger* asked. "If so, of what value will your consideration of postwar Jewish problems in Continental Europe be if there will be hardly any Jews left on the Continent?" A columnist for the AJCongress's own *Congress Weekly* acknowledged that "Jews, ordinary Jews with sound national instincts," had responded with "distrust, and even fear," when they heard of plans for the conference, asking, "Is this the solution for a people that stands on the brink of annihilation?"[210]

Shortly before the opening, the AJConference organizers gave in and agreed to add a Committee on Rescue to their roster of conference committees. Joint Distribution Committee chairman Paul Baerwald later described the decision as being the result of "a very insistent demand on the part of the delegates."[211] No official explanation of this policy change was presented, perhaps because the organizers were reluctant to call attention to their initial failure to include rescue on the agenda. The Independent Jewish Press Service speculated that the Bergson Group's Emergency Conference the previous month had "embarrassed" the AJConference organizers into embracing rescue.[212] The Bergson event undoubtedly provided a vivid reminder that the mainstream leadership was lagging behind on the rescue issue. The complaints voiced at JEC meetings and other gatherings of Jewish leaders, and the letters to Jewish leaders from the JTS students and other members of the Jewish community, may also have helped prod some consciences.

The JTS student activists, anxious to ensure that the rescue issue was given adequate attention, stood outside the opening session and distributed a leaflet urging delegates to focus on rescue. The leaflet began by quoting a conversation between a Jewish underground figure in the Warsaw Ghetto and a courier who would soon meet with Jewish leaders in England and the United States:

> Jewish leaders abroad won't be interested. At eleven in the morning, you will begin telling them about the anguish of the

Jews of Poland, but at one o'clock they will ask you to halt the narrative so they can have lunch....They will go on lunching at the regular hour at their favorite restaurant. So they cannot understand what is happening in Poland.[213]

The author of that jarring message from Warsaw "will never hear of the forthcoming American Jewish Conference," the students asserted. "He and his comrades of the Warsaw Ghetto have been wiped out, but there are hundreds of thousands of Jews in Rumania, Bulgaria, Hungary, and even Poland, who, though living in constant danger of death, are sustained by the hope that their brothers abroad are using every device to effect their rescue."

The students bemoaned the fact that despite the urgency of the situation in Europe, the AJConference program spoke only of postwar Jewish rights and the status of Palestine. "How can the Conference discuss the rights and status of Jews in the postwar world – we are sure the Jews of Poland would ask – when there may not be any postwar Jews?" Therefore, "[h]ow to move the [Allies] to save the remaining Jews of Europe must be item number one on the agenda of the Conference... [The Conference] must utilize all the resources – financial, political, and moral – of the various national organizations which compose it, to influence our government to act immediately."

"The spokesman from Warsaw must be proven wrong!" the students' leaflet concluded. "American Jewry cannot be out to lunch in the hour of crisis! The American Jewish Conference must see to that!"[214]

Rescue and the Palestine Issue

Unbeknownst to the public, another significant controversy was threatening to upset the American Jewish Conference. Worried that the Bergson Group's rallies and newspaper ads urging creation of a Jewish army would arouse the Arab world against the Allies, the State Department and the British Foreign Office in 1943 proposed that the president announce that all "public discussions and activities of a political nature relating to Palestine" were endangering "the war effort" and should "cease." FDR approved the plan, as did the British, and an early August declaration was planned. Rumors of the impending statement reached Jewish leaders in late July, but after a White House meeting, Rabbi Wise reported to his colleagues that the president "seemed completely in the dark" about the matter. No wonder Vice President Henry Wallace privately characterized Roosevelt as "a waterman," that is, someone who "looks one direction and rows the other with utmost skill."[215]

Some of the Jews in Roosevelt's inner circle, such as Treasury Secretary Henry Morgenthau, Jr., saw the proposed Anglo-American statement as an attempt "to deprive U.S. citizens of their constitutional liberties." Others, such as presidential speechwriter Samuel Rosenman, a prominent member of the AJCommittee, feared Zionists would ignore the declaration and thereby stir up antisemitism by making Jews appear unpatriotic. When Rosenman met with FDR on July 31, 1943, to discuss the issue, the president took the occasion to complain about the Bergson group's newspaper ads, as well as an ad by the New Zionist Organization of America, the U.S. wing of the Revisionist Zionist movement, urging the British to give up their rule over Palestine. The president asked Rosenman to pressure American Jewish leaders to curtail their efforts to create a Jewish state.[216] The Bergson Group and U.S. Congressman Emanuel Celler, belatedly learning of the plan, weighed in with objections of their own. "[T]he joint Anglo-American statement will, with its 'Silence, please' drown the clamor of the tortured Nazi victims pleading for a haven of refuge," Celler charged.

State Department officials tried to use the proposed statement as leverage on the Zionist leadership. In early August, they suggested to Wise and Goldmann that the only way to head off the statement was for Jewish leaders to postpone the American Jewish Conference or, at the very least, prevent the conference from issuing a strong declaration on Palestine. In truth, the statement was dead well before the AJConference opened on August 29. The opposition of Roosevelt's Jewish aides and the War Department, combined with unfavorable media reports and criticism in Congress, turned the proposal into a political hot potato. At a meeting in Quebec between Roosevelt and British prime minister Winston Churchill on August 22, the two leaders decided to hold the plan "in abeyance." It was never revived.[217]

But Rabbi Wise, laboring under the illusion that he had to downplay Palestine at the AJConference in order to head off the

Anglo-American statement, and hoping to keep the anti-Zionist American Jewish Committee from quitting the conference, conspicuously avoided any reference to Jewish statehood in his keynote address at the conference on August 29. This irked activist-minded delegates, including some from Wise's own AJ-Congress, who gave their time slot to Dr. Abba Hillel Silver, the Cleveland Zionist leader known for his forthright positions on Palestine. Silver delivered an electrifying appeal for Jewish statehood that "swept the conference like a hurricane," as one delegate put it. "There was repeated and stormy

Rabbi Dr. Abba HIllel Silver (seated) and Congressman Sol Bloom

applause, the delegates rising to their feet in a remarkable ovation." The assembled then sang a rousing version of the Zionist song Hatikva, which later became Israel's national anthem.[218] State Department pressure or no State Department pressure, there was now no way to prevent a Palestine homeland resolution from being introduced. "[W]e would be torn limb from limb if we were now to defer action on the Palestine resolution," Nahum Goldmann told AJCommittee delegates.[219] The resolution, calling for the establishment of a Jewish commonwealth in Palestine, passed by 498 to 4. The AJCommittee delegation left the hall and, shortly afterwards, the committee formally withdrew from the American Jewish Conference.

The Palestine vote was an overwhelming demonstration of American Jewish support for Silver's line and, in effect, a repudiation of Wise's strategy of caution. Elevated to co-chairmanship of the American Zionist Emergency Council alongside Wise, Silver set to work transforming American Zionism into a vigorous activist movement. "Since his induction as co-chairman, things have begun to happen," a columnist for the *Philadelphia Jewish Exponent* reported. "The Zionist Emergency Committee [is] now clicking on all cylinders under the leadership of Dr. Abba H. Silver..."[220] In the months to follow, Silver mobilized grassroots Jews and pro-Zionist Christians to hold rallies, write letters to public officials, and lobby Congress and the White House to support Jewish statehood. To the extent that their efforts for Palestine also called attention to the plight of the Jews in Europe, which they usually did, it could be argued that Silver's work also increased the pressure for a U.S. response to the Holocaust. Certainly Silver's followers saw it that way.

Yet in two important respects, the campaign for Zionism did not benefit the cause of rescue. First, Silver's ascent triggered a struggle with Wise that continued for nearly two years. At one point, Wise even managed to force Silver out of the Zionist leadership for some eight months. This internal Zionist battle sapped the energies of both men and their supporters and diverted considerable attention from larger issues such as the Nazi mass murder. Second, some members of Congress who were sympathetic to rescue felt uncomfortable taking a stand on Palestine because it meant criticizing an American ally, England, in the midst of a war. For some legislators, the Bergson position of downplaying the future of Palestine and focusing on immediate rescue needs was more appealing than the mainstream Zionists' presentation of Palestine as the solution for the refugee problem.

A Jewish Leader's Mea Culpa

Amidst the fireworks over the Palestine resolution, perhaps the most remarkable speech delivered at the AJConference passed almost unnoticed. Speaking on the second day of the conference, August 30, the president of the Synagogue Council of America, Rabbi Dr. Israel Goldstein, delivered the most stinging critique to date of America's, and American Jewry's, response to the Holocaust. When one recalls Goldstein's contacts with the JTS students in connection with the Sefira campaign, the similarities between his speech at the AJConference and the *Reconstructionist* article by the rabbinical students seem to indicate that the students' arguments may have influenced Goldstein's message at the AJConference. [221]

The time had come, Dr. Goldstein declared in his address, for American Jewry to undergo a *heshbon ha-nefesh*, an examination of its behavior in responding to the slaughter of Europe's Jews.

> Let us forthwith admit that we American Jews, as a community of five millions, have not been stirred deeply enough, have not exercised ourselves passionately enough, have not risked enough our convenience and our social and civic relations, have not been ready enough to shake the bonds of so-called amicability in order to lay our troubles upon the conscience of our Christian neighbors and fellow citizens.

Only "a relatively small segment" of American Jewry had participated in fast days or demonstrations, Goldstein said. "The American Jewish community as a whole has not been convulsed by the unprecedented tragedy which has fallen upon the Jews of Europe." He said the pogrom in the Russian city of Kishinev in 1903, in which 47 Jews were killed, "shook American Jewry more profoundly than the mass-murder of a million Jews in 1943." The sense of kinship between "too many American Jews" and the rest of the Jewish people "is so thin and so pusillanimous that the agony of their people instead of agonizing them into seething, restless, even reckless activity, merely saddens them. We have lamented, we have protested, but we have not sufficiently exercised ourselves."

Dr. Goldstein then launched into an extensive and unusually forthright critique of the Allies' response to the Holocaust. "The moral tragedy of our times," he said, is that "the Christian nations... lack the forthrightness and moral courage to embrace the Jewish people as their ally in the same measure as Hitler hounds the Jewish people as his foe." This "lack of moral consistency" means that "Great Britain and the United States, on the eve of their military victory, are threatened with a moral defeat."

When Allied officials in 1941 claimed that rescue of the Jews was possible only through military victory over the Nazis, "such statements might have been regarded by a generous stretch of the imagination as being naively mistaken," Goldstein said.

> Today, however, after all that has happened, the calculated murder of nearly three million Jews and the calculated Nazi

plan to exterminate before the end of the war the remaining two million Jews at their disposal, today reluctance on the part of the leaders of the democracies to employ special measures to save the remnants of a people uniquely marked for extermination, cannot be permitted to pass unchallenged even if it means that we must criticize friends in high places....It is a stark fact that unless special and drastic measures of rescue are undertaken immediately, the victory of the United Nations will come too late to do the Jews in Nazi hands any good. They will all be dead.

Goldstein blasted the "piddling ineffectiveness at Bermuda and since Bermuda." He chastised the State Department for its "self-exonerating references to the numbers of refugees who have been accommodated on our shores since 1933... as if a single additional Jewish life can be saved thereby." It was reasonable, he said, to tell the U.S. administration: "If millions of American citizens were trapped in the Nazi charnel-houses, you would find a way to rescue large numbers and without delay."

> The will to undertake a bold, great program of rescue is lacking. [Jews are offered only] a resolution of sympathy every now and then, a thread of assistance every now and then, a little help here and there, a bagatelizing, temporizing, compromising program, instead of a great passionate, moral urge to say to the doomed Jews of Europe, "To you, whom we welcome as our natural allies, who have been the first of Hitler's victims and have borne such lacerations as no other people has borne, to you we say with all our hearts, 'Wherever there is room and most of all in your mother land of Eretz Israel, let the hounded of your people find rest, respite and salvation.'"

The Synagogue Council president then outlined six steps to facilitate rescue: warnings to the Axis of postwar punishment for war crimes, and the immediate creation of a tribunal to investigate war crimes; food shipments to the Jews in the ghettoes; contacts with leaders of Nazi satellite countries to arrange the emigration of their Jewish residents; pressure on neutral countries in Europe to provide "temporary asylum" to refugees; opening Allied countries to refugee immigration; and annulment of the "illegal and immoral" British

White Paper, which "is, in effect, a death warrant for hundreds of thousands of Jews."

But few were listening. With all eyes focused on Abba Hillel Silver's triumph at the conference and the AJCommittee's withdrawal, Goldstein's remarks eluded the notice of both the news media at the time and historians in later years.

A New Battlefield

The conclusion of the American Jewish Conference, on September 2, marked the end of one critical period in the history of American Jewry's response to the Holocaust, and the start of another. During the nine months from December 1942 through September 1943, rescue advocates focused heavily on raising public awareness. They had no alternative, for when the Bergson Group and the JTS students first appeared on the scene, at the end of 1942, much of the American public knew little about the fate of Europe's Jews, and a significant portion of the American Jewish community exhibited limited interest at best. The Bergson Group's "We Will Never Die" pageant, torrent of newspaper ads, and Emergency Conference to Save the Jewish People of Europe sought to enlighten the American public; the JTS students' Inter-Seminary Conference and Sefira campaign targeted American Jewry and, to a lesser extent, America's churches.

These efforts to influence public opinion provided the crucial underpinnings for what would follow. With the rescue issue at last gaining widespread attention and sympathy, the activists were able to shift their focus to the nation's capitol. The support of American Jewry and American public opinion provided the backbone for the second, and most crucial phase of the rescue campaign: the effort to change U.S. refugee policy.

Now the Bergson Group occupied center stage by itself, and the JTS activists moved to the sidelines. The rabbinical students did what they were capable of doing, and they did it at the time it was most needed. "We were not in a position to lobby Congress or meet with senior government officials," Noah Golinkin recalled. "That was the Bergson Group's role. We felt as if we did what we could."[222] Unexpectedly, however, another Golinkin was about to step into the limelight, however briefly.

The rabbis coming out of Union Station at the beginning of the march.

The Day the Rabbis Marched

"Clear the way for those rabbis!"[223]

That was the first, and probably last, time those words were heard from the Station Master at Washington, D.C.'s central railway hub, Union Station. The crowd before him was unlike any that had ever been seen in the central train station of the nation's capitol. The date was October 6, 1943, three days before Yom Kippur, and more than four hundred rabbis had come to plead for U.S. government action to save Jews from Hitler.[224]

There had never before been a "march on Washington" by American Jews. Other interest groups had staged marches or protest rallies in front of the White House or elsewhere in the nation's capital, but American Jewish organizations had never felt sufficiently passionate about an issue, or sufficiently secure of their place in American society, or sufficiently convinced that it was politically necessary, to do so. As we have seen, the steady stream of reports about the mass killings and the failure of the Allies to intervene prodded some Jewish activists, in April 1943, to begin thinking of Washington as the site for a protest. The JTS students urged the Joint Emergency Committee for European Jewish Affairs to hold what they called "a March on Washington," consisting of Jews and Christians from around the country converging on the nation's capitol for a day of lobbying members of Congress for rescue action.[225] In a similar spirit, Nahum Goldmann had urged the JEC at its April 18 meeting to sponsor a mass meeting in Washington of "1,000 to 2,000 representatives of all Jewish organizations, to publicize the refusal of the Allies to have our large program discussed at the Bermuda Conference." At the same meeting, United Palestine Appeal director Henry Montor proposed mobilizing groups of Jews from around the country to come to Washington to lobby Congress and a U.S. Labor Zionist official made a similar suggestion at the JEC's August meeting.[226]

By the autumn of 1943, the Bergsonites were convinced that as long as refugee policy remained exclusively in the hands of the State Department, there was little chance of saving more than a token handful of Jews. That led them to the idea of seeking the creation of a new government agency whose sole purpose would be to rescue refugees. Since this demand directly conflicted with the Roosevelt administration's concept of "rescue through victory," the administration was certain to oppose it. The only possibility of advancing the proposal was to mobilize congressional and public support. Fowler Harper, a solicitor general in the Interior Department who was active in the Bergson Group, drafted a congressional resolution urging the president to establish a rescue agency. To keep the issue in the public eye and demonstrate to Congress that rescue was a matter of intense concern in the Jewish community, the Bergsonites decided to stage a march to the White House, by rabbis, to be held three days before the holiest day on the Jewish calendar, Yom Kippur.

Rabbi Mordechai Ya'akov Golinkin

Bergson's friendly contacts with leaders of the Va'ad ha-Hatzala, the New York City-based Orthodox rescue group, made it possible to enlist the Va'ad to handle the actual legwork of recruiting participants. Most of the rabbis who took part in the protest were from the New York area, but others came from Philadelphia and Baltimore, and some from as far away as Chicago, Cleveland, Cincinnati, Pittsburgh, Columbus, and Connecticut. From Worcester, Massa-

Two of the marchers. At left is Rabbi Avraham Kalmanovitz.

chusetts, came Rabbi Mordechai Ya'akov Golinkin, father of JTS student activist Noah Golinkin. Traveling to Washington by train in 1943 was quite a time-consuming task for those coming from New York, as most of the participants were; even more so for those coming from more distant locales such as Worcester. To do so in such close proximity to Yom Kippur, when the typical congregational rabbi ordinarily would have been consumed with preparations for the holiday, was all the more arduous.

The marchers included some of the most prominent rabbinical figures in the American Jewish community, such as Rabbis Eliezer Silver and Israel Rosenberg, co-presidents of the Union of Orthodox Rabbis; Rabbi Solomon Friedman, president of the Union of Grand Rabbis; Rabbi Bernard Dov Leventhal, known both as the Chief Rabbi of Philadelphia and one of the leaders of the Orthodox rabbinate nationwide; and two younger scholars soon to become the leading halachic figures in America: Rabbi Moshe Feinstein and Rabbi Joseph B. Soloveitchik.[227]

According to an internal Bergson group document, some Jewish Congressmen, led by Rep. Sol Bloom (D-NY, who had been a U.S. delegate to the Bermuda conference), "had done all they could to dissuade the Rabbis from making their bearded appearances in Washington. At a certain moment they almost succeeded [in dissuading the rabbis] but Mr. Bloom spoiled the soup by telling one of the Rabbis, as an additional inducement for not going, that it would be very undignified for a group of such un-American looking people to appear in Washington. This created a lot of resentment and in the end instead of 250 Rabbis on whom we counted, we had to cope with 400."[228]

On the steps of the Capitol, Rabbi Eliezer Silver reads the marchers' petition aloud. Vice President Henry Wallace is at left.

The rabbis, most of them wearing long black coats and black hats, marched from Union Station to the Capitol, accompanied by marshals provided by the Jewish War Veterans of America. They were met on the steps of the Capitol by members of Congress and Vice President Henry Wallace, who, *Time* reported, "squirmed through a diplomatically minimum answer" to their plea. Wallace's vague statement expressed "grief" at the plight of the Jews but made no reference to the possibility of rescuing any of them. Two of the marchers then read aloud from the group's petition: "Millions have already fallen dead, sentenced to fire and sword, and tens of thousands have died of starvation... [H]ow can we stand up to pray on the holy day of Yom Kippur, knowing that we haven't fulfilled our responsibility? So we have come, brokenhearted, on the eve of our holiest day, to ask you,

The rabbis in front of the Lincoln Memorial.

our honorable President Franklin Roosevelt... to form a special agency to rescue the remainder of the Jewish nation in Europe."[229]

The protesters proceeded to the Lincoln Memorial, where they recited prayers and sang the national anthem, then marched to the gates of the White House, expecting a small delegation would be granted a meeting with President Roosevelt. Instead, to their surprise and disappointment, they were met by presidential secretary Marvin McIntyre, who told them the president was unavailable "because of the pressure of other business." Actually, the president's schedule was remarkably open that afternoon, but rather than meet with the leaders of the march, Roosevelt departed the White House through a rear exit.

The real reason FDR declined to meet the rabbis was that he had been urged to avoid them by Samuel Rosenman, who was embarrassed by the protesters and feared the march might provoke antisemitism. In his diary, presidential aide William D. Hassett noted that Rosenman told the president on the morning of the march that "the group behind this petition [is] not representative of the most thoughtful elements in Jewry. Judge Rosenman said he had tried – admittedly without success – to keep the horde from storming Washington. Said the leading Jews of his acquaintance opposed this march on the Capitol."[230] Wise publicly condemned "the orthodox rabbinical parade" as a "painful and even lamentable exhibition." He derided the organizers as "stuntists" and accused them of offending "the dignity of [the Jewish] people."[231]

If the president thought he could avoid this controversy by avoiding the rabbis, he was mistaken. The next day's newspapers told the story. "Rabbis Report 'Cold Welcome' at the White House," declared the headline of a report in the *Washington Times-Herald*. A columnist for one Jewish newspaper angrily asked: "Would a similar delegation of 500 Catholic priests have been thus treated?" The editors of another Jewish newspaper, the Yiddish daily *Forverts* (Forward), reported that the episode had affected the president's previously-high level of support in the Jewish com-

Samuel Rosenman

munity: "In open comment it is voiced that Roosevelt has betrayed the Jews."[232]

Rabbi Mordechai Ya'akov Golinkin and his fellow-protesters left Washington that day believing that since they were not granted an audience with the president, their mission to the nation's capitol had been a failure. As a result, in the years to follow, virtually none of the rabbis who participated found occasion to discuss the march in public. In many instances, they did not even mention it to their own children or grandchildren. Although not in any way regretting they had taken part, they saw it as unworthy of mention because, they believed, it had achieved nothing. [233]

The Struggle for Rescue Reaches the Halls of Congress

The rabbis' march actually achieved a great deal. The Bergson Group's intention in staging the protest was to attract media attention and make an impression on prominent members of Congress. This would make the idea of a rescue agency the subject of discussion in Washington circles and help generate sympathy on Capitol Hill. The march accomplished both aims. Within weeks, Representatives Will Rogers (D-CA), Joseph Baldwin (R-NY) and Sen. Guy Gillette (D-Iowa) introduced a resolution authored by the Bergsonites, urging the president to create a rescue agency.[234]

Rep. Sol Bloom, chairman of the House Committee on Foreign Affairs, tried to stall the resolution by insisting that it be the subject of hearings, a process normally reserved for legislation, not a resolution, which was only a recommendation. Bloom, a staunch supporter of the administration's refugee policy, regarded the Gillette-Rogers resolution as a personal slap in the face. To support the resolution, Rogers called as witnesses such prominent personalities as New York City Mayor Fiorello La Guardia. Bloom countered with Rabbi Stephen Wise, who asserted in his testimony that the resolution was "inadequate" because it made no reference to settling refugees in Palestine. Bergson and Rogers had deliberately omitted Palestine because some members of Congress would not support a resolution challenging British policy in Palestine. "I understand that there are differences of opinion in Jewish circles," a frustrated Rogers wrote to Wise and other Jewish leaders afterwards. "But sincerely, gentlemen, those differences should be forgotten when a case of rescue is concerned."[235]

Wise's opposition was not just a matter of a difference of opinion. It was also a reflection of Wise's fear that he was being usurped. Wise felt strongly that he was best qualified to lead refugee advocacy and strongly resented the Bergson Group's effort to, in effect, assume the leadership of the rescue campaign. Indeed, at the same time Wise was opposing the Gillette-Rogers resolution, he was tightening his control over rescue policy within the Jewish community. Alarmed by the forceful proposals made by delegates to the Joint Emergency Committee, Wise brought his ally, the Hadassah organization, into the JEC in order to create a majority to shut down the JEC altogether. In early November, by a vote of five to four, the JEC dissolved itself and turned over its functions to the Wise-dominated American Jewish Conference, which at the end of its inaugural event had transformed itself into a permanent organization.[236]

In the end, a blunder by Rep. Bloom and Assistant Secretary of State Breckinridge Long spoiled the administration's strategy for blocking the resolution. On November 26, testifying before the Foreign Affairs committee as to why a separate rescue agency was unnecessary, Long declared: "[W]e have taken into this country since the beginning of the Hitler regime and the persecution of the Jews, until today, approximately 580,000 refugees."[237] Long's testimony was given behind closed doors, but wavering congressmen subsequently asked him to release it publicly, because they believed it would justify their decision to shelve the Gillette-Rogers resolution. Long, with Bloom's support, agreed. Long's statistics made the front page of the *New York Times* on December 11, 1943[238] and seemed to sway key members of Congress – until, a few days later, his figures were exposed as false. The actual number of refugees admitted was not more than 250,000, and many of them were not Jews. Long's errors set off a firestorm of criticism from the media, mainstream Jewish organizations and members of Congress.[239] The controversy deeply embarrassed the administration and provided additional momentum to the campaign for U.S. rescue action.

Blowing the Whistle

While the battle over rescue was raging in the halls of Congress, an equally momentous struggle was underway behind the scenes at the Treasury and State departments. Aides to Treasury Secretary

Morgenthau discovered that senior State Department officials had been deliberately obstructing opportunities to rescue Jewish refugees, blocking the transmission of Holocaust-related information from Europe to the United States, and trying to cover up evidence of their actions. State Department officials took these steps because they feared the rescue of large numbers of Jews would put pressure on the United States to open its doors to them. As one official privately explained: "There was always the danger that the German government might agree to turn over to the United States and to Great Britain a large number of Jewish refugees. In the event of our admission of inability to take care of these people, the onus for their continued persecution would have been largely transferred from the German government to the Allied nations."[240]

On Christmas Day, 1943, Morgenthau aide Josiah E. DuBois, Jr. composed an 18-page report which he titled "Report to the Secretary on the Acquiescence of This Government in the Murder of the Jews." In careful, detailed, lawyerly language, DuBois exposed the State Department's record of obstruction. The report's searing conclusion: State Department officials "have been guilty not only of gross procrastination and willful failure to act, but even of willful attempts to prevent action from being taken to rescue Jews from Hitler... Unless remedial steps of a drastic nature are taken, and taken immediately... to prevent the complete extermination of the Jews [in Hitler's Europe], this Government will have to share for all time responsibility for this extermination." DuBois pressed Morgenthau to bring the matter directly to the president, and warned the Treasury Secretary that if he did not act, DuBois would resign in protest and publicly expose the scandal.[241]

All this took place just as the controversy over Breckinridge Long's testimony was exploding on Capitol Hill and the rescue resolution was advancing in the Senate. In late December, the Senate Foreign Relations Committee, under the acting chairmanship of Senator Elbert Thomas of Utah – a staunch Bergson supporter – unanimously adopted the Gillette-Rogers resolution. "It is not a Jewish problem alone," the Senators wrote in the preamble to the resolution. "It is a Christian problem and a problem for enlightened civilization. We have talked; we have sympathized; we have expressed our horror; the time to act is long past due."[242] It was precisely this concept – that everyone, not just Jews, should be concerned about the mass murder – that had guided the Bergson Group, as well as the JTS students, throughout their campaigns for rescue.

Surveying the political landscape as 1944 began, Morgenthau could easily see that attitudes toward the Jewish refugees had changed drastically during the past year. A public that had been almost completely indifferent to the persecution of Europe's Jews was now increasingly sympathetic to their plight. A congress known as a bastion of anti-immigration and anti-foreign sentiment was embracing the cause of rescue. A Jewish community that was intimidated and divided was now aroused and pressing for U.S. intervention on behalf of European Jewry. Morgenthau understood that this was the moment to push forward. The pressure in Congress and the shift in public opinion, he told his aides, gave him the leverage he needed to convince the president that "you have either got to move very fast, or the Congress of the United States will do it for you." With election day just ten months away, the last thing the president wanted was a public scandal over the refugee issue. On January 16, 1944, Morgenthau presented FDR with an abbreviated version of the DuBois report and a proposal to establish a government rescue agency. Within days, Roosevelt issued an executive order creating the War Refugee Board.[243]

U.S. Intervention, at Long Last

Josiah DuBois was named General Counsel of the War Refugee Board, and his Treasury colleague John Pehle became its Executive Director. Despite receiving little government funding, they and their small but dedicated staff advanced the cause of rescue with determination and creativity. They energetically employed unorthodox means of rescue, including bribery of border officials and the production of forged identification papers and other documents to protect refugees from the Nazis. The WRB's agents saved the lives of 48,000 Jews by arranging for them to be moved from Transnistria, where they would have been in the path of the retreating German army, to safe areas in Romania. About 15,000 Jewish refugees, and about 20,000 non-Jewish refugees, were evacuated from Axis-occupied territory, and at least 10,000 more were protected through various WRB-sponsored activities. The Board orchestrated a series of condemnations and threats from the U.S., the Vatican, and other world leaders against the Hungarian government to bring an end to the deportation of Hungarian Jews to Auschwitz. The Board arranged for the sheltering of Jews in places such as Budapest, where Swedish diplomat Raoul Wallenberg saved lives with the funds and assistance of the board. It also persuaded Roosevelt to admit one token group of 982 refugees outside the quota system–"a bargain-counter flourish in humanitarianism," the journalist I. F. Stone called it. Historians estimate that the War Refugee Board's efforts played a major role in saving about 200,000 Jews and 20,000 non-Jews during the last fifteen months of the war. The board's work demolished the Roosevelt administration's long-standing claim that there was no way to rescue Jews except by winning the war.[244]

Chapter 4

EPILOGUE

Noah Golinkin in the 1950s.

Noah Golinkin was the first of the JTS student activists to graduate, in June 1944. He held pulpits in Nebraska, Pennsylvania, and Connecticut, before becoming spiritual leader of the Arlington-Fairfax Jewish Center in Virginia in 1950. One year later, he married Devorah (Dolly) Perlberg who became his partner for over fifty years. Golinkin later founded the Board of Jewish Education of the Jewish Community Council of Greater Washington, D.C., and served as its director from 1965 to 1970. Then he moved to

Knoxville, Tennessee for eight more years as rabbi of the Heska Emunah synagogue, before assuming his final pulpit, Beth Shalom Congregation in Columbia, Maryland, from 1978 until his retirement in 1986.

A spirit of activism permeated Golinkin's career. He took part in numerous civil rights marches, including one in which he was seated on the podium next to the Rev. Martin Luther King, Jr. He lobbied energetically for the integration of the Arlington school system and for fair housing in Arlington and Washington, D.C. An early activist for Soviet Jewry, he was one of the initiators of the daily protest vigil across from the Soviet Embassy in Washington D.C., which was held from 1970 to 1991. Golinkin once led the cast of a local production of "Fiddler on the Roof" on a march for Soviet Jewry through the streets of Knoxville. Golinkin was also the originator, in 1989, of the custom, still observed by a number of synagogues and Jewish organizations, to plant yellow tulips on Holocaust Remembrance Day as a reminder of the yellow star that Jews were forced by the Nazis to wear on their clothing, and of Dutch Christians who helped saved Jews.[245]

During the final decades of his life, Golinkin devoted himself to the spread of Hebrew literacy. Fearing that the Hebrew language would become, as he put it, "as little known to American Jews as Latin is to most Catholics," Golinkin created the Hebrew Literacy Campaign in 1963. In twelve weeks, every adult in his synagogue in Arlington could read the prayer book, a feat which earned his synagogue the Conservative movement's Solomon Schechter Award. In 1978, Golinkin founded the Hebrew Literacy Program in cooperation with the Federation of Jewish Men's Clubs. In 1986, Golinkin initiated the Hebrew Reading Marathons which taught adults how read Hebrew in one day. He and Devorah personally taught over 150 marathons throughout North America. Golinkin authored three textbooks – *Shalom Aleichem, Ayn Keloheynu* and *While Standing on One Foot* – that enabled adults to learn how to read Hebrew in twelve sessions or in one day. Between 1978 and 2010, approximately 200,000 adults learned to read Hebrew using his textbooks. Rabbi Noah Golinkin passed away on 25 I Adar 5763 (February 27, 2003).

Jerry Lipnick (left) with his brother Bernie and wife Joan
in Minneapolis, around 1962.

Jerry Lipnick graduated from the seminary a year later than Noah Golinkin, in 1945. He accepted a one-year position at Congregation Beth Shalom in Wilmington, Delaware, followed by another one-year post at Congregation Beth Jeshurun, in Houston, in both instances replacing rabbis who were called to serve abroad as army chaplains. In the autumn of 1946, Lipnick was offered his own pulpit, Congregation Beth El in Utica, NY, where he and his wife, Joan, would remain for fourteen years. He subsequently served, for briefer periods, as spiritual leader of Adath Jeshurun, in Minneapolis, and the Jacksonville (FL) Jewish Center. From 1969 to 1976, Lipnick was director of education for the B'nai B'rith Youth Organization in Washington, D.C., overlapping briefly with Noah Golinkin's years in Washington before Golinkin moved to Tennessee.

Lipnick's days as a youthful student activist of the 1940s were often echoed in his rabbinical career. In Utica, for example, he responded to local government corruption by co-founding the Citizens Association of Greater Utica and chairing its Law Enforcement Committee. "A rabbi, priest or minister who on occasion rolls up his sleeves and bares his muscles, is an inspiring sight to see," the *Utica Daily Press* editorialized upon the Lipnicks' departure from the community. "Rabbi Lipnick is this sort of man and we are sorry to lose him. Minneapolis may also have civic feet of clay and the good people out there will find him a willing ally if they need him in the constant struggle against evil, crime, yes sin and worst of all, apathy."[246]

In Minneapolis in the early 1960s, Lipnick was outspoken in support of black civil rights, traveling twice to Hattiesburg, Mississippi to take part in civil rights protests and participating in Minnesota's delegation to the October 1963 March on Washington. As a symbol of mourning for the deaths of four black children killed in the bombing of a church in Alabama, Lipnick and other civil rights activists wore a black ribbon on their lapels for thirty days. In a memorable sermon quoted elsewhere in this volume, he noted the poignant connection between that ribbon and the JTS students' ribbon of 1943.

During his years in Washington, Lipnick was an active participant in the vigil at the Soviet Embassy. "He made it a religious duty to be there every day," his old classmate Rabbi Wilfred Shuchat later recalled. "Even during the months of his illness [related to the rheumatic fever he suffered as a child], when mobility was difficult for him, he made superhuman efforts to make an appearance at the vigil as often as possible." This, Shuchat said, was typical of Lipnick's "radical concern for his fellow man," a sentiment born of his anguish over American Jewry's inadequate response to the Holocaust. "It was this hurt that was the great motivation for his participation, selflessly, in all areas of social action and concern."[247] Jerry Lipnick passed away on 25 Adar 5737 (March 15, 1977), at age 59.

Moshe "Buddy" Sachs holding his first great-granddaughter
in Jerusalem in 2006.

Buddy Sachs likewise applied his activist spirit and experience during his subsequent career. His first pulpit, as a student rabbi, was Oheb Zedeck Congregation, in Pottsville, Pennsylvania, a position he secured thanks in part to an effusive letter of recommendation from JTS registrar Prof. Moshe Davis, who cited Sachs's "extra-curricular work in conjunction with the Committee for European Jews" and co-authorship of the essay in *The Reconstructionist* as evidence that Sachs "has been one of our most active and sincere students that we have had in many years." One of the first projects he initiated at Oheb Zedeck, in September 1943, was a memorial service for European Jewry. "We solemnly pledge to do all possible to save those who can still be saved," Sachs's script for the program declared. "Let Jewry refuse to be silent and comforted in this crisis. Let not its mourning pass until the day of redemption of our people throughout the world."[248]

Upon graduating from JTS in 1945, Sachs enlisted in the army as a chaplain, where he was stationed in Okinawa. He was also stationed for a time in the Philippines, where he was able to assist Jewish refugees who had fled there from the Nazis. (In defiance of the State Department, the U.S. High Commissioner for the Philippines, Paul

McNutt, arranged for the admission of some 2,000 European Jews during 1938-1939.)[249]

Sachs was a devoted Zionist, and as a teenager had been active in the Labor Zionist youth movement Habonim-Gordonia in his native Baltimore. In 1947, he and his wife Frances traveled to British Mandatory Palestine, where he enrolled in a Hebrew University doctoral program in Jewish Thought with the famed philosopher Martin Buber. At the same time, he and Frances enlisted in the Haganah, the largest Jewish underground militia in Palestine. During the 1948 Arab siege of Jerusalem, Sachs, still officially on duty as a U.S. army chaplain, organized a Passover seder for American servicemen in the city's Talpiot neighborhood, led by future Nobel Laureate S. Y. Agnon. Sachs jokingly told the participants that theft of the afikoman "would be punishable by court martial."[250]

Returning to the United States in 1949, Sachs held several rabbinical positions in Illinois before settling in as the spiritual leader of the St. Louis Park congregation, in Minneapolis, Minnesota, from 1956 to 1974, during five of which years he was just down the street from his old friend Jerry Lipnick. An innovative program that Sachs designed for teenagers to teach younger children how to read from the Torah is still widely used in synagogues in Minnesota. An activist spirit guided Sachs throughout his life as it did the lives of his JTS comrades. In the 1960s, he traveled to Birmingham, Alabama, to join the Rev. Martin Luther King, Jr. in civil rights marches. Sachs founded the Minnesota Soviet Jewry Committee, which was instrumental in persuading U.S. Senators Hubert Humphrey and Walter Mondale to take an active interest in the plight of Soviet Jewry. In 1974, at the University of Minnesota, Sachs finally completed a Ph.D. in Psychology.

The Sachses then settled in Israel, where he worked first in the development town of Beit Shean with juvenile delinquents, and later as a private therapist. Sachs's letters from Jerusalem in 1947-49 were later published as a book, *Under Siege and After*, and transcripts of his 1970s telephone conversations with Jews in the Soviet Union were published in a volume entitled *Brave Jews*.[251] He passed away in Jerusalem on 11 Av 5769 (August 1, 2009).

The JTS Activists, American Jewry, and the Holocaust

The American Jewish community was psychologically unprepared for the Hitler persecutions, and its leaders did not easily rise to the new challenge. Many precedents existed for seeking U.S. intervention on behalf of Jews mistreated abroad, but American Jews had never faced anything remotely resembling the barbarism of the Nazis, nor had they ever needed to do so in the midst of an economic depression and widespread isolationism and nativism. Jewish fears of provoking antisemitism further contributed to the American Jewish failure of will. During the 1930s, leaders of major Jewish organizations hesitated to press their demands lest they be accused of dragging America into war; during the 1940s, when America was in the war, they feared antisemites would accuse them of undermining the war effort. In the case of Stephen Wise, his passionate attachment to President Roosevelt's policies sometimes clouded his political judgment and inhibited a vigorous response to the Nazi genocide. Jewish leaders genuinely agonized over the suffering of European Jewry, yet many of them found it difficult to shake off business-as-usual attitudes and modes of political action that were more suited to an earlier era. Moreover, they were often unable to rise above religious, political, and personal rivalries. These conflicts sapped the Jewish leaders' energies and undermined their effectiveness in the public arena. The periodic flare-up of grassroots dissatisfaction and dissident activism, such as that of the JTS students, offers a glimpse of what might have been had the mainstream Jewish leaders been able to think outside the box.

The JTS student activists did not have the numbers or resources to directly influence American public opinion or U.S. foreign policy. The Bergson Group, with its full-page newspaper advertisements, high-impact lobbying in Washington, and dramatic public protests, filled that role. What the students did possess was creativity, passion, and determination, and they used those qualities among the constituencies they knew best, American Jewry and religious seminarians. They showed their creativity by organizing the Inter-Seminary conference. They demonstrated their passion in the emotionally compelling articles and letters they composed. They exhibited their determination by pressing Jewish leaders until one major organization, the Synagogue Council of America, heeded their pleas. Once the resources of the Synagogue Council were at their disposal, the students were able to reach a vast audience and thereby help influence American Jewish opinion and, to a lesser extent, American Christian opinion as well.

The JTS students' timing also played an important role in their achievements. When no forceful response from the mainstream Jewish leadership followed the confirmation that systematic mass murder was underway, a vacuum was created. The JTS students strove to fill that vacuum during the crucial period between December 1942 and August 1943. Grassroots dissatisfaction with the Jewish organizations' response to the crisis was beginning to manifest itself, especially in the Jewish press. Jewish public opinion was already beginning to shift in the direction that the JTS students wanted to see it go. Their efforts accelerated that shift and supplemented the Bergson Group's efforts to make the rescue issue a high priority on the Jewish agenda. Keeping it atop the Jewish agenda in turn helped make it an issue of greater concern to the American public at large and to policy makers in Washington.

Tiny in number, but persistent and imaginative, the students demonstrated that it was possible, even without funds, office, or a staff, to make a real difference in the shaping of American Jewry's response to the Holocaust.

REFLECTIONS ON
THREE REMARKABLE STUDENTS

Remarks delivered at the sixth national conference of
The David S. Wyman Institute for Holocaust Studies,
Fordham University School of Law,
New York City, September 21, 2008

A STORY THAT MUST BE TOLD

Prof. David G. Roskies

Until late November 1942, most people who lived outside Nazi-occupied Europe and were concerned about the fate of the Jews were in agreement that the only way to save the Jews within Nazi territory was the win the war. Then suddenly the secret was out: Hitler was waging another war, which he was coming perilously close to winning – the Final Solution.

"Never Again!" was the defiant response given by Rabbi Stephen S. Wise when he published a symposium in January 1943, subtitled "Ten Years of Hitler". Like other symposia, this one too was an imagined community of disparate people making common cause. Among those who made their voices heard was the novelist Fanny Hurst, who lamented this "bloody anniversary," while the Unitarian minister and antiwar activist John Haynes Holmes spoke of "the darkest decade." Seven months later, the Institute of Jewish Affairs, the scholarly arm of the American Jewish Congress, published a booklet entitled *Hitler's Ten-Year War on the Jews*. It was filled with factual reports, arranged region by region, and concluding with terrifying statistical summaries. Table III gave the final tally of Jews who had already died "by extermination" in Nazi-occupied Europe as 3,030,050. A second printing came out in September, 1943.

Beginning in late November 1942, small groups were formed in Mandatory Palestine, Great Britain, and the United States, whose sole purpose was to mobilize public opinion on behalf of the remaining Jews of Europe.

In Palestine, they enlisted as their *cri-de-guerre* the Psalmist's appeal to God (Ps. 83:2): *Al domi!* Do not be silent! In Great Britain they called themselves The Screamers. In the United States, the Committee for a Jewish Army of Stateless and Palestinian Jews changed its name as it changed its mission, henceforth to be known as the Emergency Committee to Save the Jewish People of Europe. Insiders still knew them as the Bergson Group. And finally, at the Jewish Theological Seminary of America, never known for its political activism, there appeared a European Committee of the Student Body.

Signing himself "R.B.," the initials of Rabbi Binyamin, the Hebrew writer Yehoshua Redler-Feldman issued this proclamation on December 17, 1942:

"To All,

"The 'Do Not Be Silent' Group in Jerusalem wishes hereby to inform you that it has begun activities of various kinds; if, for all the hesitations and doubts, there is one chance in a thousand, in ten thousand, to rescue those who are condemned to death, we must use all means at our disposal. Jews of every stripe and in every locale! Organize yourselves at once into active cells! Let us not lose a precious moment in overly cautious delays! We are dispatching messengers and information wherever they are needed."

The Screamers were led by the Hungarian-born journalist and novelist Arthur Koestler. "We, the screamers," he wrote in the *New York Times Magazine*, "have been at it now for about ten years." Comparing himself to the Biblical prophets Amos, Hosea, and Jeremiah, Koestler sought a psychological explanation for his failure to bridge the gap between "knowing" and "believing," between the "tragic plane" of history and the "trivial plane" of everyday life, or between what I would call wartime and Jewtime. He titled his trenchant essay "On Disbelieving Atrocities."

The master of outrage was the Hollywood scriptwriter, Broadway playwright, and man-about-town, Ben Hecht. After months of back-room politics aimed at blocking its publication, Hecht's global indictment finally appeared as a display ad in the *New York Times* on September 14, 1943. Billed as a "Ballad of the Doomed Jews of Europe" and written in doggerel, the last stanza read:

> Oh world be patient
> it will take
> some time before the murder crews
> Are done. By Christmas you can make
> Your Peace on Earth / without the Jews.

Twenty-nine year-old Noah Golinkin, who arrived here from Vilna in 1938, was the driving force behind the "European Committee" that organized itself at the Rabbinical School of JTS. Together with his classmates Jerome Lipnick and Moshe Sachs, they issued a manifesto, "Retribution Is Not Enough," which was published with editorial endorsement in *The Reconstructionist* on March 5, 1943.

What did these four groups have in common?

Each was organized by refugees and recent arrivals.

Each group understood that extraordinary times demanded extraordinary measures. It exploited the mass media, especially radio broadcasts, and the free press; organized public fasts and days of mourning, mass rallies, and protest pageants; and most important, forged new alliances. Inreach was insufficient; to effect change, it was incumbent upon the Jews to reach out to the Gentiles.

In short, each group did battle against apathy, business-as-usual, and disbelief.

The war on the Jews, as the American Jewish Congress had been the first to call it, required of the Jews a commensurate response, however numbing the numbers, however great the geographical divide, however insurmountable the psychological barrier.

As we listen to the presentations this afternoon, we should be listening with two sets of ears:

– Listening for the plot: the main and secondary characters; the ups and downs; the chronology.

– The deep structure; the big picture.

Here are three questions we might want to keep in mind:

First: how is this a quintessentially American story? How did these three twenty-something rabbinical students change the way that American Jewry conducted its business in the public arena? How does this represent a paradigm shift from everything that came before in American Jewish history?

Second, what were the obstacles that had to be overcome in that time and in a world that was divided between the free zone and the Jew zone? And finally this question: What are the obstacles that we face even today in making this proud chapter a part of our historical narrative? Why has it taken so long for this story to be heard?

Let me speak for myself. I have been teaching at JTS for 33 years. As an outsider to JTS, I always kept my ears open and was quick to absorb the culture of the institution. JTS has a very rich folklore. If you have lunch with Rabbi Morty Leifman, you can hear much of it from a living font of institutional memory. In 33 years, I never heard any mention of the JTS student initiative. Were it not for Rafael Medoff's pathbreaking essay published in *Holocaust and Genocide Studies* in 1997, I would not have known the story and would not be here today chairing this session.

What is it about this story that challenges our preconceptions?

Even as we look back to commemorate and celebrate this remarkable initiative, we might ask ourselves: Is there not a blind spot in our perfect hindsight? Is there not a dark side to this story that we are unwilling to confront?

WHY NOAH GOLINKIN FOUGHT
TO SAVE THE JEWS OF EUROPE

Rabbi Prof. David Golinkin

My father Rabbi Noah Golinkin z"l (1913-2003) lived a long and very productive life.[252] In my remarks today, I would like to answer one important question: Between late November 1942 and August of 1943 my father – together with his two good friends Jerry Lipnick z"l and Moshe (Buddy) Sachs [z"l] – spent most of his time fighting to save the Jews of Europe. But why? Why would a refugee who had just arrived in the United States in June 1938 decide to arouse Jewish and Christian pressure on FDR and the State Department to save the remaining Jews in Europe? Wouldn't it have been easier to learn English, get married, and get settled in America before "taking on" the government of the United States in a mass campaign which had never been done before by a Jewish organization?

At first glance, one could reply that my father and his two friends were simply fulfilling a number of basic *mitzvot* and teachings about helping fellow-Jews who are in danger. However, this would not really answer the question. After all, *all* rabbis and Jewish leaders in the United States in 1942-1943 were familiar with these basic Jewish teachings, yet most did little or nothing to save the Jews of Europe from death.

Therefore, I would like to suggest four reasons why my father, Rabbi Noah Golinkin z"l, devoted his heart and soul to the rescue of European Jewry in 1942-1943:

First, he was following in the footsteps of *his* father Rabbi Mordechai Ya'akov Golinkin z"l (1884-1974). My Zeyde, in addition to being a rabbi, a *talmid hakham* and an *Av Bet Din*, was also an activist who was willing to roll up his sleeves on numerous occasions in order to save lives, teach Judaism and Zionism, obtain kosher meat, or defend the rights of non-Jews.

In 1913, he became the *Av Bet Din* and de facto Chief Rabbi of Zhitomir, capital of the Volyn (Volhynia) district of the Ukraine, where he presided over the rabbinic court, delivered sermons every Shabbat afternoon, and developed a youth organization called *Tiferet Bahurim* for 1200 young men. He also developed a good relationship with the Governor of Volyn. As a result, he was able to persuade the governor to exempt from the Russian draft the yeshiva students of Novaradok who had fled to Zhitomir, and he also prevented a blood libel in Zhitomir at the time of the Beiliss blood libel in Kiev in the fall of 1913.

After the February 1917 revolution, my grandfather, together with Rabbi Shlomo Aronson of Kiev (later of Tel Aviv) and Rabbi Judah Leib Zirelson of Kishinev, formed an organization called *Aḥdut*, which defended the religious and cultural rights of the Jews of Russia. After the October revolution of 1917 and the subsequent pogroms of Petlyura,[253] my grandfather and his family fled to Vilna where he worked at a number of Jewish institutions. He became an active member of the religious Zionist movement *Mizrachi*, traveling all over Poland to preach on its behalf. He also raised funds for the newly created *Va'ad Hayeshivot* and for *Yeshivat Hakhmei Lublin*.

My grandfather then served as rabbi of Dokshitz near Vilna where he founded a Yavneh religious Zionist day school and traveled to other cities to found Yavneh schools. From 1936 to 1939 he served as chief rabbi and *Av Bet Din* of the Free State of Danzig, where he supervised the kashrut on the many ships embarking from Danzig and Gdynia. Since the Nazis forbade kosher slaughter, he arranged *sheḥitah* in the Polish town of Ossawa. After most of the Jews of Danzig fled before the Holocaust, Golinkin escaped to the United States in 1939 where he served as rabbi of Worcester, Massachusetts until his death.

On October 6, 1943, Golinkin participated in the historic march on Washington in which 400 Orthodox rabbis marched through the streets of Washington demanding that the Roosevelt administration help save the Jews of Europe.[254]

After the Holocaust, my grandfather also served as *Av Bet Din* of the Orthodox Rabbinical Court of Justice (*Bet Din*) of the Associated Synagogues of Massachusetts for over twenty years until his death. In that capacity, he presided over a number of cases which achieved national prominence. In 1968, his *Bet Din* spent months mediating between a Jewish slum landlord in the South End of Boston and his poor tenants. In the final agreement, reached in August 1968, the landlords agreed to repair and maintain the apartments according to city codes and the tenants pledged to maintain the properties once the repairs were made. The ruling concluded: "Our aim is clear, it is justice for all concerned. 'Justice justice shalt thou pursue.' " (Deut. 16:20). The case was reported in the *Wall Street Journal, Look*, the *Boston Globe, Newsweek, Hadassah Magazine* and other publications. In March 1969, the rabbis fined the landlords $48,000 for noncompliance and then the landlords sold most of the buildings to the Boston Redevelopment Authority, which assigned them to the Tenants' Council for management.

In 1969-1970, the Boston *Bet Din* spent ten months studying the subject of civil disobedience and conscientious objection in light of the Vietnam War. In January 1970, they issued a 54-page responsum to the seven major questions which had been submitted by students and academicians.

In 1972, the *Bet Din* began to prepare a responsum regarding the *kashrut* of animals in light of the drugs and chemicals used in raising cattle and processing meat products. This responsum was never completed due to the deaths of Rabbi Golinkin and Rabbi Samuel Korff, the Rabbinic Administrator. Yet, for a brief time, the Boston *Bet Din* showed that a rabbinic court could function as an activist court which could go way beyond the domain of family matters.[255]

Thus, in light of my grandfather's activism, it is not surprising that my father was an activist who could not sit by and watch passively as the Jews of Europe were killed.

Second, for my father, antisemitism and killing Jews were not remote, historical events. For the first 25 years of his life until he arrived in the U.S. in June 1938, Ukrainian and Polish antisemitism were a constant threat to my father and his family, and nearly cost them their lives.

Around the year 1920, when my father was about seven years old, the Petlyura massacres began. He heard shots of people being killed in their courtyard in Zhitomir. The family ran away from the White Russians to a town called Lishtin or Lishchin where they hid in a dark room and were told not to cough or sneeze lest they be detected by the pogromists.[256] They then went to Zvil on the Russian side of the border and finally via Rovne, Poland, to Vilna.

My father spent the years circa 1922-1938 in or near Vilna which was also a hotbed of antisemitism.[257] When he studied law at the Stefan Batory University of Vilna, he and the other Jewish students were told that they had to sit on "ghetto benches" on the left side of every lecture hall. The Jewish students refused to do so; they preferred to stand in the back of the classroom. Periodically, the Polish university students would riot and beat up the Jewish students. On one such occasion, my father was chased across the campus by a group of antisemitic students. When he found a policeman, the latter refused to come to his aid.[258] Similarly, he once went to visit his parents in Danzig, which was mostly German and strongly antisemitic. There he was chased through the streets by a Nazi and took refuge in a store. Thus, unlike many native-born Americans, my father believed that the Germans and their Polish and Ukrainian allies were perfectly willing and able to murder large numbers of Jews.

Third, my father learned through his own experience that it was possible for Jews to get visas to the United States, despite the antisemitism in the State Department. He himself wrote to the rabbinical school of Yeshiva College in February 1937, asking to be admitted as a full time student there,[259] which would enable him to receive a U.S. visa. He was assisted by a Danzig resident named Mr. Schiffman, whose American relative, one Mrs. Schulsinger of Newark, served on the national board of Hadassah, and she asked the college's president, Dr. Bernard Revel, to invite my father to study there. After arriving in the U.S., my father arranged with Mrs. Schulsinger for an Orthodox congregation in Newark to compose a fictitious contract inviting Zeyde to serve as their rabbi.

Zeyde and Bubbe arrived in America in May 1939. Since my father's sisters, Rivka and Rachel, were not minors, they were not allowed to go with their parents. Rivka and Rachel went from Danzig, in western Poland, to Vilna, in eastern Poland, and there they were trapped when the area was occupied by the Russians in September 1939.

My father and grandfather began to lobby members of Congress from Massachusetts in order to obtain visas for Rivka and Rachel. Rep. John McCormack of Massachusetts was up for election to be Democratic Majority Leader in 1940 on the same day that my father and grandfather came to Washington D.C. to meet with him. When, after a lengthy wait in McCormack's office, my father learned what was happening, he apologized for imposing. "Your business is just as important as our business" was the reply of a senior staff member.

Rivka and Rachel were issued visas to leave Russia to go to the U.S., but the visas had to be picked up in person at the American Embassy in Moscow. Traveling was severely restricted in Communist Russia. They had to get permission to travel within Russia from Vilna to Moscow. They waited in line every day from late 1939 until early 1941 at the American Consulate in Vilna just to be allowed to take a train to Moscow. When they finally reached Moscow, the American Consul in Moscow saw the pile of correspondence from Massachusetts congressmen and senators requesting permission for Rivka and Rachel to travel from Vilna to Moscow. He asked them: "Are you related to Senator Lodge of Massachusetts?"

They had to travel to America going east, the long route, as World War II was being fought in Europe to the west. They traveled by railroad across Siberia to Vladivostok, crossed over to Japan, traveled by ship across the Pacific to San Francisco, then by rail through Chicago to Worcester. Rivka and Rachel arrived in Worcester on June 22, 1941, the same day Germany invaded Russia. Had they still been in Vilna on that date, they probably would have been killed in the Holocaust.

Thus, between 1937 and 1942, my father learned that it was very difficult to obtain a visa to the U.S., but it was possible if you persevered and never took no for an answer.

Finally, it is clear from my father's biography from 1942 until he passed away in 2003 that, as in the case of Jerry Lipnick and Buddy Sachs, the students' campaign for European Jewry was not an isolated phenomenon. All three of them spent their lives fighting for Israel, civil rights, and Soviet Jewry.

While still at JTS, my father founded the Young Zionist Action Committee, an umbrella organization of New York City Zionist youth groups which he headed until he moved to Lincoln, Nebraska in 1944. In the 1950s and 1960s, my father wrote and preached continually on behalf of civil rights. As a leader of the Ministerial Association of Arlington and the National Conference of Christians and Jews, he fought for the integration of the Arlington School system and for fair housing in Arlington and Washington. In 1963, he marched on Washington and heard Martin Luther King proclaim "I have a dream!"

In the late 1960s and 1970s, he organized numerous demonstrations on behalf of Soviet Jewry. He organized a citywide youth assembly in Washington. He convinced a group of teenagers in Washington to undertake a "Fast for Freedom" which became a daily vigil in front of the Soviet Embassy, which lasted for many years. In 1971, he organized a march through the streets of Knoxville, Tennessee, with the mostly non-Jewish cast of "Fiddler on the Roof."

Finally, he spent much of his time beginning in 1978, and all of his time beginning in 1986 after retirement, teaching Jewish adults how to read Hebrew via the Hebrew Literacy Campaign and the Hebrew Reading Marathons. Indeed by 2010, 200,000 Jewish adults had learned how to read the siddur using his books *Shalom Aleichem, Ayn Keloheynu*, and *While Standing on One Foot*.

Thus, my father's efforts to save the Jews of Europe in 1942-1943 seems to have been the result of four major factors: the example of his own father; his first-hand experience and understanding of antisemitism; his success in saving his own parents and two sisters – though not his brother Eliyahu[260] – from the jaws of death; and his own innate need to perfect the world in the Kingdom of God.

And what did my father himself think of the efforts of the European Committee during the Holocaust? A hint of an answer was discovered in August 2009 after Rabbi Buddy Sachs passed away in Jerusalem. His son Noam Zion found a copy of Haskel Lookstein's book *Were We our Brothers' Keepers?*[261] in his father's library. In that book, Rabbi Lookstein heaped lavish praise on the three young JTS students and on their manifesto "Retribution is Not Enough." This is what my father wrote on the title page of the book:

> Dear Moshe,
>
> You and Jerry Lipnick and I tried to be our Brother's Keepers. We didn't succeed, but we tried.
>
> Noah[262]

If success meant to save millions of Jews, they did not succeed. But they did succeed in three areas:

– They were part of the activist campaign that ultimately helped force President Roosevelt to set up the War Refugee Board in January 1944, and that agency helped save 200,000 Jews and 20,000 non-Jews from certain death.

– Noah and Jerry and Buddy taught us that the basic Jewish principles alluded to above are not mere slogans but are basic principles which must guide the lives of all Jews: "I am my brother's keeper" (see Genesis 4:9); "Do not stand idly by the blood of your fellow" (Leviticus 19:16); "All Jews are responsible for one another" (*Shevuot* 39a); "When one delays even a moment in redeeming captives – where it is possible to hasten – he is considered as one who spills blood" (*Yoreh Deah* 252:3).

– Finally, they taught us that one person, or in this case, three people, can change the world and make the world a better place.

We hope and pray that Noah and Jerry and Buddy will serve as role models for all Jews – and especially young people – for generations to come.

127

A LETTER FROM RABBI MOSHE "BUDDY" SACHS

Mishael Tziyon

I am here representing my grandfather, Moshe "Buddy" Sachs. I visited his home in Jerusalem about a month ago, to write down a message from him that I would recite this afternoon. I found him sitting in his living room surrounded by books, old newspapers, magazines, and his notes from the period. He was crying. It's not easy for a grandson to see his grandfather crying, and it's not something that I have seen my grandfather do often. I was wondering why he was crying, until I realized that he was crying because they didn't do enough, because of what happened during the Holocaust. It didn't matter that it happened more than sixty years ago; there he was, on his couch in Jerusalem in the State of Israel in the year 2007, and he was crying over what they hadn't achieved in 1942 and 1943. My grandfather's life story, like Noah Golinkin's and Jerry Lipnick's, was spent trying to make up for what they felt was their responsibility or what they tried to do and failed.

In 1945, he served as a chaplain in Okinawa as part of the United States Army. From 1947 to 1949, he was fighting in Jerusalem for the Haganah. In the 1960s, as a rabbi in Minneapolis, he fought for Soviet Jewry and marched for African-American rights as part of the civil rights movement. In 1976, when he made aliyah, he lived in Jerusalem but worked in the development towns of Beit Shean and Beersheba trying to help immigrants become part of Israeli society. He never stopped. And now, when he is too old to do that much, he worries about the Philipino worker we hired to worry about him. Here is his message, which he titled "A Period of Broken Hearts and Deaf Ears: The Failure of American Jewish Leadership as we at the JTS Study Body Experienced It – My Recollections":

Dear friends, scholars, spiritual leaders,

I speak today not only in my name but also in the name of those who have passed away, my good friends Rabbi Jerome Lipnick and Rabbi Noah Golinkin of blessed memory. They loved the Jewish people and struggled so hard to overcome the silence of American Jewish leadership. Let them be honored by this Conference which you have arranged at this distinguished center of learning.

The atmosphere over the period in which our community did its work was one of disbelief and desperation. Despite the mood at the times, Hashomer Hatzair had produced a short book describing the concentration camps as if they were centers of Jewish culture.[263] They obviously had received reports from Europe that were inspired by German and communist propaganda designed to tell the American public that all was well in Eastern Europe, that in the concentration camps there was opportunity for music, study, and all those positive activities that one should expect in a humane society. Probably very few, even in the West, believed that story, but I confess that I believed it – so deep was my naive hope that all would be well.

But in the winter of 1941-42, my colleagues and I were informed of the horrific reality of the Shoah. Rabbi Max Gruenewald was a young German refugee scholar who was working for the World Jewish Congress gathering their reports of what was happening to the Jews across Europe. By sheer chance Rabbi Gruenewald was given residence by the Seminary and had received me as his new roommate. In conversation over many nights, he informed us students of what he knew. As we heard more about it, the Nazi decision to destroy the Jewish people shocked us as it did the entire student body. In response, we set up a committee of three to spread the word of the impending destruction in Europe. Our committee spent its time going from New York office to New York office, meeting with Jewish leaders one by one. Sometimes the reaction to our work was at least positive, but on most occasions our cause was pushed away as we were told America must win the war against the Nazis before it can take any position. Our response was if we don't act now there won't be any Jewish community left to save. But the American Jewish leadership did not sense our dread and did not respond with appropriate desperation.

The first significant response to our efforts came from the Labor Zionist movement and in particular from Hayim Greenberg, with whom we met and shared the little information we had. Greenberg was the editor of the widely read *Jewish*

Frontier, an English-language journal, and concurrently editor of the *Yiddisher Kemfer*, a Yiddish-language journal. In November 1942, both journals appeared with black frames and published in great detail what was going on in Europe.[264] I still have a copy of that issue. This was the first popular public Jewish clarion call. Within the journal, the editor wrote that they had omitted publishing for one month because the subject matter was so overwhelming that they needed to provide real documentation country by country, yet still American Jewish leaders did not sense the dread and did not respond with the appropriate desperation.

In frustration with the continuing silence, our committee sent an article to *The Reconstructionist*. In that article, we issued what we considered a bitter denunciation of American Jewish leadership and called for actions in the synagogues and Jewish community institutions to raise awareness of the distress of European Jewry.[265] Following this, the Synagogue Council of America gave us some support, they let use their office, an assistant, and a mimeograph machine. And yet the majority of the American Jewish leadership did not sense our dread and did not respond with appropriate desperation.

In early 1943, in an effort to break the barriers of silence, we turned to our fellow Jewish students at the Jewish Institute of Religion and to Christian students who were studying at the Union Theological Seminary across the street. We held a conference which publicized and called for action[266] and still American Jewish leadership did not sense our dread and did not respond with appropriate desperation.

As the summer of 1943 began, American Jewry became more and more involved in the procedures it had set up to hold what they called the American Jewish Conference. There had been elections in every major city and in most places the Zionist leadership had been victorious – thus the American Jewish Conference was a showpiece of Zionist commitment. The conference was held at the Biltmore Hotel and I remember the excitement and the joy as the delegates and the observers celebrated their victory over the American Council for Judaism, an anti-Zionist group. However, our student committee was not satisfied and leafleted the morning session of the conference in order to influence its decisions.[267] The conference resulted in two important decisions. First, it supported a program for a national Jewish home in Palestine; second, it passed a resolution calling for a national program with the purpose of saving European Jewry. We students left with a sense of great delight, both in the commitment to Palestine and in the commitment to awaken American Jewry to the horrors of the Shoah.

Subsequently our student group was scattered as we were sent to serve in various Jewish communities whose rabbis had been drafted into the American army. This signified the end of the work of the European Committee as I remember it, but also the beginning of our lifelong work in synagogues and Jewish communities across America.

We are proud to have had this small part in the historical endeavor to save European Jewry. With the modesty appropriate for judgments of the past we allow ourselves to confirm the opinion of yesteryear and express the feeling that American Jewish leadership failed our people in the period of the Shoah.

We all stand in memory of Rabbis Jerome Lipnick and Noah Golinkin who I was honored to call my colleagues, who devoted everything day and night to informing the world about the Shoah.

JEROME LIPNICK'S TWO BLACK RIBBONS

Rabbi Jonathan Lipnick

My father, Jerome Lipnick, was born in Baltimore, Maryland in 1918 and died at the age of 59 in 1977. His life embraced the close of World War I, the Great Depression, World War II, the Holocaust, the beginning of the nuclear age, the establishment of the State of Israel, the Vietnam War and the civil rights movement. While living in Washington D.C. in the late 1970s and right before his death, my father's lunchtime was spent standing vigil in front of the Soviet Embassy to protest the oppression of Soviet Jewry. My uncle, Rabbi Bernard Lipnick, my father's younger brother, wrote about his brother Jerome that "these events were not merely the backdrop of Jerome's life, they were the stuff out of which he drew the meaning and the challenges of his career."

When my father passed away, our family decided to gather his essays and articles that were written mostly for the synagogue bulletins where he served and we put them into a book, *From Where I Stand: From the Writings of Jerome Lipnick*.[268] We thought that through his words, his grandchildren that he did not live to see would get a very real idea of who he was and what inspired him. He frankly was inspired by engaging in the issues of the day. In 1943, about six weeks after "Retribution is Not Enough" was published, Jerome wrote a letter to his brother Bernie on his 17th birthday. Dated April 28, 1943, it reads:

> Dear Bernie,
>
> Tomorrow is your birthday, 17 years old. You're growing up but you've been grown up for a long time. You know by this time what is right and what is wrong. I'm glad to see that you're casting your lot with the right – most of the time anyway. You've got a good start. I want to leave you just one word – and that is consecration. Consecrate yourself Wipsey to fight for the rights of the oppressed – for the underdog, for the persecuted. Consecrate yourself to fight for the freedom of your brother Jews abroad, and for your negro brothers within. Consecrate yourself to build America as a place where all groups can retain their own individuality, their own hopes and ambitions.

Consecrate yourself to help build ארץ ישראל for only from there can תורה be spread to a תורה- less world. Consecrate yourself to be a nice guy, to labor for others, to give to others, to live for others. And never slacken in your determination no matter how black the future, how small the dividends. Today the future is black for the world and for the Jew in particular and goodness pays little. Enclosed is a black ribbon – wear it. It's not for mourning – don't be afraid. It's for protest against those who permit the Jews to die today without anyone lifting a hand to help. You've got to learn how to show your dissatisfaction, your disgust at all the hypocrisy and sham and lying which daily confronts you – and not to be ashamed. You can't be just a complainer, a beefer, you must also be a builder. Before you build anew however, you have to destroy what stands in the way. Wear your Jewishness proudly, your disagreements proudly and as for your consecration, keep that as your propelling drive, but wear it modestly.

Your brother,

Jerome[269]

I recall one Pesach seder growing up when my father pulled out a map of the world and started identifying all the countries where people were still enslaved by their governments. The challenge at that seder was that we were going to do something about it. For my father, the task to redeem the world was a lifelong commitment and struggle.

In looking back on his student initiatives with his fellow classmates, I was struck by an article my father wrote in a synagogue bulletin published in 1963 entitled "Two Black Ribbons." Here's what he wrote:

> As I fasten the black ribbon to my lapel with a straight pin, I thought back twenty years to an afternoon in New York when a friend and I trudged up and down Broadway in New York in search of black ribbon and pins. Ribbons were scarce. It was during the war but we succeeded in locating several stores, enough for our needs, but we were lacking in pins with which to secure the black ribbons, our symbols of mourning. We found a box of pins, however, in a small home laundry establishment directly across the street from the Seminary and paid the man a

pretty price for them. We convinced him that ours was a greater urgency and that he would be performing a mitzvah and perhaps help to save a few lives by letting us have them.

Several of us at the Seminary conceived a grandiose idea that if every Jew in America would wear a black ribbon on his lapel we could arouse American public opinion to the immediacy of rescuing the remnants of European Jewry from slaughter by Hitler. The idea we thought would sweep the country and once America was alerted, who could stand in the way of saving this beleaguered group of men and women.

Hard as it was to find the black ribbon and pins, it was even harder to find the Jews to wear them. To be wearing a black ribbon while your parents were still living, it was an open invitation, as it were, to the Angel of Death. What could ribbon do in the face of such a calamity? The idea never got very far. We wore the ribbons for a while and then we took them off.

Several years later I discovered the box of pins in a drawer. I never saw so many pins, they seemed to increase in number, for we had paid a heavy price. Each pin was a dagger to pierce our hearts and to mark our failure for by this time the statistics of those who had perished in Europe were made known to us. Six million. Who could have believed it. Had we succeeded we could have aroused public opinion. It might have made a world of difference.

I thought of all of this as I pinned the black ribbon to my lapel several Sundays ago at the invitation of Bayard Rustin, leader and organizer of the March on Washington. Word had been circulated by Mr. Rustin that a national day of mourning would be observed for those four children who had been killed in the bombing of a church in Birmingham and those two others who had met their death by shooting. Black ribbon was suggested as our symbol of mourning. How could I disassociate this act from an old remembrance and from the recollection of its futility?

The Minneapolis delegation to the March on Washington pledged themselves to wear the ribbon for a month. A few people asked me what the ribbon was for, if I had lost anyone in my family, but most people were polite and respectful and did not wish to invade my privacy. The inquiries were few.

The other day I took the ribbon off. The thirty days were up and I put it aside. I shall deposit this black ribbon, the ribbon of the six kids in a manila folder in my filing case beside another black ribbon, the ribbon of the six million which I have saved these twenty years. If only we could have saved more people. I hope and pray that in this country, the land of sanity and decency, that those standing in the way of the negro's march to freedom will move aside. Please move aside that no more lives will have to be sacrificed and wasted.

Minneapolis, Minnesota, October 20, 1963[270]

According to my mother, Joan Lipnick Abelson, it was the Holocaust that moved my father to activism throughout his career. She felt that he took this initiative in 1943 as a personal failure and that is why it was so important for him to act on injustice wherever he saw it.

Had my father been alive today, I often think about what the issues of his concern and attention would be. He would have been at the forefront of articulating a thoughtful and strategic American Jewish communal response to Darfur and would be extraordinarily proud of the work of Ruth Messinger, the American Jewish World Service, and all of the Jewish organizations that have stepped up to this issue of the day. He would be fighting for health care reform here in America. He would be advocating for the full and equal rights of all of Israel's citizens. He would be working towards the end of poverty and homelessness here in America, and would be overwhelmed with emotion knowing that one of our presidential candidates is an African-American.

The message that my father would deliver to his grandchildren today would be the same serious message he imparted to his younger brother, Bernie: Consecrate yourself, do the sacred work of making the world more peaceful, just and equitable. I think those were the lessons that I learned from my father, Jerome Lipnick, *zichrono livracha.*

There is one message, one dictum that is said every Pesach which is the master story of the Jewish people that celebrates the liberation of moving from enslavement to freedom. *Bekhol dor v'dor ḥayav adam lirot et atzmo ke'ilu hu yatza mimitzrayim,* In every generation one is required to see oneself as if he or she personally left Egypt. My father had the uncanny ability to see the lives of downtrodden people and to put himself in the position of others. It was the way of human relationships that was so real for my father in his rabbinate. Not only on the national scene, but just the inter-relationships of the people that he would meet on the street where one lives.

VISION, ACTIVISM, AND COURAGE:
INDISPENSABLE ATTRIBUTES OF THE JTS STUDENTS

Cantor Abe Golinkin

The purpose of this article is to offer new perspectives into what motivated the JTS students — beginning with some insights about my father, and then looking at the motivating forces that guided the Student Committee as a whole.

My father, first and foremost, was an activist, like his namesake Noah of the Bible. The biblical Noah rescued his generation from the physical destruction of the Flood. My father, Noah, likewise tried to rescue his generation at two critical points in recent Jewish history — first from physical destruction, and later from cultural destruction. Each time, he analyzed the situation, recognized what needed to be done, and was willing to lead the way in getting the job done.

During the Holocaust, my father arranged for the rescue of his immediate family — his parents and his sisters — as did the biblical Noah, who rescued his immediate family. However, the biblical Noah did not rescue anyone else. My father, Noah, was not content with rescuing just his own family. Through the committee that he organized, Noah, the activist, was instrumental in helping to bring the Holocaust to the attention of the American Jewish community, and advocating for rescue.

The bottom line is that Noah Golinkin and the JTS Student Committee helped to elevate the cause of Holocaust rescue onto the national agenda of the American Jewish community.

* * *

Later in his career, over a 25 year period starting in 1978, he led the way to help rescue more than 200,000 American Jewish adults from Jewish oblivion and likely assimilation, by bringing them back into the synagogue with the National Hebrew Literacy Campaign that he founded, with the sponsorship of the Federation of Jewish Men's Clubs. He recognized the danger that widespread Hebrew illiteracy posed to the future of the American synagogue, and he made it his life's mission to resolve the problem on a massive scale.

137

Known among his colleagues as "the pioneer of Hebrew Literacy in America," he authored three Hebrew Literacy textbooks for adults, which have been used by congregations nationally to teach the reading of prayer book Hebrew. As a rabbi who could have retired, he chose instead — while in his 70s and all through his 80s — to conduct eight-hour, one-day Hebrew Reading Marathon classes, which he taught, along with my mother, Devorah Golinkin, in more than 150 cities throughout the United States and in Canada.

Once again, the bottom line is similar. Through one man's sheer perseverance and refusal to give up, Noah Golinkin, the activist, succeeded in elevating Hebrew Literacy onto the national agenda of the American Jewish community.

* * *

Others have written about the specific actions taken by the JTS Student Committee. This article would like to offer a new perspective by framing their actions in the context of "speaking truth to power."

The members of the Student Committee took upon themselves a real-life "mission impossible" — to save European Jewry. It was like David versus Goliath, yet they refused to take the attitude that "It's too hard, so why should we even try?" How were they able to pursue this "mission impossible?" What kept them going?

The students had three indispensable attributes that kept them going:

First, the JTS students had the *vision* to see clearly the situation of European Jewry, something that others were either unaware of, or unwilling to see. They then had the foresight to envision a plan that spelled out what needed to be done about it.

Second, the JTS students had *activism* in their blood. They challenged the American Jewish community to follow the "Program of Action" which they proposed in 1943. They had the inner conviction of the rightness of their cause, even if it required, in my father's words, "the persistent prodding of the powers-that-be."

Third, the JTS students had the *courage* to confront the leaders of the Jewish establishment of their time. In spite of the resistance they encountered, they did not take no for an answer, until the establishment began putting some of their proposals into action.

It was these three attributes – *vision, activism,* and *courage* – that motivated the students to "speak truth to power." They were a group of students in their twenties who had the *chutzpah* to tell it like it is. If the emperor had no clothes, they were not afraid to say so to his face.

The students had the *vision* to bring into focus for their leaders the urgency of the crisis when they quoted the *Shulḥan Arukh,* the authoritative Code of Jewish Law, to spur the Jewish leaders to action. The *Shulḥan Arukh* says: "When one delays even a moment in redeeming captives – wherever it is possible to hasten – he is considered as one who spills blood." The students implored: "This dictum indicts us. We must act now!" They spoke truth to power.

The students were *activists* like the biblical Mordechai, the voice of conscience, who challenged Esther, who was in a position of authority, to come to the aid of her people in their time of crisis. Mordechai implored: "And who knows, that for just such an occasion, you were put in a position of influence?" They spoke truth to power.

In their *Reconstructionist* article in March 1943 (see Appendix J), the students had the *courage* to question their leaders: "What have the rabbinical bodies representing the Orthodox, Conservative, and Reform groups attempted, in order to impress upon their congregations the necessity for action now? What have they, or any other responsible organizations within American Jewish life, undertaken to awaken the conscience of the American people?" They spoke truth to power.

* * *

Looking at the actions of the Student Committee from another perspective, chronologically, a fascinating pattern seems to appear. The timeline of their activities can be seen to illustrate the students' progression: from *vision* — to *activism* — and finally to *courage*.

In the first stage, in December 1942, they approached Rabbi Stephen S. Wise with their *vision* of how to respond to the unprecedented crisis. When he rejected them and turned down all of their proposals, rather than becoming frustrated and giving up, they became more determined than ever.

In the second stage, in February 1943, they proceeded to the next step with their *activism* when they convened, on their own, an Inter-Seminary Conference – an idea that Rabbi Wise had rejected. The Conference reached out to hundreds of Jewish and Christian seminary students and faculty, to get the word out about the plight of European Jewry.

In the third stage, in March-April 1943, with the success of the Conference, they became emboldened to demonstrate their *courage*, when they challenged the entire Jewish establishment with their article in *The Reconstructionist*. They immediately followed up by approaching the umbrella organization of American Jewish con-gregations, the Synagogue Council of America, to implement the ideas contained in their article. Their courage was rewarded when the SCA president, Rabbi Israel Goldstein, endorsed their ideas, and the SCA adopted the students' plan for a "Six-Week Period of Mourning and Intercession" on behalf of the Jews of Europe, between Passover and Shavuot of 1943.

* * *

The bottom line is that, motivated by their *vision, activism,* and *courage*, the JTS Student Committee helped awaken a segment of the complacent American Jewish establishment and challenged the national Jewish leaders to push forcefully for the rescue of European Jewry.

In summary, it was these three indispensable attributes that enabled the JTS students to help elevate the cause of Holocaust rescue onto the national agenda of the American Jewish community.

THE RALLY THAT ALMOST WASN'T

Rabbi Dr. Haskel Lookstein

The American Jewish community's response to the Holocaust was, tragically, characterized not by unity but rather by divisiveness and discord. A recently discovered document concerning my father, Rabbi Joseph Lookstein z"l, helps shed some additional light on this sad reality.

On November 24, 1942, in Washington D.C., Rabbi Stephen S. Wise held a news conference announcing to the world the broad outlines and statistics of Hitler's Final Solution to the Jewish Problem. Two million dead and four or five million – depending on one's estimate of the number of Jews under Nazi control – to be murdered. The general press covered the story, sometimes on the front pages. The lead editorial in the *New York Times* on December 2nd described the horrifying details. The Jewish press screamed in pain.

But after a few weeks, the suffering of European Jewry no longer dominated the news and was not front and center in the Jewish press either. More importantly, American Jewry did not react vigorously. Business went on as usual. Rallies were few and far between. The proposals for rescuing those who could be saved were marginalized and life more or less went on. It seemed as if American Jews were fiddling while European Jews were burning.

There were notable exceptions to this pattern. One such exception was a series of concrete proposals drawn up by three rabbinical students at the Jewish Theological Seminary in 1943.[271] Some of these proposals were adopted by the Synagogue Council of America, the umbrella group for Orthodox, Conservative, and Reform synagogues in the United States. The Synagogue Council then circulated these proposals among thousands of synagogues from coast to coast.[272] The main purpose of these proposals was to raise the consciousness of American Jews about the plight of their brethren in Europe.

How did synagogues around the country respond to this call? The newsletter of Kehilath Jeshurun, the synagogue led by my father, reports how he and his congregation responded:

141

The Synagogue Council of America decreed a six week period of mourning for the millions of our brethren slain on the continent of Europe. Rabbi Lookstein announced this fact at the Yizkor Services [on the last day of Pesach]. Black ribbons were distributed to our worshippers who were asked to wear them during this period. We are asked also to observe a partial fast on Mondays and Thursdays during that period and to donate the monies otherwise spent on food to the United Jewish Appeal. In addition, at the close of the main meal in every home, a special prayer should be recited by all members of the family. A copy of that prayer is enclosed with this *Bulletin*.[273]

The Synagogue Council of America also called for a series of rallies in synagogues and churches around the country to be held in late May toward the end of the sefira period.

In New York City, it was the responsibility of the New York Board of Jewish Ministers, of which my father was then president, to carry out the call of the Synagogue Council of America for a rally that would be attended by hundreds of rabbis. One might assume that at this point, the very peak of the Holocaust, it would not be difficult to find a synagogue in New York City to host such a rally. But a document discovered by The David S. Wyman Institute for Holocaust Studies reveals a very troubling episode.[274]

The document is a memorandum written by Rabbi Ahron Opher, who was the staff member at the Synagogue Council in charge of trying to get synagogues to hold the rallies and other activities.

Rabbi Opher begins by reporting that at the last meeting of the New York Board of Jewish Ministers, it was unanimously agreed to hold a rally of rabbis to call for rescue of the Jews in Europe. Twelve rabbis were chosen to speak at the rally – four Orthodox, including my father; four Conservative, and four Reform. The event would consist of "prayer, cantorial selections, biblical responses and sermons devoted to the theme of the Period of Mourning and Intercession on behalf of the Jewish martyrs."

The Board of Ministers put together a list of several local synagogues where the rally might be held, and left it to Rabbi Opher to work out the details.

The first possible host whom he called was Rabbi Herbert Goldstein, head of the West Side Institutional Synagogue, a modern Orthodox synagogue on the upper West side of Manhattan. Rabbi Goldstein replied "that he was anxious to accept the offer of the Committee, regarding the use of his synagogue, but that he would have to consult his board about it." Fair enough, but then he added "that inasmuch as his board had just had a meeting, it would be some time before another meeting could be called, and he asked that we wait."

As the rabbi of a synagogue, I appreciate the importance of consulting with the board before making a major decision, but there are times when a matter is so urgent that you have to find a way to move forward. Rabbi Opher, not unreasonably, "suggested that since immediate action was necessary, Rabbi Goldstein call a meeting of his House Committee to pass on the question." I am sorry to tell you that, according to the document, Rabbi Goldstein said he "feared that the House Committee would not want to decide such an important matter without presenting it before the entire board." Rabbi Opher said he would call someone else.

A few minutes later, Rabbi Opher called Rabbi Dr. David de Sola Pool, head of another modern Orthodox synagogue in Manhattan, the Spanish and Portuguese Synagogue. The answer he received was a little better, but still not quite what he was hoping for. Rabbi Pool said "Unofficially, yes," but "he would have to consult his president. Rabbi Opher urged him to do so as soon as possible since time was pressing and it was planned by the Synagogue Council to call similar convocations in all the larger communities in the country." Rabbi Pool promised to get back to him the next morning.

But then Rabbi Goldstein called back to ask what sort of progress Rabbi Opher was making. When he was told that Rabbi Pool was considering the proposal, Rabbi Goldstein said he might be able to have an "expedited board meeting" to consider it, after all. Naturally Rabbi Opher had to tell him that since he had already made the offer to Rabbi Pool, he would have to wait to hear back from him, and if Rabbi Pool said no, then they could consider holding it at Rabbi Goldstein's synagogue.

Incredibly, Rabbi Goldstein replied "that would be impossible, since if Dr. Pool said no, his answer too, would have to be no." We can only speculate as to why that was; it is not explained in the memo.

The next morning, Rabbi Pool called back with good news: the Spanish and Portugese Synagogue would agree to host the meeting, although, curiously, they insisted that the rally would be sponsored only by the New York Board of Jewish Ministers and the Synagogue Council of America, but not by the Spanish and Portugese Synagogue itself.

That was fine with Rabbi Opher, who quickly put out a press release to the news media announcing the rally, and also mailed letters to 150 rabbis around the country, urging them to hold similar rallies.

Half an hour later, the phone rang. It was Rabbi Herbert Goldstein again. Upon being informed that the Spanish and Portugese Synagogue agreed to host the rally he said, somewhat ominously, "that he knew some people in Dr. Pool's synagogue who would object..." Rabbi Opher replied "that he could not see why anyone should object to a group of leaders in Israel gathering in an hour of deep grief and sorrow to pray and invoke God's aid and intercession."

A good point, I think. I would have said the same thing myself.

But Rabbi Goldstein replied "that some Orthodox are like Catholics in this respect," meaning, apparently, that some Orthodox Jews would not want to have non-Orthodox rabbis speaking in their synagogue. Rabbi Opher, who by the way was a Reform rabbi, answered, "that it is then the duty of the rabbis to guide them in tolerance, and that seemed to him to be the whole purpose of such an organization as the New York Board of Jewish Ministers and the Synagogue Council of America. He added that this was a matter of *Pikuach Nefesh* [saving a life], and that it required the united effort of all Israel to awaken the religious conscience of the country."

It soon turned out that those intolerant Orthodox Jews to whom Rabbi Goldstein was referring were not only in Dr. Pool's synagogue, but in Rabbi Goldstein's as well. A few days later, Rabbi Opher spoke to Rabbi Goldstein again about the whole matter, at which point Rabbi Goldstein said that he personally would have liked to host the rally, "but that some members of his Congregation would have preferred to have the convocation a purely Orthodox service without any non-Orthodox rabbis participating..."

Rabbi Opher pointed out that, first of all, the New York Board of Jewish Ministers had unanimously agreed to have a rally at which rabbis of all streams would speak. Second, he pointed out that if the program were changed to exclude the non-Orthodox, "much damage would be done to the causes of *pikuach nefesh* and *pidyon shvuyim* [the redemption of captives]." Third, noting that Rabbi Goldstein himself was scheduled to serve as the next president of the Synagogue Council, Rabbi Opher added that "he feared very much for the survival of the Synagogue Council of America if its next president failed to cooperate in the effort to bring about a measure of unity in Jewish life in this darkest hour of our history."

The next day, another phone call, this time from an officer of the Spanish and Portugese Synagogue, to inform Rabbi Opher that "the Board of that congregation had overruled the decision of its Rabbi and president, and revoked their agreement to hold the convocation in the Spanish and Portuguese Synagogue."

So there you have it. Board members of two major Orthodox synagogues in New York City felt that preventing non-Orthodox rabbis from speaking in their synagogues was more important than holding a rally to publicize the need to prevent Jews from being taken to Nazi gas chambers.

I do not want to be judgmental regarding the actions of Rabbi Goldstein or Rabbi Pool, who were very important and respected rabbis in the American Jewish community. I know how difficult it can be for a rabbi to deal with unreasonable board members. But I admit to feeling disappointed that these rabbis did not regard this as the moment to really use their influence and leverage to insist on holding the rally, given the dire situation in Europe.

But I am glad to report to you that this was not the end of the story. Rabbi Opher's memorandum concludes with this sentence: "Rabbi Opher, thereupon, phoned Dr. Lookstein and arranged to hold the convocation in the Synagogue of Kehilath Jeshurun."

Now we turn to the minutes of the Board of Trustees of Kehilath Jeshurun, my father's – and my – synagogue, for May 20, 1943:

It begins, "The Rabbi announced" – notice the word "announced" – he did not put it up for a vote, he did not give his board members the option to try to vote it down, because he understood the urgency of the matter. He announced

> that on Monday, May 24, a special meeting for Prayer and intercession would be held in our synagogue at 10:30 AM.[275] This meeting is being sponsored by the New York Board of Jewish Ministers and would be participated in by rabbis of all groups – Orthodox, Conservative and Reform. He said there had been some objection to this meeting by some of the older rabbis but that when the real purpose of it was explained they withdrew their objections. The Rabbi asked our Board members to act as ushers. Among the speakers would be, besides our own Rabbi, Dr. Stephen S. Wise, Israel Goldstein, David de Sola Pool, Louis I. Newman and many others.

I do not know who those "older rabbis" were that had objections, or what their objections were. I know only that my father got them to withdraw those objections. Not only did the board not try to overrule my father but, as we see, he "asked" them to serve as ushers at the rally!

This story of one event provides important insights into one of the reasons for the muted response of American Jews to the Holocaust while it was happening. The community simply could not work together in unity. Rabbi Stephen S. Wise, leader of the American Zionist movement, could not work together with the non-establishment Bergson Group that was pressing for the creation for a U.S. government agency to rescue Europe's Jews. Non-Zionists and Zionists were fighting each other. And some Orthodox Jews could not put aside their differences with Conservative and Reform Jews during European Jewry's darkest hour in order to engender support for whatever relief and rescue work could be done. Hitler had no difficulty in seeing all Jews unified as victims. How tragic that Jews themselves could not work together to meet that terrible threat.

But how fortunate that there was one Orthodox rabbi who rose to the occasion.

The rally took place on May 24, 1943. Between 300 and 400 rabbis took part. The event received extensive media coverage, from the *New York Times* to newspapers in Toronto and Texas. Hundreds of thousands of newspaper readers learned about the slaughter of the Jews in Europe and the protest by American rabbis.

Many of those newspapers – although not the *New York Times* – quoted from an unusually strong declaration issued by the rabbis, in which they charged that the Allies' response to the Holocaust was one of "evasion and helplessness."[276] This was not the sort of language that American Jews normally used when referring to the policies of President Franklin D. Roosevelt. The hour was late, but many Jews were beginning to realize that to save the remnants of European Jewry, they would have to start using language and tactics that were out of the ordinary. They would have to put aside old ways of thinking and find appropriate ways to respond to the tragedy. I am proud that my father, Rabbi Joseph Lookstein z"l, was one of those who realized this before it was too late.

LESSONS FOR JEWISH LEADERS

Rabbi Prof. David Ellenson

Human beings are largely creatures of habit. That is, the judgments that individuals make and the actions they take at a contemporaneous moment are based in no small measure upon previous experiences.

In relationship to World War II and the deeds and decisions of many Jews during this period of horror and destruction for the European Jewish community, one need only think of Elie Wiesel's classic work *Night* to demonstrate this point. At the very beginning of this memoir that takes place in 1944, members of his home community in Sighet, Hungary, are depicted as being incredulous – despite the warning given them by Moshe the Beadle – regarding the possibility that their transport from their homes would mean they were going to be sent quite literally to death camps as opposed to – however horrible they were – concentration camps. Indeed, the residents of Sighet take Moshe to be a lunatic.

In historical perspective, their unawareness of the death camps and their seeming refusal to acknowledge the executions that fate had in store for them seems beyond belief. How could these Jews, living in the heart of Nazi-dominated central Europe, have been unaware so late in the war that destruction and murder lay in wait for them? Yet, the overwhelming majority – with the exception of a "madman" – clearly did not.

In order to understand how this could have been, it is instructive to turn to a remarkably insightful essay written a number of years ago by the eminent historian Ismar Schorsch, former chancellor of the Jewish Theological Seminary. Entitled "On the History of the Political Judgment of the Jew," this essay attempted to explain why the Jews of Germany had been so myopic in terms of the reality that surrounded them in Nazi Europe.[277] Schorsch indicated that there had unquestionably been a history of virulent antisemitism in Germany in particular and Europe in general for centuries prior to the Holocaust. However, prior to the Shoah, there had never been a bureaucratically organized and systematic policy of complete and total extermination of a people. The point that Professor Schorsch derives from this, in assessing the "political judgment" of American and German – and by extension all central European – Jews of that era, is that the "misjudgments" of these Jews was based in part upon the fact that there was no historical precedent for the systematic policy of genocide that the Nazis carried out. However horrible the pogroms and discriminations inflicted upon European Jews in the past had been, there had always been an end to them. In short, a policy of complete genocide directed against the Jewish people, as opposed to the worst type of antisemitic activity, represented a terrible yet novel escalation in the history of European anti-Judaism, one unimaginable in its scope for the Jews of those days.

From the Schorsch essay, I would draw the following lesson as we today measure our assessments of, and reactions to, the disappointing record of Rabbi Stephen Wise, on the one hand, and the praiseworthy and heroic actions of the three Jewish Theological Seminary students, on the other, in their responses to the Holocaust.

There is no question in my mind that those students better appreciated the nature and dimensions of the crisis than did Rabbi Wise. However, a judicious treatment of our topic requires us to keep in mind that the unprecedented nature of the crisis that confronted the world and American Jewish community during those years may have been responsible – in part – for what I see as the failure of Rabbi Wise during that period.

Nevertheless, I acknowledge that such an explanation is at best only partially satisfactory. After all, Rabbi Wise was devoted to the Jewish people throughout his career and it was he who had organized the first massive public protests against Nazi acts of anti-Jewish discrimination during the 1930s. In addition, there was no greater champion of Zionism and devotee of the Jewish people – *Klal Yisrael* – than Rabbi Wise. By the time the students approached Rabbi Wise to enlist his support for their activities, he already knew that the ovens of the death camps were open and that the crematoria were destroying hundreds of thousands – millions – of Jewish lives. Why then did he not respond differently to the requests that were placed before him?

Given the character and record of commitment to *Am Yisrael* that Wise displayed throughout his lifetime, it is not simple to answer this question. Nevertheless, I would suggest that there are two factors about Rabbi Wise that should be kept in mind as we attempt to comprehend his inaction at this time. One was that he possessed a complete and absolute love and respect for President Franklin Roosevelt. From this perspective, Rabbi Wise was like hundreds of thousands of other American Jews. Indeed, if I look at my own family and I consider my grandparents, who were all East European immigrants to this country, one of my major childhood memories is that there was a clock in my grandfather's den where an American and an Israeli flag stood side by side. Next to the Israeli flag, there was a picture of Theodor Herzl. A picture of Franklin Delano Roosevelt stood next to the American flag.

This iconographic memory is revealing, for I do not think the attitude of love and unbridled admiration my grandfather had for both Herzl and Roosevelt, Israel and America, were rare among American Jews. His clock bespeaks the devotion and reverence that most American Jews felt for Franklin Delano Roosevelt and the reality is that Stephen S. Wise, probably more than any Jewish leader, had a close personal relationship with President Roosevelt. I am certain he believed absolutely that Roosevelt had the best interests of the Jewish people at heart. His personal relationship with the president undoubtedly blinded him to the value of the proposals made by the students and he probably could not accept the fact that Roosevelt would not do everything in his power to aid the Jewish people – or that if Roosevelt did fail to act, it was because Roosevelt must have perceived that such actions would impede the larger goal of winning the war.

Another factor that surely accounts for Wise's negative response to the students was undoubtedly the antipathy he felt towards Ze'ev Jabotinsky – an antipathy that is well-known and can hardly be exaggerated. Wise's angry response to the students' proposal about "evacuating" Jews from Poland, in that horrifically disappointing meeting he had with the students in December 1942, harkens back to a speech Jabotinsky delivered before the Royal Commission meeting in the British House of Lords on February 11, 1937.[278]

As a seminary head in the leadership of the American Jewish community, who bears responsibility for the education and formation of the leaders of the Reform movement, I believe there is much that is instructive for us in that speech by Jabotinsky, and much to be learned from Wise's reaction to the remark by Jerome Lipnick that he felt echoed Jabotinsky.

The Royal Commission was debating the conflicting Jewish and Arab demands regarding the future status of Palestine. This was eleven years before the creation of the State of Israel. Appearing before the commission, Jabotinsky stated that the plight of European Jewry was desperate and that the Jewish people had the right to return to their ancestral homeland in Palestine. Jabotinsky emphasized that it was quite literally a matter of life and death that confronted our people at that moment.

In a characteristically fiery and literary speech, Jabotinsky alluded to the Dickens novel *Oliver Twist* and said to the commissioners, "I would remind you of the commotion which was produced in that famous institution when Oliver Twist came and asked for 'more.' He said 'more' because he did not know how to express it; what Oliver Twist really meant was this, 'Will you just give me that normal portion for a boy of my age to be able to live.'" Jabotinsky then added, "I can assure you that you face here today, in the Jewish people with its demands, an Oliver Twist who has, unfortunately, no concessions to make."

Of course, today we all know the tragic history of that moment. The Peel Commission did not sufficiently open the borders of Palestine to Jewish immigration and, as a result, millions of our brothers and sisters who would have been rescued had the State of Israel existed or had the borders been opened, instead perished in the fires of the Shoah.

To use the talmudic idiom, "*Mai nafka mi-nei* – what do we learn from this?" On the one hand, for the reasons cited above, I cannot simply 'condemn' Rabbi Wise. After all, Rabbi Wise was surely a great man and an exemplary leader of our people in so many ways and on so many occasions. As an historian, I can understand the factors that led to his negative response to the student delegation. At the same time, in my capacity as head of a major seminary, I believe that the lesson for responsible leaders to draw from this episode is that in exercising leadership, one should never be blinded to the truth of a posture even when that stance is advanced by one who is generally an opponent.

To draw upon another historical episode that illuminates the crux of this position, I would recall a disagreement that took place in 1872 between Rabbi Esriel Hildesheimer, the head of the Orthodox Rabbinical Seminary in Berlin, and his colleague Rabbi Samson

Raphael Hirsch of Frankfurt, the great leader of Jewish neo-Orthodoxy.[279] Their debate at that time dealt with the question of whether an orphanage should be established for Jewish orphans in Palestine. The only orphanages that existed then in Jerusalem were Christian ones. Heinrich Graetz, who was then a professor at the Jewish Theological Seminary in Breslau, had taken a trip to Jerusalem. When he saw that Jewish orphans in the Holy City were being placed in Christian institutions, he proposed constructing a Jewish orphanage there and sought help from Jewish leaders in Europe – including Hildesheimer and Hirsch – in realizing this ambition.

However, Rabbi Hirsch opposed the creation of a Jewish orphanage because he said this proposal was put forward by the "heretic" Heinrich Graetz, a man whose religious views Hirsch considered anathema. Hildesheimer wrote back that he too found Graetz's religious views abominable, but he added, *"Ha'emet hu ha'emet afilu im hu betzad mitnagdenu* – The truth is the truth even if it is stated by those who are our opponents." Hildesheimer therefore supported the creation of this Jewish orphanage, while Hirsch remained steadfast in his opposition.[280] The orphanage was not constructed, and Jewish orphans in Jerusalem remained prey for Christian missionaries. I tell this story because in the episode involving the three JTS students, a major factor motivating the response of Rabbi Wise closely paralleled that of Rabbi Hirsch in his response to the proposal put forth by Graetz. Indeed, I suspect that Wise's opposition to the plan the students advocated stemmed in no small measure because he saw the students as advancing a posture akin to that of his opponent Jabotinsky. This may well explain why Wise moved viscerally in the other direction when the students came before him with their request.

As we stand today here in New York City, aware that tomorrow the president of Iran, Mahmoud Ahmadinejad, will be here, we should remember the admonition, *"Z'khor yemot olam* – Remember the events that have occurred in the past." Noah Golinkin, Jerome Lipnick and Moshe Sachs, whose deeds we recall today, stand before us as heroes. They answered the demands of the hour and did all in their limited power to attempt to save their fellow Jews in Europe during the dark days of the Holocaust. They obeyed an injunction Rabbi Hildesheimer issued in the 1860s in regard to the Jews of

Ethiopia, when he wrote, "These people are our flesh and blood. They are our brothers and we have an obligation to rescue them and to bring them back to life."[281] While one of our greatest leaders failed, for perhaps understandable reasons, to respond with the wisdom the students displayed more than sixty years ago, those of us who exercise leadership today must learn from their example. Their love for the Jewish people shines out to us in a commanding and instructive way today.

Writing the Student Activists Back into History: A Note on the Historiography of American Jewry's Response to the Holocaust[282]

Dr. Rafael Medoff

For many years following the Holocaust, there was very little public or scholarly discussion concerning the American Jewish community's response to news of the Nazi genocide. Consequently, the efforts undertaken by the JTS student activists were unknown.

In the late 1960s and early 1970s, however, scholars began exploring the American government's response to the Holocaust. The first books on the subject, such as Arthur Morse's *While Six Million Died* (1968), David S. Wyman's *Paper Walls* (1968), and Henry Feingold's *The Politics of Rescue* (1970) included a few references to the Jewish community's response. This helped open the door to wider discussion of the topic.

Meanwhile, activists in the Soviet Jewry protest movement, which by the early 1970s had become a major phenomenon in American Jewish life, were citing the community's inadequate response to the Holocaust as a reason for a more vocal posture with regard to the plight of Jews in the USSR. The 1973 Yom Kippur War also contributed to the surge of interest in this issue. The cold treatment of Israel during and after the war by much of the international community reinforced a sense among many American Jews that they needed to respond more actively than the 1940s generation.

Hollywood, too, played a role in this process. The film *Voyage of the Damned* (1976), about the ill-fated voyage of the *St. Louis*, sparked more than a few conversations about the lack of an effective American Jewish response to Roosevelt's rebuff of the ship. Laurence Jarvik's documentary, *Who Shall Live, Who Shall Die* (1979), also focused attention on American Jewry and the Holocaust.

The 1970s was the period when Holocaust survivors began to find their voices. After many years of reluctance to discuss their experiences, many survivors began speaking in schools, granting interviews to the news media, and participating in events connected to Holocaust Remembrance Day (*Yom HaShoah*), which was being observed in a rapidly-increasing number of Jewish communities. Survivors were often highly critical of American Jewry's response to the Holocaust and stimulated discussions about the topic.

Finally, one should take into consideration the impact of the rise and fall of the American Jewish Commission on the Holocaust, better known as the Goldberg Commission. This privately-constituted group of Jewish leaders, survivors, and intellectuals undertook, in 1981, to assess U.S. Jewry's response to the Nazi genocide. In a drama that was played out on the front page of the *New York Times* and other major news media, the commission collapsed in a bitter dispute over a draft report by its research staff that some commission members considered excessively critical of the wartime Jewish leadership. Off and on for nearly two years, the work of the commission generated furious debates in the Jewish community over the question of American Jewry's response to the Holocaust, including the first extensive discussions about the role of the Bergson Group.

While recognition of the Bergson Group's achievements was often obstructed by partisan politics and the lingering rivalries of yesteryear, the efforts of the three Jewish Theological Seminary students fell victim to a simple lack of accessible information. There was no organized collection of materials about them in any major Jewish archive. Their story only began to come to light in 1985, when Haskel Lookstein mentioned the students' *Reconstructionist* article in his pioneering study, *Were We Our Brothers' Keepers?*[283] My own study of American Jewry and the Holocaust, *The Deafening Silence* (1987), also included several paragraphs about the JTS students.[284]

In the years to follow, my research increasingly focused on the minority of Americans, and American Jews, who spoke out for rescue. I sought out and interviewed Noah Golinkin, Moshe "Buddy" Sachs, and many of their rabbinical school classmates. I examined the archives of the Jewish Theological Seminary and Union Theological Seminary. I reviewed the records of the Synagogue Council of America to trace the students' influence on the council's response to the Holocaust. The result was an essay, " 'Retribution Is Not Enough': The 1943 Campaign by Jewish Students to Raise American Public Awareness of the Nazi Genocide," which appeared in 1997 in *Holocaust & Genocide Studies*, the scholarly journal published by the United States Holocaust Memorial Museum.[285]

Little by little, the story of the JTS students committee has begun to enter the mainstream narrative of the Holocaust. Prof. Marsha Rozenblit, writing on "The Seminary during the Holocaust Years" for the official two-volume history of JTS in 1997, included four paragraphs about the student activists, as well as the first (and so far, only known) photograph of the students' rescue conference.[286] The new edition of the *Encyclopaedia Judaica* (2007) included an entry, by this author, on Noah Golinkin, focusing on his Holocaust activism.

With the publication of this book, the history and impact of the JTS students' campaign is at last presented in great detail, and in the context of the American Jewish response to the Holocaust that the students helped influence.

APPENDICES

Appendix A
The Rabbinical Students' Memo to Rabbi Wise,
December 17, 1942 (see p. 35)

December 17, 1942

<u>Memorandum for Dr. Stephen S. Wise</u>

Presented by a joint student committee of:-
The Jewish Institute of Religion
Yeshiva College
The Jewish Theological Seminary of America

I. Statement:

Students of the above schools are aroused by the gravity of the European catastrophe and volunteer their services to do whatever may possibly be done to help.

For this we deem it necessary to clarify several questions and make tentative suggestions.

II. Questions:
1. What is being to;-

   a. Stop the killings in occupied Europe.
   b. Evacuate Jews from occupied Europe and places in Europe in imminent danger of invasion.
   c. Facilitate immigration of refugees to--- Sweden, Turkey, Switzerland, Virgin Islands, Alaska, U.S.A., Palestine, or other countries.
   d. Arouse public opinion to action
      (1) Press, radio
      (2) Churches, universities, etc.
      (3) American Congress

III. Tentative suggestions how we may help:

1. To arouse public opinion.

   a. Activate alumni of our institutions to organize Jewish and interfaith meetings for protest and petition to higher churchmen, public officials, Congressmen etc.
   b. Acquaint non-Jewish seminaries with the facts in order to get a joint proclamation of protest and specific demands.
   c. Acquaint faculties and student bodies of universities and colleges with the situation in order to get public action.
   d. Form an emergency general Jewish youth council to consider youth action.
   e. Present our own views and demands to influential Jewish organizations e.g. American Jewish Congress.

159

Appendix B
The Schedule of the Inter-Seminary Conference,
February 22, 1943 (see pp. 46-53)

1943

~ INTER-SEMINARY CONFERENCE ~
Monday, February 22nd

MORNING SESSION - AT JEWISH THEOLOGICAL SEMINARY

NE corner, Broadway and 122nd Street

10:30-11:00 Registration :

11:00- 1:00 The Problem

Invocation
Hitler's Policy of Extermination - Rabbi Philip
    Bernstein, Jewish Welfare Board
What Can Be Done - Varian Fry,
    Foreign Policy Association
Discussion

1:00-2:30 Lunch (at Union T.S. & Jewish T.S. from 35¢)

AFTERNOON SESSION - AT UNION THEOLOGICAL SEMINARY

SW corner, Broadway and 122nd Street

2:30-4:15 The Experts Speak

The European Church - Dr. Henry Smith Leiper
    American Representative, World Council of Churches
Providing Food - Howard Kershner
    American Friends Service Committee
Avenues of Emigration - speaker to be announced
What the Church and Synagogue Should Do - Dr. Willard
    Johnson, Nat. Conference of Christians and Jews
Discussion

4:15-4:45 Recess

4:45-5:40 Palestine as an Immediate Refuge

Prof. Robert Gordis, Jewish Theological Seminary
Rabbi M.J.Schachtel, West End Synagogue, New York

5:40-6:15 Recess

EVENING SESSION - AT JEWISH THEOLOGICAL SEMINARY

6:15-7:00 Dinner - All conferees will be the guests of the School
    of Religious Studies (the Interdenominational
    Institute)

7:00-7:45 Report of Resolutions Committee and Discussion

7:45-8:00 Worship Service

8:00-8:30 Our Common Heritage - Professor Louis Finkelstein,
    President, Jewish Theological Seminary

(Session closes at 8:30)

- -

There will be a twenty-five cent registration fee to
cover the expenses of the Conference

Appendix C
Ecumenical Prayers Recited at the
Inter-Seminary Conference, February 22, 1943
compiled by Irwin Gordon (see p. 52)

(see p. 52)

WORSHIP SERVICE
INTER-SEMINARY CONFERENCE
February 22, 1943

1) Responsive Reading:

Save me, O God; for the waters are come in unto my soul.

I sink in deep mire, where there is no standing; I am come into deep waters, where the floods overflow me.

I am weary of my crying: my throat is dried: mine eyes fail while I wait for my God.

They that hate me without a cause are more than the hairs of mine head: they that would destroy me, being mine enemies wrongfully, are mighty: then I restored that which I took not away.

O God, thou knowest my foolishness; and my sins are not hid from thee.

Let not them that wait on thee, O Lord God of hosts, be ashamed for my sake: let not those that seek thee be confounded for my sake, O God of Israel.

Because for thy sake I have borne reproach; shame hath covered my face.

I am become a stranger unto my brethren, and an alien unto my mother's children.

For the zeal of thine house hath eaten me up: and the reproaches of them that reproached thee are fallen upon me.

When I wept, and chastened my soul with fastin, that was to my reproach.

I made sackcloth also my garment; and I became a proverb to them.

They that sit in the gate speak against me; and I was the song of the drunkards.

But as for me, my prayer is unto thee, O Lord, in an acceptable time: O God, in the multitude of thy mercy hear me, in the truth of the salvation.

Deliver me out of the mire, and let me not sink: let me be delivered from them that hate me, and out of the deep waters.

Let not the waterflood overflow me, neither let the deep swallow me up, and let not the pit shut her mouth upon me.

161

2

Hear me , O Lord; for thy lovingkindness is good: turn unto me according to the multitude of thy tender mercies.

And hide not thy face from thy servant; for I am in trouble: hear me speedily.

Draw nigh unto my soul, and redeem it: deliver me because of mine enemies.

For the Lord heareth the poor, and despiseth not his prisoners.

Let the heaven and earth praise him, the seas, and every thing that moveth therin.

For God will save Zion, and will build the cities of Judah: that they may dwell ther, and have it in possession.

The seed also of his servants shall inherit it: and they that love his name shall dwell therein.

2)   The following traditional Jewish prayer in memory of those who have died in sanctifying the Name of God has become hallowed through countless periods of Jewish martyrdom. In it, is expressed the religious view of man who, when "he departs this earth, puts off his outer coverings and continues to live by virtue of his soul, which is immortal."

O merciful God, who dwellest on high and yet art full of compassion, keep in Thy divine Presence among the holy and pure, whose light shineth as the brightness of the fernament, the souls of those who sacrificed their lives for the Sanctification of Thy Holy Name. O may their souls be bound up in the bond of life so that their memories stir us to serve Thee and our fellow men in truth, kindness, and peace. Amen.

3)   Responsive Reading:

Cause us, O Lord our God, to lie down in peace, and raise us up, O our King, unto life. Spread over us the tabernacle of thy peace; direct us aright through thine own good counsel; save us for thy name's sake; be thou a shield about us; remove from us every enemy, pestilence, sword, famine and sorrow; remove also the adversary from before us and from behind us. O shelter us beneath the shadow of thy wings; for thou, O God, art our Guardian and our Deliverer; yea, thou, O God, art a gracious and merciful King; and guard our going out and our coming in unto life and unto peace from this time forth and for evermore,

3

4) Unison:

The Lord is my shepher; I shall not want.

He maketh me to lie down in green pastures; he leadeth me beside the still waters.

He restoreth my soul: he leadeth me in the paths of righteousness for his name's sake.

Yea, though I walk through the valley of the shadow of death, I will fear no evil: for thou art with me; thy rod and thy staff they comfort me.

Thoue preparest a table before me in the presence of mine enemies; thou anointest my head with oil; my cup runneth over.

Surely goodness and mercy shall follow me all the days of my life; and I will dwell in the house of the Lord for ever.

5) Song

The God of Abraham praise, All praised be His Name.
Who was, and is, and is to be, And still the same!
The one eternal God, Ere aught that now appears;
The First, the Last: beyond all thought His timeless
years.

His spirit floweth free, High surging where it will:
In prophet's word He spoke of old-He speaketh still.
Established is His law, And changeless it shall stand,
Deep writ upon the human heart, On sea, or land.

He hath eternal life Implanted in the soul;
His love shall be our strength and stay, While ages roll.
Praise to the living God! All praised be His Name
Who was, and is, and is to be, And still the same!
Amen.

Appendix D
The Resolutions Adopted at the
Inter-Seminary Conference (see pp. 52-53)

A Metropolitan Interseminary Conference
Called to Discuss the Plight of European Jewry Today

February 22, 1943

REPORT OF THE RESOLUTIONS COMMITTEE

We, as Christian and Jewish theological students, regard it as our sacred obligation to call upon the American public to be informed of the grave danger which threatens the peoples of Europe, and the Jewish people in particular. Acting in accordance with the highest principles of mercy, compassion and justice, the people of the United States should urge that immediate aid be granted to these unfortunates so that they, too, may continue to live on this earth which God has given to us all. We believe that it is the duty of the Church and the Synagogue, and their leaders, to try to mold the opinion of America so that all may realize the religious importance of such action as we shall describe.

We believe that it is the duty of the American people to demand that the governments of the United States, Great Britain, and the other United Nations proclaim that, at least for the duration of the emergency, the lands of the United Nations will be opened to all the refugees who can be saved from Europe. We feel that every necessary move must be made, in so doing, to prevent the infiltration of Axis spies, even to the establishing of internment camps for the refugees. But we do not believe that the possibility of sabotage can be used as an excuse for condemning many thousands of people to remain under threat of death by starvation or slaughter.

We believe that America especially should show an example to the rest of the world by its willingness to accept refugees immediately.

We believe that Palestine in particular, with all its possibilities, should be opened for all those refugees who can be brought to the Holy Land. The American government should exert its influence on the British government to the above end.

We believe that it is the duty of the American government in particular, and of the United Nations as a whole, to negotiate:

a) with the German government, through neutral governments, to exert every possible effort to release Jews and political prisoners from occupied Europe;

b) with the Balkan powers, Hungary, Roumania, and Bulgaria, to try to persuade these lands to release their Jewish populations;

c) with Denmark, to seek to release the Jewish population there which is threatened with imminent Nazi persecution;

d) with Spain, to seek to free those detained in prisons and concentration camps to reach Palestine, America, and other lands of greater safety and opportunity.

164

Interseminary Conference Resolutions, p. 2

We believe that the saving of children is particularly important. Efforts must be made again and again to help the movement of children from Spain, France, and the Balkans to Palestine, America, and other asylums.

We believe that every effort should be made immediately, within the limits of military necessity, to provide food for the relief of the starving peoples of Europe, especially the children.

The Conference recommends the continued study of Palestine as the Jewish homeland as part of the long range solution to the Jewish problem.

. . . .

The Conference Committee is called upon to give widespread publicity to these resolutions among churches and synagogues from the pulpit and through the religious press.

We hereby establish a temporary Post-Conference Committee to be appointed by the Conference chairman for the implementation of these resolutions.

We hereby establish a permanent Interseminary Conference of Christian and Jewish Seminaries to meet on common problems.

The Conference shall work with the National Conference of Christians and Jews; the size and membership of the Interseminary Conference Committee shall be decided by the outgoing Conference Committee.

. . . .

We extend our thanks to the hosts of the Conference, the Union Theological Seminary, the Jewish Theological Seminary of America, and the Institute of Religious Studies; to the National Conference of Christians and Jews for their cooperation, and to the speakers who have helped to make this conference a success.

We extend our thanks to Mr. Herbert Bräutigam and his committee for their work in preparing this conference.

. . . .

Adopted unanimously by delegates of:
Biblical Seminary
Drew Seminary
General Theological Seminary
Jewish Institute of Religion
Jewish Theological Seminary
Moravian Seminary
New Brunswick Seminary
Princeton Theological Seminary
Union Theological Seminary
Yale Divinity School
Yeshivah College

Appendix E
One of the Newsletters Distributed by the JTS Students
after the Inter-Seminary Conference (see pp. 58-59)

March, 1943

The Challenge

AM I MY BROTHER'S KEEPER?

THE CONFERENCE IS N O T OVER

It's been over a month now since the Inter-Seminary Conference convened, and there is a possibility that some of us have allowed the matter which called us together to slip from our minds. Somehow or other after the sessions many of us actually felt that the danger which faced European Jewry would disappear because of the impact of our deliberations. But since our conference the United States and its allies have not taken any action whatever to save the five million Jews of Europe who can be saved. However, additional voices have since been added to our own--the Federal Council of the Churches of Christ has issued a fine statement which embodies many of the actions which we would like to see initiated.

But our government is yet unmoved by any body of resolutions set up on the printed page. It will only act if it knows that these resolutions are written down upon the wills of the vast American public who are really interested in saving those of our spiritual community who are destined for death.

Elsewhere in this issue of "The Challenge" you'll find the resolutions and digests of the speeches delivered at our meeting, but the Inter-Seminary Conference is not over yet. It shall not be over until we have succeeded in salvaging at least one life from the slaughter house which is Europe.

Before that can be done the challenge must be extended to each of the members of our congregations, to our communities, to our neighbors, and to our friends; and we must not cease from our God given task until there is sent abroad in this land an ever swelling chorus of "We are our brother's keeper."

FEDERAL COUNCIL URGES ACTION

A three-point program of aid for European Jews has been approved by the executive committee of the Federal Council of the Churches.

The points:

1. That the Department of Research and Education issue a statement giving the best possible judgment concerning the facts of the situation for the information of the American churches.

2. That we appeal to our government to give full consideration to the following proposals:

a. To offer financial assistance for the support of refugees that neutral governments (for example, Switzerland, Sweden, Spain, Portugal and Turkey) may receive from areas under Nazi control, as a result either of infiltration across their borders or of repatriations with the Axis powers, with the expectation that, after the war, such refugees would be repatriated.

b. To provide places of temporary asylum in which refugees whom it may be possible to evacuate from European countries may be removed.

3. As a special occasion for the expression of Christian solicitude, the Federal Council, through its Executive Committee, designates Sunday, May 2nd, as a "Day of Compassion" for the Jews of Europe. The council invites all Christian people to join in constant intercession--and unitedly on May 2nd-- for the victims of racial and religious persecution.

The statement urged that Christians in America oppose all tendencies to anti-Semitism in this country and pray that the spirit of racial good will and justice be strengthened among all men throughout the world.

Editorial by J. Herbert Brautigam, Jr. (see p. 59)

THE UNION REVIEW

"To give expression to the best of student Christian thought and to promote further thought and action in the service of Christ."

Vol. IV.   MARCH, 1943   No. 2

On Implementing Brotherhood

The Interseminary Conference on the plight of European Jewry was a success. Eleven seminaries in the metropolitan area accepted the joint invitation of the student bodies of Union and of the Jewish Theological Seminary of America to plan and participate in a one-day conference; 167 students registered. A distinguished panel of speakers presented the immediate situation in compelling terms. Dr. Louis Finkelstein, the distinguished president of our neighboring seminary, gave a moving and prophetic address on 'Our Common Heritage', which is in fact our mutual responsibility.

The response was spontaneous and unanimous. So fruitful had been the fellowship, that it was planned to make this interfaith venture among the Protestant and Jewish seminaries in and around New York an annual institution. So demanding is the situation in Europe, that a forthright declaration was adopted: "Acting in accordance with the highest principles of mercy, compassion, and justice, the people of the United States should urge that immediate aid be granted to these unfortunates, so that they too may continue to live on this earth which God has given to us all. We believe it is the duty of the church and synagogue and of their leaders to try to mold the opinion of America so that it may realize the religious importance of such action as we shall describe." There followed a conservative program of immediate relief, the expediting of emigration from Europe, and the coöperation of the United Nations in setting up places of refuge.

This responsibility was echoed a few days later, by Bishop Tucker, the president of the Federal Council, speaking at a mass meeting in Madison Square Garden. "If we the people of America really believe in the brotherhood of man, as we profess to do, we will not only be moved to indignation by the brutality of these persecutions but we will also be moved to demand that everything possible to bring it to an early end shall be done at the earliest possible moment."

But can we say that the conference, or the mass meeting were in fact successful? Having emoted we have returned to our normal routines. In the three weeks since, *what have we done?* In the three months since the United Nations published its documentation of Hitler's campaign for the systematic extermination of the Jews in Europe, what have the United Nations done? Two million Jews have died, deliberately murdered; five million more face the same fate. And we confront the situation with a kind of moral paralysis.

We all accept the responsibility and the necessity, but we do not know what to do about it. Perhaps unconsciously, the framers of the conference resolutions hit the exact point: "We believe it to be the duty of [the religious] leaders to try to mold [public] opinion." We usually begin our campaigns by besieging Congress, and end them there, thus absolving ourselves. But the fact of the matter is—and this was the key to what several of the speakers said—that public opinion in the United States is not willing to support a program of action for the relief of Europe's Jews, particularly one that involves any changes in our immigration policy. Indeed, in our own country anti-semitism is increasing, an index of social unrest, and the churches have no recourse except to deplore it.

This is a matter of life and death. It is literally a *matter of hours and days.* Can the Church speak forth in any but hollow tones of moral generalities, or can it make demands on the conscience and opinion of America that will make it possible to help those of our spiritual community who suffer?

J.H.B., Jr.

Appendix G
The Yeshiva College Student Newspaper,
March 4, 1943 (see pp. 59-60)

עַל שֶׁבֶר
בַּת עַמִּי"

The Commentator

"פְּלַגֵּי מַיִם
תֵּרַד עֵינִי..."

Special Issue Jointly Sponsored by Yeshiva College Student Council
and Students' Organization of Yeshiva.

VOLUME XVII. NEW YORK CITY, THURSDAY, MARCH 4, 1943 No. 1

"Out of the Depths Have I Cried Unto Thee, O Lord!"

PSALMS CXXX:1

"SAVE US, O LORD .."
An Editorial

Ten years ago in Germany there came into power a man who did not believe in man—or G-d. This man was the epitome of everything against which enlightened mankind had been fighting since the dawn of civilization, and his first official act was the sacrificing on his altars of animalic cruelty, debauchery, and supreme hatred the Jewish citizens of his state.

Yet, the world kept silent.

His slaughter benches became redder and redder with the blood of this people. The drops accumulated and became raging torrents, and as the years went on they bore ghastly witness to the extermination of a portion of mankind.

Yet, the world kept silent.

The tidal wave of chaos and havoc overflowed the sluice gates, and this flood of fury poured out all over Europe, tearing out everything in its path—appeased for the moment only when mixed with Jewish blood. Rob the Jew! Kill the Jew! Exterminate the Jew!

Yet, the world kept silent.

The Jew As the Symptom of World's Ills — The world did not realize that this stigmatized Jew was its pulse. It did not realize that rot and decay were setting in, that when the Jew suffers it is always symptomatic of a greater and far more deadly illness. And even when, finally, the world decided to take up arms, "expediency" prevented it from demanding justice for the first heroic soldiers who fought this monster.

"It might be said it is a Jewish war", furtively whispered so-called leaders of freedom. "It might lead to embarrassing complications if we bring the Jew into the limelight", worried so-called fighters of liberty. Blasted appeasement and weak-kneed cowardice was all that it was! While the world was sacrificing itself on an altar of "expediency", the Jewish people was being sacrificed for all humanity, and that same indifferent world is now paying dearly for turning its eyes away, for saying "Peace, Peace" when there was no peace.

Conditions have now reached a head—late enough to be sure. With the blood of two million murdered Jews screaming out for revenge, rumblings of protest and demands for action are finally issuing forth. The stomach of human decency is vomiting in revolt!

We, the students of Yeshiva College and The Rabbi Isaac Elchanan Theological Seminary, have dedicated ourselves to the task of making those rumblings **Our Sacred Duty As Future Leaders** stronger and stronger. We have taken upon ourselves the sacred duty of making every human being with a spark of mercy and righteous indignation bring pressure upon the leaders of the United Nations to guarantee for our brethren a fifth freedom—the freedom to live. Or if to die, to die as human beings, and not as helpless lambs being led to the slaughter.

This publication is our initial attempt. Through it we hope to create a militant nucleus—on the campus, from the pulpit, on the floors of Congress, in the schoolroom, on street corners, wherever a thinking being can be found—which will storm the gates of our leaders and demand that abstruse principles be translated into dynamic reality.

Whether we shall succeed or not depends wholly upon the reader. If what is presented in the ensuing pages is read with the proper measure of mind and heart and soul, we will succeed; if not, this will but be a hollow voice in the wilderness of indifference.

Yet, it goes still deeper. We are students of a theological seminary. Our lives are bound up in the work of the Lord. We hope some day to become leaders of Jewry, to mould a good and spiritual people.

But we, the living, cannot rest while our brethren are dying. The words in our holy books become blurred because of the burning tears which blind us. And although we know that the ultimate decision rests in the hands of G-d, we also feel that it is incumbent upon us to let our brothers know that we are not forgetting them in this, their darkest hour—to let them know, that besides our prayers, we are trying our utmost to make mankind itself create out of their black misery a new humanity and a real civilization.

Students Condemn Nazi Atrocities; Demand Action

"We ask that the United Nations extend a strong hand to the Jewish people which is being martyred by Nazi brutality. Justice, mercy and human decency demand that this action be taken."—Abraham Zuroff.

"We must not be deluded into thinking that ours is but a feeble and ineffectual protest. With concerted efforts, we can effect action."—Jacob Walker.

Resolution Urges United Nations Lend Succor to Jews

Representing all the departments of the Rabbi Isaac Elchanan Theological Seminary and Yeshiva College, an overflow crowd of students, alumni, and faculty members assembled Tuesday morning, Feb. 23, and condemned the Nazi atrocities against the Jews. A vigorous protest was lodged against the United Nations' silence in the face of "the brutal obliteration of a whole people."

The assembly gave its unanimous approval to a strongly-worded resolution urging the American government to assume the lead in effecting the rescue of the European Jews now facing extinction. In addition, the resolution urged that the Palestinian immigration laws be annulled to allow the Jewish refugees from persecution "a haven in the Jewish National Home."

Retaliation for Atrocities — "The government of the United Nations must impress the Germans that acts of atrocities against the Jews will result in immediate retaliation," the statement continued. "We appeal to the leaders and statesmen of the justice-loving nations of the world to act now while there is yet time.

Preceding the adoption of the resolution, Abraham Zuroff '41, president of the Students' Organization of Yeshiva, briefly outlined the state of the European Jews today. "The record shows," he stated, "that over two million Jews have already been ruthlessly slaughtered. The Nazis have conceived and executed a satanic program beyond the grasp of the decent human mind. ...What is needed now is action, not pity, action, not sympathy!"

Walker Urges Action — Discussing the immediate problem of "what can be done by the individual student," Jacob Walker, president of the Yeshiva College Student Council, declared: "Our own beloved country is, thank G-d, still a democracy and public opinion is still a powerful force. The voice of decent, justice-loving people must be heard." The speaker concluded with a spirited plea to the gathering to send letters to its representatives in Congress, protesting America's indifference to the plight of the Jews.

Solomon Gopin, representing the alumni of the institution, then read the resolution which was unqualifiedly accepted.

TEXT OF RESOLUTION

We, the students of the Rabbi Isaac Elchanan Theological Seminary, and of the Yeshiva College, raise our voices in solemn protest against the iniquitous silence and callous passivity on the part of the United Nations, in the face of total annihilation of all the Jews on the continent of Europe.

Hitler and his accomplices in crime have committed themselves to a policy of barbarous extermination, the magnitude of which is unparalleled in the annals of human history. Millions of Jews have already met a martyred death in the German slaughterhouses; millions more are facing imminent destruction at the hands of the ruthless Nazi butchers.

We, citizens of a free country where the torch of freedom still burns with unabated intensity, cannot resign ourselves to the belief that the conscience of mankind has become so morally numb as to view with equanimity the total obliteration of a people. For the Jews do not bleed alone. Israel's wounds are the wounds of all mankind.

In view of the aforementioned we demand that:

1.) Immediate negotiations be started through the good offices of the Vatican or a neutral country, for the immediate release of all Jews imprisoned on the continent of Europe.

2.) That the gates of Palestine, the Jewish national home, be thrown open to these innocent victims as a haven of refuge. All restrictions on immigration must be lifted!

3.) That the governments of the United Nations impress the Germans that acts of atrocities against the Jews will result in immediate retaliation.

We appeal to the leaders and statesmen of the justice loving nations of the world to act now while there is yet time. Recent reports from reliable sources indicate that thousands of Jews can be saved from the inferno created by the Nazi hordes.

If the United Nations fail to act now, they will have placed an indelible stigma on themselves second only to the barbarism of the instigators and perpetrators themselves. Mere expressions of pity, sympathy, and commiseration are but empty gestures and a hollow mockery if they are not translated into concrete action.

In regaining the lost soul of the world let us not, G-d forbid, discover that in the process, we have, by our own indifference, lost our own.

T. A. Joins In Protest

Gordon Speaks At Mass Assembly

More than 300 students of the Talmudical Academy assembled last Wednesday afternoon, Feb. 24, in the Harry Fischel Synagogue to appeal for action on the part of the United Nations which will alleviate the suffering of as many persecuted European Jews as possible.

The principal speaker at the assembly was Irwin Gordon '43, Vice-President of the College Student Council who, after outlining the atrocities which the Jews had suffered in Nazi-dominated

Europe, stressed the urgency of immediate action to save the "remnant of Israel."

Continuing his address, Gordon stated, "Hitler is willing to make peace with the Poles, the Czechs, and the Greeks; for the Jews there is no peace but the eternal peace of the grave." He

Student Leaders Act

The following steps have been taken by your leaders since the student assembly:

1. A dramatic appeal was sent out to student leaders of three hundred colleges and universities by our Student Council president. The appeal, which includes the resolution adopted at the mass meeting, also offers a seven point program to be adopted at these campuses.

2. A delegation of students represented the College at an inter-seminary conference last week. The aim of the conference was to discuss fully the plight of the Jew. A resolution was adopted condemning the atrocities and urging the lowering of the barriers to immigration to Palestine.

3. Copies of the College resolution were sent out to hundreds of Anglo-Jewish newspapers.

further pointed out the importance of public opinion which must be brought to bear on our government in order to insure effective action.

The next speaker, Sam Oakman, president of the G. O. of the Talmudical Academy told the students of concrete ways and means in which American public opinion could be aroused.

Appendix H
Letter from Editor of *The New Palestine*
to the JTS Students, April 28, 1943 (see p. 61)

OFFICIAL PUBLICATION OF
THE ZIONIST ORGANIZATION OF AMERICA

The New Palestine
The American Zionist Fortnightly Devoted to Jewish Affairs
1720 SIXTEENTH STREET, N. W.
WASHINGTON, D. C.

April 28, 1943
One Day Closer To Victory. .

Mr. Noah Golinkin
The Jewish Theological Seminary of America
3080 Broadway
New York City

Dear Mr. Golinkin:

I have read with considerable interest the "Program of Action"
drawn up by the European Committee of the Student Body of the
Jewish Theological Seminary of America. It is a most timely
and statesmanlike document, and I hope it will receive the
attention it deserves in the circles of the "mighty".

If followed, this program would certainly create a stir. It
amounts, in effect, to American Jewry standing upright, seizing
civilization by both shoulders, and shaking hard. Only such a
shaking will be of any help today.

When I note the progressiveness, the imagination, and the
energetic spirit displayed in your memorandum I feel that
perhaps it would not be such a bad idea if all leaders of
American Jewry were to abdicate and a committee of students
from the respective Rabbinical seminaries were to take over
for a period of six months. It's quite an idea, isn't it?

Sincerely yours,

Carl Alpert
Carl Alpert
Managing Editor

CA:eg

P.S. Please give my regards to Jerry Lipnick.

C.A.

Appendix I
Jerry Lipnick's Sermon About Amalek,
March 7, 1943 (see pp. 61-62)

Jerome Lipnick
March 7, 1943

— עמלק —

1. Midrash — אמר לפני תמחת ... אלהים ה' הגית והיה
   באול אבנית ישראל ובגד ג. ברית :עולה פסוק ישראל אבכית אבגית באול
   ואמרו סתירה את את יצחק פקד. אלף פתוך אמרו
   אלהים פקד והיה הגית דכרית אמרו לפר אמ.

2. Explanation — When the Israelites left Egypt they
   were attacked by the Amalekites. God, therefore,
   told Moses that when the Israelites entered Palestine
   they should do three things. They should choose for
   themselves a king, establish a temple, and blot
   out, that group which which ~~was~~ a constant threat
   to their life as a nation (mentioned in the Midrash
   by אלף) and as a religious group (mentioned in the
   Midrash by פ' בהירם). In other words blotting out
   the remembrance of Amalek, was the guarantee for
   group survival.

   Today the United Nations ~~are~~ supposedly
   fighting a war against a modern Amalek who
   threatens their ~~their~~ survival and the survival
   of all of the peoples of earth. They are fighting this
   war for the freedom of all peoples as they
   state in the Atlantic Charter. Also

   Franklin Roosevelt — Jan. 6. 1942
   "Our own objectives are clear, the objective
   of smashing the militarism imposed by War Lords

upon their enslaved peoples: We are fighting today
for security and progress and for peace, not only for
ourselves but for all men, not only for one generation,
but all generations. We are fighting, as our fathers
fought to uphold the doctrine that all men are equal
in the sight of God"

If this war then is to be a war for
the freedom of all peoples, a war for democracy then
it the United Nations should certainly grant the Jewish
people the right to continue as a nation and as a
religious community.

3. Proposition — A criterion of the extent to which the
United Nations are sincere in their struggle for
democracy is the extent to which they are ready to
permit Jews to continue as a nation and as a religio·
community.

4. Definition + Why do we say criterion?
Analysis   The strength of any chain is to be
judged by its weakest link. We cannot deny that the
position of the Jew in the world today is indeed weak.
After all the hate and scorn and persecution which
have been our lot through the centuries few have
come to regard us a nation which yearned to
return to the land of Palestine. We have been so
downtrodden and humbled that few have gone out of the

way to consider our plight. Especially today have we been so ground into the dust in Hitler dominated Europe that many believe that we deserve nothing better. We have no armies or natural resources to trade for recognition.

To permit the Jews to continue as a nation and as a religious community would be a true indication that this is a democratic struggle for all of humanity. ⟵ This should be explained analytically.

~~Analysis~~ –

What is the position of the Jew in the world today

a) In the lands of the United Nations he is participating with his fellow citizens in the conduct of the war and in helping to wipe out Amelek.

b) In Palestine he is producing and creating and contributing to the war effort as a Jew. He wants to do even more to help wipe out Amelek than he permitted. ie. Jewish army.

c) In the Nazi-dominated countries he is being exterminated. In Spain he is in concentration camps In North Africa he still suffers from anti-Jewish laws. About half the Jewish people in the world today have either been killed or are threatened with death.

Application — If the United Nations are fighting for freedom then certainly they should be fighting to save the lives of those, whom they are willing to give that freedom. The saving of the 5,000,000 Jews of Europe should not be a post-war aim; it should be engaged in immediately. So far the United Nations have in no way defined the place of the Jew in the post-war world. If the United Nations are sincere in their fight for democracy they should immediately.

a) Undertake to rescue those Jews who are endangered and who can be saved from Bulgaria, Rumania, Spain, and Hungary, etc.

b) Open the doors of Palestine for unlimited immigration

c) Feed starving civilian populations. Excuse for exterminating Jews is that there is not enough food to go around.

d) Attempt to deal directly with stopping the extermination program by publicizing the atrocities and promise reprisals

If the United Nations are sincere in their fight for democracy they should when this war is over:

a) Grant the Jews recognition as a

174

national group. and Palestine ~~must become~~ as a Jewish state integrated into the structure of a democratic society. It should be open for unlimited immigration. The White Paper must be repealed, of course. The Arab problem will be dealt with equitably.

b) If the Jews of Europe choose to return to their native lands they should form a religious community such as they do in the United States and England with the allegiance to the country in which they live. If minority treaties are made then the Jews should enjoy the same rights as any other minority. The minority treaties should be enforced.

c) This must become a present war aim.

Conclusion : לא כזו. נבין. נציב בישראל קטון

שבט ה ישראל.

The United Nations if they are sincere must recognize the justice of the Jewish claim to be a nation and a religious community. even though we are small in the eyes of the world.

Appendix J
Manifesto by the JTS Students in
The Reconstructionist, March 5, 1943 (see pp. 62-65)

THE

Reconstructionist

Vol. IX.   Adar I, 28, 5703   March 5, 1943   No. 2.

Retribution Is Not Enough

The following statement by a committee of students of the Jewish Theological Seminary presents a serious challenge to American Jewry and particularly to the American Synagogue. There may be disagreement as to some of the methods proposed by this committee, but its recommendations certainly merit public discussion that may lead to action.

Editors.

WE Jews who live in the staid serenity of America have failed to grasp the immensity of the tragedy which has befallen our people, and this failure is perhaps the greatest part of the tragedy. Were the entire Jewish populations of Boston, Cincinnati, Baltimore, Philadelphia, Chicago, San Francisco, Cleveland, St. Louis, Los Angeles, and Detroit slain, it would be little over half the number of those who have already been annihilated in Europe. What have the rabbis and leaders of these cities, or of New York, done to arouse themselves and their communities to the demands of the hour? What have the rabbinical bodies representing the Orthodox, Conservative, and Reform groups attempted in order to impress upon their congregations the necessity for action now? What have they, or any other responsible organizations within American Jewish life, undertaken to awaken the conscience of the American people?

The United Nations, we are told, have promised retribution for these killings; but this retribution will be meted out *after* the war. We do not want retribution for Jews who have already died. We prefer help for those Jews who yet live. These protests are meaningless and ineffectual. Have any of the United Nations offered refuge to Hitler's victims? Have they taken any steps beyond protest to indicate that they are really concerned in stopping the bloodshed? In failing to act speedily, they have become partners in these horrible crimes.

As Jews and as American citizens it is our sacred duty to call upon the United Nations, and in particular upon our own

country, to come to the aid of European Jewry *now;* and never for a moment must we relax our efforts until that help comes!

"The Nation" and "The New Republic" have been the only publications which have outlined plans for positive and immediate action to ameliorate the position of European Jewry. It seems almost incredible, but the Anglo-Jewish press has done little beyond documenting the tales of horror. Most of us, it appears, have already given up European Jewry in our hearts; others have acquiesced in their helplessness; and those who have not, have chosen the solutions which offer the least difficulties—and the least results. But in order to save five million human beings who have been doomed to die we must take bold and ambitious measures. Here are some of the things we should do:

1. Rescue Jews from Spain and Portugal and other countries threatened with Nazi invasion. Denmark and Bulgaria have expressed a willingness to permit Jews to leave their borders if proper arrangements can be made. These refugees might be brought to Allied countries in order to relieve the war labor shortage which is growing steadily worse.

2. Put pressure on the United Nations to obtain refuge for Jews in the neutral countries of Sweden, Turkey, and Switzerland. Urge that the United States allow Jews to settle in the Virgin Islands since they do not come under the immigration quota. If the United States will not change its immigration laws, then efforts should be made to establish

176

internment camps here for those refugees until the war ends. Jews who are in concentration camps in North Africa must be released, and the anti-Jewish laws there must be abrogated.

3. Put pressure on the United Nations to open up Palestine for large scale immigration. So that refugees in haven countries would not become permanent additions to their populations, guarantees should be made that they will go to Palestine after the war.

4. Request that the United Nations reconsider their blockade of Europe in order to permit the feeding of starving Jewish populations. Perhaps a program similar to the one now successfully operating in Greece could be carried out.

5. Put pressure on the United Nations to recognize a Jewish army to be composed of Palestinian and stateless Jews. The right should be given to refugees who are not subject to American draft laws to form separate commando units under the leadership of the United States army.

6. Put pressure on the United Nations to fully publicize the atrocities against the Jews to the German people and to the peoples of Europe by leaflets and shortwave broadcasts. So far, little has been done to arouse local populations in opposition to these mass murders.

To achieve such far-reaching goals we need mass action on a nation-wide scale, mass action that involves bucking the people and the American government. But bucking injustice is our religious duty!

We should therefore like to suggest that the religious leaders of America initiate the program of positive action along the lines we present here. Since the synagogue is the one institution in American Jewish life which can reach the greatest number of Jews, the synagogue should take the lead in this all-out effort to ameliorate the condition of European Jewry. Action

should not be limited to synagogues, however. All Jewish organizations of whatever character should participate in this program designed (a) to make Jews and non-Jews aware of the policy of extermination; (b) to move them and the duly constituted bodies which represent them, both as Americans and as Jews, to present uniform demands to the United Nations to save as many lives as possible now:

1. An "Aid European Jewry Now" week should be proclaimed throughout America to be observed by Orthodox, Conservative, and Reform Jews and those Jews unaffiliated with the synagogue. During this week special services should be held and programs arranged to stimulate activity for immediate help.

2. A Shivah Day, or its equivalent in Reform temples, should be observed in prayer and mourning in *all* synagogues, to be held on a Sunday when maximum communal participation can be expected. The day of prayer and mourning which took place on December 2 was unsuccessful. Most Jews became aware of the observance only after it was over. This time we should pray and mourn for a purpose —to call for concrete assistance from the United Nations and from our own country in particular.

3. During the entire week usual synagogue activities should be suspended and special programs dealing with how to save Jews should be arranged. Centers and Y's and all Jewish organizations such as B'nai B'rith, Hadassah, Habonim, etc., should undertake similar programs.

4. Large interfaith meetings should be held simultaneously throughout the country. There should be one meeting in each city, and in the large cities one in each section, where uniform demands for action should be made to the United Nations and our own government.

5. An Emergency Committee for European Jewry, representative of the

various organizations within American Jewish life should be created, with sub-committees in *each* city and in each local organization. These committees should use all the means of publicity available—radio, press, film advertisements, etc., to arouse public opinion to demand speedy action. They should approach every type of Gentile and non-sectarian organization—political, religious, humanitarian, and social—and urge them to lend their support. A central steering committee should conduct negotiations. The Congress of the United States must be induced to take a stand.

6. In order to make Jews ever conscious of their responsibility to work incessantly until help is offered European Jewry, a uniform prayer followed by a minute of silence should be recited wherever Jews gather in numbers of ten or more—at parties, weddings, meetings,

etc., until the end of the war.

7. A uniform prayer, such as an extra Kaddish, should be recited by the entire congregation in all synagogue services until the end of the war. In this way we would mourn those Jews who have no one left to mourn for them, and we would always remind ourselves of our obligations to those Jews in Europe who still live.

The lives of five million Jews hang in the balance. It is up to us to do everything possible to save them *now*. Each day's delay means thousands of lives lost. When the final tabulation of those murdered has been published will American Jewry be able to say: "*Yadenu lo shafku et hadam hazeh*" (Our hands have not shed the blood")?

NOAH GOLINKIN
JEROME LIPNICK
N. BERTRAM SACHS

Book Notes

MAJOR TRENDS OF JEWISH MYS-TICISM, by Gershon G. Scholem. *Jewish Institute of Religion, New York, and Schocken Publishing House, Jerusalem.**

RELIGION is mysticism, indefinable exactly as that term is. The religious soul feels the presence of the Beyond which beckons him, and to reach this distant shore is the constant object of his striving. The omnipresent dualisms—mind and matter, soul and body, here and there, now and eternity—are resolved by the experience of meeting with the living God, eternal, infinite and holy. Judaism from its very

* Dr. Levy's contribution to the Chicago Fellowship Number, unfortunately postponed for lack of space.

beginning was saturated with mystic doctrine. Prophet and psalmist, lawgiver and priest, haggadist and halakist—all tried to enter the sacred arcanum where the riddle of existence would be solved. They made the daring leap of faith across the abyss which spans thought and being, to use philosophical terminology, and their courage was regarded. They found God and peace, the only answer to man's questionings.

Jewish Mysticism (with a capital M) is the Jewish way to the divine. Jewish history and thought determine the peculiar character of this discipline which varies from age to age, as for example, in ancient Gnostics and early modern Hasidim. The classic form of Jewish esoteric doctrine is the Kabbalah which, in its origins,

Appendix K

Editorial in *The Reconstructionist*, March 5, 1943

(see p. 67)

Vol. IX.   Adar I, 28, 5703   March 5, 1943   No. 2.

8

SAVE EUROPEAN JEWRY NOW!

WE HEARTILY ENDORSE the demand for immediate practical action voiced by the Seminary students in the article "Retribution Is Not Enlough," printed elsewhere in this issue, to save those Jews who still can be saved from the policy of utter and ruthless extermination which Hitler has decreed for all Jews in Nazi-occupied European lands.

A kind of paralysis has seized American Jewry. There is one section of American Jewry which seems to be wholly indifferent to the tragic plight of our European brethren, either because of plain ignorance of the facts, or out of fear of raising an undue clamor about what erroneously seems to them to be a specifically Jewish tragedy. Nothing too bitter can be said about such Jews. The rest of American Jewry, stricken dumb by grief, seems to have accepted resignedly the fate of European Jewry. There has been some fasting and much weeping and fervent praying, but no such concerted and ceaseless hammering at the conscience of mankind as will make the United Nations act with force and immediacy to stop the mass slaughter and to save those who can be saved.

If our inaction cannot be avoided, it can at least be understood, in the light of our sorrow and our hopelessness. But how explain the indifference, amounting almost to callousness, of our own country and of the other United Nations? The plight of Lidice aroused a continent, and other Lidices arose to take its place. Yet the hell of Lidice was but a spark compared to the gehenna of Warsaw, and Warsaw was only one of many such gehennas. Why are the nations silent and lift no hand to snatch the remaining Jews from certain death? The problem is not

(*Continued on Page 24*)

179

and there found access to Jewish learning, frowned upon by Orthodox educators, who opposed the teaching of Torah to girls. But Mrs. Schenierer had realized that, in the precarious situation of East European Jewry, the spirit of Jewish womanhood was the dam that might save it. First in her modest home, then in an apartment, she taught her young students, and finally moved to the seminary where I spent unforgettable days. The Friday night service was conducted by Mrs. Schenierer; no men were present. Advanced students gave proof of their ability in lectures or rather sermons on the *sidra*. The entire school organization from kindergarten to seminary took care of about 30,000 students, many of them so poor that they later paid back their tuition out of their meager salaries.

Every summer former students were reunited in study camps in the Carpathian mountains, and the spirit of devotion and faith, in the presence of often insurmountable odds, kept this unique organization full of its amazing vitality. It was not the spirit of ascetic nuns. Mrs. Schenierer herself, and many of the teachers that had been educated by her were married, and they were always fully aware that their teachings might, at any moment, meet the supreme test. Even in the comparatively normal conditions of Jewry in Poland between the two great wars, the existence of the Beth Jakob school organization had the startling effect of a miracle, a flame kept alive by will power and burning faith only. Its sublime victory should be remembered as a pledge of the ultimate victory of the spirit over might and power.

DORA EDINGER

(*Continued from Page* 8)
a Jewish problem; it is an American problem. If we American Jews do not act quickly, we shall be guilty not only as Jews but as Americans, and as human beings.

It may not be feasible to carry through the whole program outlined by the Seminary students, but we must do everything humanly possible in this situation. We must do nothing less than our best, and we must do it now. Nothing must stand in the way of organized united action on the part of all American Jews to save European Jewry. Let us proceed along all lines, and let us proceed at once!

Correspondence

A Kindly Rebuke

Sirs:

Please do not misunderstand me. I value your magazine very highly, but I do wish that you would reprimand those who disagree with you in a more kindly manner. I would rather have the opposition from within, and, as you know, before water can become clear, it has to flow over many rocks and stones. Believe me to be sincere.   HARRY ALTMAN,
Hollywood, Calif.

Dr. Pool Answers His Critic

Sirs:

I have before me the review of *The American Jew*, published in your issue of January 8th. I take no exception to your reviewer's strictures on the chapter I wrote insofar as they are based on honest differences of opinion and judgment. But I must point out that your reviewer has misconceived the whole function of the chapter assigned to me. Mine was not the task of interpreting various philosophies and approaches in Jewish religious life. This was the purpose of the chapter allotted to Rabbi Milton Steinberg. It was my less pleasant duty to give a factual presentation of the functioning of the Orthodox, Conservative, and Reform Synagogue in the historic American Jewish community. My chapter, therefore, in all honesty could not close its eyes to the weaknesses inevitable in the practical application of ideas to life. Your reviewer's criticisms should have been directed against these weaknesses, not against the recording of them.

I regret also to have to add that much of your reviewer's criticism is based on clear misquotation and misinterpretation of my words.
DAVID DE SOLA POOL,
Rabbi, Shearith Israel, New York, N. Y.

Appendix L
The Synagogue Council of America's Press Release
about the Sefira Campaign, April 9, 1943 (see p. 68)

1973

From Synagogue Council of America — Mailed, Friday, April 9
Committee for Emergency Intercession
607 W. 161 Street, New York City

Tel. Washington Heights 7-3725

FOR RELEASE ON RECEIPT

SYNAGOGUE COUNCIL OF AMERICA PROCLAIMS A
SIX-WEEK PERIOD OF "MOURNING AND INTERCESSION"
FOR EUROPE'S JEWS; JEWS URGED JOIN CHRISTIAN
OBSERVANCE MAY 2 AS DAY OF COMPASSION

The Jews of America will mourn the loss of 2 million
European Jews exterminated by Hitler and make urgent pleas for
governmental action to rescue as many as possible of those remaining in Nazi-held Europe, during a six-week "Period of
Mourning and Intercession", proclaimed by the Synagogue Council
of America.

This Period will start on the closing day of Passover,
April 26-27 (in orthodox and conservative synagogues, it is
April 27, in reformed temples, April 26), which is a customary
day of memorial in Jewish life, and continues until the ob-
servance of Shavuoth, June 9. This extends over the Safirah
Season, traditionally a period of mourning.

The program is under the direction of a specially ap-
pointed Committee for Emergency Intercession of the Synagogue
Council of America, of which Rabbi Israel Goldstein, of
Congregation B'nai Jeshurun, is president. Its members are
Rabbi Milton Steinberg of the Park Avenue Synagogue in New York
City, chairman; Dr. Joseph Lookstein, president of the Rabbinical
Council of America; Rabbi Max Maceaby of the Free Synagogue
of Mount Vernon, and Rabbi Ahron Opher, of the Hebrew Tabernacle,
who is secretary.

2. Period of Mourning and Intercession for Europe's Jews.

A special Memorial Service in synagogues throughout the
land on the last day of Passover will usher in the Period of
Mourning and Intercession. The week following will be a week
of mourning to be observed in the tradition of Shivah (mourning
for the dead). It will culminate on Sunday, May 2, the Day
of Intercession, which has also been designated by the
Federal Council of Churches of Christ in America, for observance by Protestants throughout the country, as a "Day of
Compassion of the Jewish Victims of Nazi Barbarism".

A resolution adopted on March 16, by the Federal Council
of Churches, setting this day, urges "the Christian people
throughout the country to give their moral support to whatever
measures afford promise of rescuing European Jews", and appeals
to our government to give full consideration to plans of rescue.

Such plans are now being presented to the government by
the newly created United Jewish Emergency Relief Committee,
composed of representatives of the American Jewish Committee,
The American Jewish Congress, B'nai B'rith, the Jewish Labor
Committee, the Zionist Emergency Committee, the Agudas Israel,
the Union of Orthodox Rabbis and the Synagogue Council of
America.

Special events on May 2 will include interfaith gatherings
with prominent Jews and Christians as the speakers, and a
nation-wide radio broadcast sponsored by the National Conference
of Christians and Jews. The combined voices of Protestants,
Catholics and Jews will be raised in behalf of the Jews of
Europe, against whom Hitler is carrying out a systematic policy

182

3. Period of Mourning and Intercession for Europe's Jews.

of ruthless extermination.

During the six-week Period of Mourning and Intercession synagogues in every part of the country will conduct special memorial services. Jews are being asked to observe Mondays and Thursdays as partial fast days, to limit occasions of amusement, and to make extra contributions to the United Jewish Appeal, which is engaged in rescue work for European Jews. Special prayers are to be recited and moments of silence observed at home and in public meetings. Certain days in the Jewish calendar which are traditionally observed as semi-festival days during this period will be accepted. Frequent religious gatherings will be organized by the leading rabbis in communities throughout the nation.

In announcing the Period of Mourning and Intercession, the Committee for Emergency Intercession declared:

"The sword of extermination is being wielded mercilessly over our people in Nazi-held Europe. Every voice which escapes through the walls of that vast tear and blood-drenched prison echoes the death cry of tortured, massacred, despoiled, humiliated and enslaved Jews.

"'Tell them that we are all dying' was the most recent message smuggled out of the Polish ghetto. 'Let them rescue all those who will still be alive when the report reaches them'.

"What is our response to this cry? Most of us have realized our helplessness as individuals to awaken the consciousness of America and the United Nations to the stake of humanity in the fate of European Jewry, and we have hoped

4. Period of Mourning and Intercession for Europe's Jews.

and striven for a united and untiring outcry that would stir them to taking immediate measures of rescue and relief.

"While attempting to arouse the religious and humanitarian conscience of the Christian world, it is of utmost importance that we awaken the religious spirit of our people to respond to this greatest calamity that has fallen upon our brethren.

"Penitence, prayer and charity remove the evil decree, 'Uthshiva uthfila utzdaka maavirin eth roa hagzera'. To translate this sacred doctrine into concrete and meaningful action the Synagogue Council of America is summoning all the religious leaders of American Jewry".

# # #

Appendix M
Part of the SCA Packet of Materials, April 19, 1943

(see pp. 68-70)

SYNAGOGUE COUNCIL OF AMERICA
COMMITTEE FOR EMERGENCY INTERCESSION
607 WEST 161st STREET, NEW YORK, N. Y.

TELEPHONE WASH. HEIGHTS 7-3725/3461

RABBI AHRON OPHER, SECRETARY

CONSTITUENT ORGANIZATIONS

UNION OF AMERICAN HEBREW CONGREGATIONS   CENTRAL CONFERENCE OF AMERICAN RABBIS
UNION OF ORTHODOX JEWISH CONGREGATIONS   RABBINICAL ASSEMBLY OF AMERICA
UNITED SYNAGOGUE OF AMERICA   RABBINICAL COUNCIL OF AMERICA

RABBI ISRAEL GOLDSTEIN, Pres.
RABBI HERBERT S. GOLDSTEIN, Vice-Pres.
RABBI ISAAC LANDMAN, Vice-Pres.

CHARLES P. KRAMER, Hon. Sec.
MAX FINK, Treas.
BENJAMIN KOENIGSBERG, Cor. Sec.

Committee for Emergency Intercession
RABBI MILTON STEINBERG, Chairman
RABBI JOSEPH H. LOOKSTEIN
RABBI MAX MACCOBY

April 19, 1943.

Dear Colleague:

We are sending you herewith the following items which may be helpful to you in your observance of the Period of Mourning and Intercession:

1. Suggestions for Service of Intercession, which you may adopt for the service of May 2nd, and any special service which you might conduct during this period.

2. A prayer for home use, which you may wish to multigraph and make available to all your congregants and friends, that they may recite at home after the major daily meal, particularly on Mondays and Thursdays.

3. A prayer for use at public gatherings during the Sefirah Season, which you may wish to recommend to the presidents of your affiliated and non-affiliated organizations.

4. A leaflet published by the National Conference of Christians and Jews, which you may find helpful in your public addresses and which you may want to distribute among your Christian friends. You may get more copies of this leaflet by writing to the National Conference of Christians and Jews, 381 Fourth Avenue, New York City.

Some synagogues in the East are planning to have a black drape or stripe on the Holy Ark as well as special candles lighted at all services, in memory of the victims, except on days when tradition forbids mourning.

The New York Times of April 19th, commenting editorially on the Anglo-American Conference at Bermuda on the refugee problem, said in part: "It appears to be pitifully inadequate...... After witnessing the Nazi mass murders for years, these two leading exponents of humanitarian ideals are still wholly in the dark as to what to do...... The present conference is strictly limited to 'exploratory consultations', with the result that the ultimate help that may grow out of it may well prove to be 'too little and too late'".

185

continued:

2.

The United Jewish Committee for Emergency Relief has presented to our government a concrete twelve point program of action. This constitutes the official demands of American Jewry. The Synagogue Council, which is a constituent of the United Emergency Committee, has undertaken a nation-wide program of galvanizing the religious conscience of the country to effectuate these demands.

Religious Jewry has a duty to act as well as to pray. The mitzvoth of saving lives, Pikuah Nefesh, and redeeming the captives, Pidyon Shevuyim, are paramount in Jewish tradition. The synagogue has a unique function in the endeavor of saving lives - - it should be our task to implement the work of the United Emergency Committee by endeavoring:

    a. To arouse our government to take decisive action to save
       European Jewry.
    b. To win the support of public opinion for this program.
    c. To emphasize continually and tirelessly that Jews CAN be saved
       now, that we need not and dare not wait until the end of the war.

Things To Be Done:

1. Publicize as widely as possible the Period of Mourning and Intercession, so that Christians as well as Jews will know the concern of religious America over the fate of our European brethren. Stress the need for help as well as sympathy. Secure time on the radio. Urge editorials in the local press.

2. Organize a permanent synagogue committee to work continually with the Committee for Emergency Intercession of the Synagogue Council.

3. Initiate a letter writing campaign by members and affiliates of the synagogue, to Congressmen and the White House. (A sample letter was enclosed in our communication of April 14th).

4. Persuade the local Christian clergymen of their religious duty to bring their influence to bear upon their congregations to intercede on our behalf with Congress and the State Department.

5. Organize local committees to contact all civic, labor and political organizations to adopt resolutions, (similar to the sample attached to our April 14th communication) and send them to their representatives and to the press.

6. Convince all important civic, political and social leaders to make public statements supporting the demands of the United Emergency Committee.

7. Adopt the symbol of mourning as the mark of all Jews for the Sefirah Period. The wearers must be ready to explain its meaning to non-Jews. Women's organizations of each synagogue will gladly provide these ribbons which should be distributed with proper ceremony during the Yiskor Service.

continued: 3.

The synagogue must remember that it is easy to forget. One week, even
six weeks of activity, is not enough! The "exploratory" conference in
Bermuda is not enough! We cannot be silent until the massacres are
stopped or until the exodus of Jews from Nazi Europe is complete.

And may the Lord establish the work of our hands.

                              Faithfully yours,

AO:DKR
                              Rabbi Ahron Opher, Secretary
                              Committee for Emergency Intercession

SUGGESTED PROGRAM FOR
SYNAGOGUE OR ORGANIZATION MEETING

Synagogue Council of America

1. The Star Spangled Banner.

2. Opening - Special prayer suggested by the Synagogue Council,
   followed by a minute of silence.

3. Opening remarks by the Chairman.

4. Responsive reading: "Tachanun" Penitential Prayer - (Bloch
   Standard Prayer Book, p. 77-9)

5. Report on the situation of the Jews of Europe at the present
   time, and the activities under way to offer them succor and
   rescue.

6. Selections from the statements of Church leaders regarding the
   Nazi program of persecution and extermination.
   a. Protests Against Vichy's Treatment of Jews - Contemporary
      Jewish Record: December, 1942.
   b. The Rt. Rev. Henry St. George Tucker, President, Federal
      Council of Churches - Congress Weekly, March 5, 1943.
   c. Resolution of the Church Peace Union, - 70 Fifth Avenue,
      N.Y.C.
   d. Appeals of the Archbishops of Canterbury, York, and Wales
      to the British Government.

7. Presentation of the Thirteen Point Resolution drawn up by the
   Joint Emergency Committee for European Jewish Affairs.

8. Discussion, led by communal leader or rabbi.
   The religious duty of trying to save lives.
   What can we and our community do to help effect the program of
   the Joint Emergency Committee to aid the Jews of Europe?
   Resolutions, letters to government officials, contributions to
   UJA, etc.

9. Reading: The Valley of Dry Bones (Ezekiel, chap. 37, 1-14)
   or, Comfort Ye, Comfort Ye, My People (Isaiah, chap. 40).

10. Close with appropriate Hymn or song.

SYNAGOGUE COUNCIL OF AMERICA

* *
* COMMITTEE FOR EMERGENCY INTERCESSION *
* 607 West 161st Street, New York *

SUGGESTIONS FOR SERVICE OF INTERCESSION - May 2, 1943

A. REGULAR MORNING SERVICE

B. SUPPLEMENTARY SELECTIONS WHICH MAY BE USED OR ADOPTED BY EACH
RABBI TO SUIT HIS CONGREGATION'S LITURGICAL REQUIREMENTS

    1. INVOCATIONS (select one or more)
       a. Blow the horn (p. 1)
       b. Our king, our God (p. 1)
       c. Our brethren, the house of Israel (p. 6)

    2. RESPONSIVE READINGS (select one or more)
       a. O Lord, hear my prayer (p. 2)
       b. O Lord, God of Israel (p. 3)
       c. From all sickness (p. 8)

    3. UNISON READINGS (select one or more)
       a. May it be Thy will (p. 3)
       b. May it be Thy will (p. 4)
       c. To Thy tranquil abode (p. 7)

    4. SPECIAL READINGS (select one or more)
       a. Merciful Father (p. 5)
       b. From the depth (p. 6)
       c. O God, who dwellest on high (p. 4)

    5. PSALMS (select one or more)
       20, 69, 70, 74, 79, 80, 109

    6. MEMORIAL PRAYERS (select one)
       a. O God full of compassion (p. 7)
       b. The Special Memorial Prayer issued
         for the Concluding Day of Passover

    7. CONCLUDING PRAYER (select one)
       a. Teach us oh Lord (p. 8)
       b. O God, the life that is rooted in
         Thee (p. 5)

- - - - - - - - - -

Edited, translated and prepared
by Rabbi Ahron Opher

189

Appendix N
Prayers for the SCA Sefira Campaign, April 19, 1943

(the first two were authored by Noah Golinkin; see pp. 69-70)

PRAYER TO BE USED AT MEETINGS DURING THE PERIOD OF MOURNING
AND INTERCESSION, FOLLOWED BY MINUTE OF SILENCE

Arranged by the
Synagogue Council of America

אֵלִי אֵלִי לָמָה עֲזַבְתָּנִי?

לָמָה יְיָ תַּעֲמוֹד בְּרָחוֹק, תַּעְלִים לְעִתּוֹת בַּצָּרָה?

אֱלֹהַי, אֶקְרָא יוֹמָם וְלֹא תַעֲנֶה וְלַיְלָה וְלֹא דֻמִיָּה לִי.

יְיָ אֱלֹהֵי יִשְׂרָאֵל שׁוּב מֵחֲרוֹן אַפֶּךָ וְהִנָּחֵם עַל הָרָעָה לְעַמֶּךָ;

חוּסָה יְיָ עָלֵינוּ בְּרַחֲמֶיךָ, וְאַל תִּתְּנֵנוּ בִּידֵי אַכְזָרִים,

קוּמָה אֱלֹהִים רִיבָה רִיבֶךָ כִּי עָלֶיךָ הֹרַגְנוּ כָל הַיּוֹם נֶחְשַׁבְנוּ כְּצֹאן טִבְחָה.

כִּי הִנֵּה אוֹיְבֶיךָ יֶהֱמָיוּן וּמְשַׂנְאֶיךָ נָשְׂאוּ רֹאשׁ; אָמְרוּ: לְכוּ וְנַכְחִידֵם מִגּוֹי וְלֹא יִזָּכֵר שֵׁם יִשְׂרָאֵל עוֹד.

כְּרַחֵם אָב עַל בָּנִים כֵּן תְּרַחֵם יְיָ עָלֵינוּ.

אֱלֹהַי! נֶעֱצַר כְּאֵבֵנוּ בְּתוֹכֵנוּ וַנֶּאֱלַם דֻּמִיָּה.

בְּתִפְלַת חֲשָׁאִי נְקַדֵּשׁ נָא אֶת זֵכֶר הַמּוּמָתִים שֶׁנִּדַּמּוּ לָנֶצַח,

תִּשָּׁמַע דְּמָמָה דַקָּה זוֹ מִסּוֹף הָעוֹלָם וְעַד סוֹפוֹ.

תִּזְעֲזַע אֶת נִשְׁמוֹת בְּנֵי הָאָדָם וְתַגִּיעַ עַד כִּסֵּא כְבוֹדֶךָ.

My God, my God, why hast Thou forsaken me?

Why hidest Thou Thyself in times of trouble?

Oh my God, I call by day, but Thou answerest not; and at night, but I find no relief.

Oh Lord God of Israel, turn from Thy wrath, and hold back this evil against Thy people.

Have compassion on us, Oh Lord, in Thine abundant mercy, and deliver us not into the power of the tyrants.

Arise, oh God, plead Thine own cause: for Thy sake are we killed all the day, are we treated as sheep at the slaughter.

For lo, Thine enemies are in an uproar, and they that hate Thee have lifted up their head. They have called, "Come, let us blot out their existence, that the name of Israel may be no more."

As a father hath compassion upon his children, so have Thou compassion for us, oh Lord.

Our anguish is locked up within us, and we are silent. In our hearts we sanctify the memory of the slain who are silenced forever. May our silence be felt to the ends of the earth. May it stir the souls of men, and reach up to Thee, O God of Mercy

Amen

190

נוסח תפילה מיוחדת מחר וברכת ומזון במשך ימי העשירה חש"ג
מוצא ע"י המועצה הכללית של בתי הכנסת בא"ב דאמריקה

בֵרַכְנוּך אֱלֹהֵינוּ שֶׁאֲכַלְנוּ וְשָׂבַעְנוּ מִטּוּבֶךָ .

אֲבָל אֵיכָכָה יֶנְעַם מָזוֹן לְחִכֵּנוּ בְּעוֹד אֲשֶׁר אֵינֵינוּ הִגֵּי יִשְׂרָאֵל

חַלְלֵי חֶרֶב וְרָעָב, מְשֻׁלָּכִים בְּרֹאשׁ חוּצוֹת?

אָנָּא יְיָ, בְּרָא בְּתוֹכֵנוּ לֵב חָדָשׁ אֲשֶׁר יֶחֱרַד וּכְאֵב אַחֵינוּ שְׂרִידֵי מָוֶת,

לֵב אֲשֶׁר לֹא יָנוּחַ וְלֹא יִשְׁקֹט עֲדֵי נוֹשִׁיט לָהֶם עֵזֶר בַּצָּרָה.

אַב הָרַחֲמִים תְּנָה בְּלִבֵּנוּ רוּחַ חֶמְלָה וָחֶסֶד, לִפְרֹס מִלַּחְמֵנוּ לָאֻמְלָלִים הַגּוֹעִים

בְּרָעָב וּבִיגוֹן, וְהַצֵּלְנוּ אֶת שְׁאֵרִית הַפְּלֵטָה, וְחָיְתָה נֶפֶשׁ נַפְשָׁם בִּגְלָלֵנוּ.

הַשְׁקִיפָה מִמְּעוֹן קָדְשְׁךָ עַל צֹאן מַרְעִיתֶךָ, חָנְנֵם וְהוֹשִׁיעֵם לְמַעַן שְׁמֶךָ, וְהָסֵר

מֵהֶם מַכַּת מַגֵּפָה וּגְזֵרוֹת קָשׁוֹת, כִּי עֵינֵיהֶם לְךָ צְפוּיוֹת.

HOME PRAYER TO BE RECITED DAILY AFTER THE MAIN MEAL
Arranged by the Synagogue Council of America.

O Lord our God, source of all blessing, we thank Thee for
the nourishment that sustains us.

But how can we enjoy our food while we know that our brothers
perish by famine and sword in the ravaged lands of the tyrant.
Create in us, O God, a new heart responsive to the agony of
our people, the suffering remnants of Israel: May we know no
rest 'til we have stretched out our hands to them in help.

Father of mercy, create in us a spirit of compassion and
loving kindness, to share our bread with the starving and to
seek rescue for those who can be saved, that they may live
because of us.

Look down, O Lord, upon Thy children, have mercy upon them and
save them for Thy name's sake, and remove from them the scourge
and the evil decrees, for their hope is in Thee.

תְּפִלַּת יִזְכּוֹר לְאַחֲרוֹן שֶׁל פֶּסַח ה'תשׁ"ג

נֻסַח תְּפִלָּה מוּצָעָה עַל יְדֵי הַמּוֹעֵצָה הַכְּלָלִית שֶׁל בָּתֵּי הַכְּנֶסֶת כָּאי"הב-דְּאָמֶרִיקָה

יִזְכּוֹר אֱלֹהִים אֶת נִשְׁמוֹת חַלְלֵי הַקְּרָב בֵּין שֶׁהֵם בְּנֵי בְּרִית וּבֵין שֶׁאֵינָם בְּנֵי
בְּרִית, אֲשֶׁר חֵרְפוּ אֶת נַפְשָׁם לָמוּת סוֹת גְּבוּרִים בְּמַעַרְכוֹת הַקְּרָב, בַּיַּבָּשָׁה בַּיָּם
וּבָאֲוִיר, בְּמִלְחֶמֶת מִצְוָה זוֹ שֶׁל כָּל הָעַמִּים הַנֶּעֱרָכִים כְּנֶגֶד מַלְכוּת הָרֶשַׁע הַמְנַאֶצֶת
שֵׁם שָׁמַיִם וּמְחַלֶּלֶת כָּל קֹדֶשׁ, הַשּׁוֹפְכוֹת כַּמַּיִם דְּמֵי אֲנָשִׁים נָשִׁים וָטַף, וְדוֹרְסוֹת
בָּרֶגֶל נָאוָה אֶת צֶלֶם אֱלֹהִים. זְכֹר נָא אֱלֹהֵי צְבָאוֹת, אֶת נִשְׁמוֹת בָּנֶיךָ שֶׁהִקְרִיבוּ
אֶת חַיֵּיהֶם עַל מִזְבַּח כְּבוֹד הָאָדָם וּגְאֻלָּתוֹ. שְׁפוֹךְ זַעְמְךָ עַל עוֹשֵׂי הָרָעָה וְהַתּוֹעֵבָה
וְהַשְּׁמִידֵם מִתַּחַת הַשָּׁמַיִם. הָחֵשׁ אֶת פַּעֲמֵי הַנִּצָּחוֹן לָאֻמּוֹת הַמְאֻגָּדוֹת, לְמַעַן שְׁמֶךָ.
הוֹצִיאֵנוּ מֵעַבְדוּת לְחֵירוּת, מִיָּגוֹן לְשִׂמְחָה וּמֵאֲפֵלָה לְאוֹר גָּדוֹל.

יִזְכּוֹר אֱלֹהִים אֶת נִשְׁמוֹת מְאוֹרֵי יִשְׂרָאֵל, חַכְמֵיהֶם וּפַרְנְסֵיהֶם שֶׁנֶּעֶוְעוּ בִּקְהִלּוֹת
הַקְּדוֹשׁוֹת בִּמְדִינוֹת אַשְׁכְּנַז פּוֹלִין, רוֹמַנְיָא, הוּנְגַרְיָא, צָרְפַת, הוֹלַנְד
בּוּלְגַרְיָא, יָוָן, יוּגוֹסְלַוְיָא, צְכוֹסְלוֹבַקְיָא, לִיסָא, אִיטַלְיָא, וּבִשְׁאָר מִשְׁכְּנוֹת הַיְּהוּדִים,
קְהִלּוֹת נוֹשָׁנוֹת בְּעֵת שִׂמְחוֹת, בְּלוֹ נְדִיכֵי עַם הוֹגֵי בְּדַעַת נְעִים, חָרְבוּ בָּתֵּי
כְּנֵסִיּוֹת בָּתֵּי מִדְרָשׁוֹת חָדְלוּ, נֶהֶרְסוּ בָּתֵּי וַעַד וּבָתֵּי עֶקֶד נִשְׂרְפוּ וְנִשָּׁדְדוּ
וּמַנְהִיגֵיהֶם גּוֹרְשׁוּ, נִרְדְּפוּ וְנִרְצָחוּ, יָרְשׁוּ זָרִים חַיָּלִם בְּרֶשַׁע הַכְּבִידוּ עֻלָּם,
בַּעֲלִילוֹת וּבְעַנּוּיִים רַבִּים דָּמוּ לְהַשְׁבִּית תּוֹרָה מִיִּשְׂרָאֵל גִּלְכְּפוּת מְאוֹר הָאֱמֶת.
זְכֹר נָא אֱלֹהֵי הַצֶּדֶק אֶת נִשְׁמוֹת צַדִּיקֵי יִשְׂרָאֵל שֶׁמֵּתוּ עַל קְדוּשַׁת שְׁמֶךָ. הַחֲזֵר
שְׁכִינָתְךָ בְּתוֹכֵנוּ. הֲשִׁיבֵנוּ ה' אֵלֶיךָ וְנָשׁוּבָה, חַדֵּשׁ יָמֵינוּ כְּקֶדֶם.

יִזְכּוֹר אֱלֹהִים אֶת הַנְּשָׁמוֹת הַטְּהוֹרוֹת שֶׁל בְּנֵי יִשְׂרָאֵל אֲשֶׁר נָפְלוּ חֶלֶל בִּידֵי
בְּרוֹאֵי אָדָם שְׁלִיחֵי מֶמְשֶׁלֶת הַזָּדוֹן, וְנִרְצְחוּ בְּעָרִיצוּת וּבְעַנּוּיִים נוֹרָאִים אֲשֶׁר
נִסְבְּחוּ נִשְׂרְפוּ נִטְבְּעוּ וְנִקְבְּרוּ חַיִּם לָאוֹר חַיִּים וּבְאִישׁוֹן לַיִל, בְּרֹאשׁ חֻצֹת
וּבְשִׁכְלֵי דְרָכִים בְּמִשְׁכָּנוֹת וּבְמִסְתָּרִים, בְּפָעֳלָם בִּמְלַאכְתָּם, בְּעָסְקָם בַּתּוֹרָה וּבְעָמְדָם
בִּתְפִלָּה וּבְמִפְנוּסָתָם מֵחֶרֶב הָרוֹעֵץ. בַּעַל הָרַחֲמִים יַסְתִּירֵם בְּסֵתֶר כְּנָפָיו לְעוֹלָמִים
וִיצְרוֹר בִּצְרוֹר הַחַיִּים אֶת נִשְׁמָתָם, בְּגַן עֵדֶן תְּהֵא מְנוּחָתָם, ה' הוּא נַחֲלָתָם,
וְיָנוּחוּ בְּשָׁלוֹם עַל מִשְׁכָּבָם, וְנֹאמַר אָמֵן.

יִזְכּוֹר יִשְׂרָאֵל וְיִתְבָּרֵךְ בְּזַרְעוֹ וְיֶאֱבַל עַל הֲדַרַת הַזָּקֵן וְעַל זִיו הָעֲלוּמִים
עַל חוּפַת הַיַּלְדוּת וְעַל חֶמְדַּת הַגְּבוּרָה וְעַל סֵתֶר הָאִמָּהוֹת אֲשֶׁר נָסְפוּ וְנֶעֶכְּרוּ
אַל יִשְׁקֹס וְאַל יִנָּחֵם וְאַל יָפוּג הָאֵבֶל עַד בּוֹא יוֹם הַגְּאֻלָּה, וְיִבְקַע כַּשַּׁחַר אוֹרִי
הַשָּׁלוֹם, הָאֱמֶת וְהַצֶּדֶק וְהָאַחֲוָה, בִּמְהֵרָה בְיָמֵינוּ וְנֹאמַר אָמֵן.

192

MEMORIAL PRAYER FOR THE CONCLUDING DAY OF PASSOVER, 5703
Arranged by the Synagogue Council of America
* * *

Congregation:
May the Lord remember the souls of the valiant men, Jews and non-Jews, who have
fallen heroically on the far-flung battle fronts of this sacred struggle of humanity
against brutality.

Rabbi:
Remember, O Lord of Hosts, the blood of Thy children, of the nations united against
the oppressors of mankind.
Strengthen with Thy might the armies which are now marching to break the power of
the merciless tyrants.
Hasten the day when the evil doers will be made powerless, so that men and nations
may go forth from slavery unto freedom, from sorrow unto gladness, from darkness
unto light. Amen.
* * *

Congregation:
May the Lord remember the souls of the sages, teachers and leaders of the holy
congregations of Israel who have perished in the ravaged lands of Europe. Age old
communities have been devastated, their guardians slain and scattered, their
sanctuaries desecrated, their houses of learning razed and their treasures burned
and looted.
Strangers have seized their heritage, seeking ruthlessly to extinguish the light
of the Torah.

Rabbi:
Remember, O Lord of Truth and Justice, the souls of the holy men in Israel who were
destroyed while sanctifying Thy name.
Restore Thy spirit in our midst.
Turn Thou us unto Thee, O Lord, and we shall be turned; renew our days as of old.
Amen.
* * *

Congregation:
May the Lord remember the souls of the sons and daughters of Israel who have
fallen prey to men of violence.
Countless numbers of them have been tortured, slaughtered and buried alive, in
daylight and in darkness, in forest and in field, taken from the pursuit of their
labors, from the study of Thy law, from their homes, while fleeing from the
pursuing sword.

Rabbi:
Remember, O Lord of Mercy, the souls of Thy martyred children, shelter them under
the cover of Thy wings, and grant them the blessedness of everlasting peace. Amen.
* * *

Rabbi and Congregation:
At this time of memorial we pray Thee, O God, that the memory of these, the dear
and beloved, shall never vanish from our thoughts.
May they live in our hearts, in our will and in our actions.
May our devotion to Thy service be rekindled as a lamp of memory to them, a light
that shall never be extinguished. Amen.
* * *

Appendix O
Letter from Jerry Lipnick to his brother Bernie,
April 28, 1943 (see pp. 132-133)

3070 Broadway
April 28, 1943

Dear Bernie,
Today [Tomorrow] is your birthday — 17 years old —
you're growing up, but you've been grown up
for a long time. You know by this time
what is right and what is wrong. I'm glad to
see that you're casting your lot with the
right — most of the time anyway. You've got a good start

I want to leave you just one word —
and that is "Consecration".

Consecrate yourself Wipsey to fight for
the rights of the oppressed. — for the underdog,
for the persecuted.

Consecrate yourself to fight for the freedom
of your brother Jews abroad, and for your
Negro brothers within.

Consecrate Yourself to build America as
a place where all groups can retain their own
individuality, their own hopes and ambitions.

Consecrate yourself to help build ארץ
ישראל for only from there can תורה be
spread to a תורה less world.

Consecrate yourself to be a nice guy
to labor for others, to give to others,
to live for others.

And never slacken in your determination
no matter how black the future, small the

194

dividends. Today the future is black for the world, and for the Jew in particular. & goodness pays little

Enclosed is a black ribbon – wear it. It's not for mourning. – don't let me be afraid It's for protest. against those who permit the Jews to die today with out anyone lifting a hand to help

You've got to learn how to show your dis satisfaction, your disgust at all the hypocrisy and sham and lying which daily confronts you. – and not to be calmed You can't be just a complainer, a beefer but also a builder. Before you build a new house you have to destroy what stands in the way.

Wear your Jewishness proudly, your disagreements proudly, and so for your consecration keep that as of your propelling drive, but wear it modestly.

Yours brother, Jerome

Appendix P
Press Clippings about the Sefira Campaign, from the
Scrapbooks of the SCA (see pp. 74-77)

SEPHIRAH SEASON PROCLAIMED AS PERIOD OF MOURNING AND INTERCESSION

The Synagogue Council of America has proclaimed a six-week Period of Mourning and Intercession, to be observed by the Jews of America on behalf of their murdered and suffering brothers. The communication of the Synagogue Council states in part: "This period is to begin on April 27th, the last day of Passover, and will be marked not only by a great outpouring of sorrow and mourning for those whom Hitler has already destroyed, but by a plan of action to rescue those still remaining in Nazi held Europe, before they, too, are annihilated."

Among the suggestions made for the observance of this period, are: (1) reading the Proclamation of the Synagogue Council of America at meetings; (2) reciting suitable prayers in Hebrew and English at all assemblies and meetings, to be followed by a minute of silence; (3) reciting special prayers at home, particularly on Mondays and Thursdays; (4) arranging special programs at meetings and assemblies; (5) wearing a black ribbon as a symbol of commisseration; (6) contributing to the United Jewish Appeal.

We urge all Jewish schools in the city to respond to the call of the Synagogue Council of America, and arrange for suitable instruction, services and programs, as well as for the wearing of the black ribbon by all pupils during this period, and contributions by them to the United Jewish Appeal.

The materials prepared in this connection by the Synagogue Council will be mailed by the Jewish Education Committee to all schools.

Der Tog - May 25, 1943

Jewish Education Committee Bulletin of Information - May 1943

RESORT JEWRY SETS SUNDAY FOR 'DAY OF PRAYER-INTERCESSION'

The nation-wide "Day of Prayer and Intercession" on behalf of the martyred Jews of Nazi Europe will be marked in Atlantic City by a joint Assembly in the Rodef Sholem Synagogue, 2016 Pacific av., at 11 o'clock Sunday morning.

All of the resort synagogues will participate and the one hour service will be conducted by Rabbis B. Reuben Weilerstein, Mosheh Shapiro and Herman Kieval and Joseph R. Narot, Chaplain Milton Aron and Cantors Jacob Barkin and Morris Schwartz.

Delegates to the four State Regional Conference of the Jewish War Veterans will attend the service as will men of the local post led by Chaplain Aron. Older students from the Religious Schools will also attend.

May 2nd has been proclaimed as the national Day of Prayer and Intercession by both the Synagogue Council of America and the Federal Council of Churches of Christ. Christians are joining Jews in prayer all over the nation. The Atlantic City public Assembly is the high light of a six-week period of mourning and devotions which was inaugurated at the special Yizkor Services on the last day of Passover. At the Assembly specific instructions will be given to each individual and to each organization as to how to conduct themselves during the period of mourning and intercession.

Atlantic City Jewish Record - April 30, 1943

196

OMAHA JEWRY WILL OBSERVE MOURNING DAY

Community - Wide Service Will Be Held on May 21st

Omaha Jewish congregations will join with synagogues throughout the land in mourning the loss of two million European Jews exterminated by Hitler and in urging saving the remaining Jews, it was announced by Rabbi Arthur J. Lelyveld, secretary of the Synagogue Council of Omaha.

Plans for the Sefira Season observance were outlined at a meeting of the Synagogue Council at the Jewish Community Center.

The city's synagogues held special memorial services for Jewish martyrs abroad on the concluding day of Passover, and rabbis devoted their sermons to the state of European Jewry and the proposed program of rescue.

On May 21 a community-wide special service of worship will be held at Temple Israel with Rabbi David Goldstein of Beth El synagogue occupying the pulpit.

Services for Children

Each congregation of the city will conduct special children's memorial services the morning of May 2.

May 2, the Day of Intercession, has been designated by the Federal Council of Churches of Christ in America for observance by Protestants throughout the country as a "day of compassion of the Jewish victims of Nazi barbarism."

Of the approximately 600 thousand Jews in Germany in 1939, the Federal Council of Churches estimated, not more than 40 thousand remained at the end of 1942.

Nebraska Jewish Press - April 30, 1943

JEWS TO MOURN DEAD AND LIVING HITLER VICTIMS

Jews of Chicago, joining with other religious groups throughout the world, began today a six-week period of mourning for the 2,000,000 martyred members of their race in Europe, and for the 3,000,000 to 5,000,000 still living there who are threatened with extinction.

The mourning will be in conjunction with the traditional Safirah period, which commences with the concluding days of Passover, today and tomorrow. The special observance has been ordered by the Synagogue Council of America, and will include prayers for the dead and the living in the Nazi-ravaged lands.

Jews of Orthodox and Reformed and Conservative congregations alike will participate in the mourning and prayer, according to the Chicago Rabbinical Association, which relayed the call of the national organization to the local temples and synagogues. Rabbi Charles E. Shulman of Glencoe, now on leave as chaplain with the armed forces, is president, and Rabbi Benjamin H. Birnbaum is vice-president.

It was announced that May 2 had been set aside as a day of intercession in behalf of the Jewish survivors of Europe. The entire population of America, Christian and Jewish alike, has been asked to participate.

Rabbi Birnbaum announced that he had communicated with all the Jewish congregations of Chicago urging observance of the mourning period, and had requested the various Christian churches to do the same.

He said also that there would be a nation-wide broadcast over the NBC network at 2:30 p. m., Chicago time, next Sunday at which a Catholic priest, a Protestant minister and a rabbi will appeal for prayer for persecuted Jews.

Chicago News - April 26, 1943

Temple School Children Plan Closing Exercises

The Sunday Religious School of Temple Adath Israel, 169th St. and the Concourse, will hold its closing exercises on Sunday. A representative from every class will speak on the accomplishments of his group. Certificates of merit and honor will be awarded to pupils who have distinguished themselves during the school year.

Conforming to the request of the United Synagogue Council of America which has set aside a period of mourning and intercession for the millions of Nazi victims in Europe, the exericses will not include the usual program of entertainment.

Above: *Bronx Home News*, May 27, 1943

Below: *San Francisco Examiner* - April 27, 1943

Memorial for Nazi Victims

State Rabbis To Offer Prayers For Victims Of Nazis

Forty Orthodox, Conservative, and Reform Rabbis of Connecticut will assemble at 10:30 Monday morning in Garden Street Synagogue for a special convocation devoted to mourning and intercession for the victims of persecution, Jewish and Gentile, in Europe. The Hartford meeting is one of many Rabbinical convocations called throughout the country at this time by the Synagogue Council of America, as part of the observance of a six weeks period of mourning for the victims of Nazi persecution.

The ceremonies on Monday will include the sounding of the Shofar, or ram's horn, the traditional call to penitence, the chanting of psalms in Hebrew, and responsive reading. Rabbi Harry Zwelling of New Britain will be the speaker. Prayers for Europe's sufferers will be made by Rabbi Abraham J. Feldman of Temple Beth Israel and Rabbi I. Solomon Rosenberg of Garden Street Synagogue. Rabbi Morris Silverman of Emanuel Synagogue will offer the prayer for a lasting victory and a just peace for all nations.

JEWS TO OBSERVE MOURNING PERIOD

R. I. Rabbinical Body Calls for Intercession for Persecuted

April 29 to June 8.

Following the lead of the Synagogue Council of America, the Rabbinical Association of Rhode Island has proclaimed the Sefirah Season, from April 29 to June 8, as a period of mourning and intercession on behalf of the persecuted and martyred Jews of Nazi-occupied countries in Europe.

The proclamation, issued by 11 spiritual leaders of Jewish synagogues in Rhode Island and Fall River and New Bedford, Mass., calls upon all members of the Hebrew faith to observe the period by fasting and attending special services dedicated to the cause of their countrymen.

In connection with the observance, a State-wide service of mourning and intercession will be held next Sunday afternoon at 5 o'clock in the historic Touro Synagogue in Newport, the oldest synagogue in America. All the rabbis of Rhode Island will unite in this service.

The Rabbinical Association also asks that the season of mourning be observed in these ways:

"To limit occasions of amusement during this season; to keep Mondays and Thursdays as partial fast days (omitting one meal, preferably the morning meal); to contribute generously to the United Jewish Appeal and other fund-raising agencies which are engaged in rescue work; to recite special prayers and observe moments of silence at home and in all public gatherings; to attend their synagogues frequently and call special assemblies, in order to demonstrate the stake of humanity and religion in the salvation of Europe's Jews."

Special services in connection with the closing of the Passover season were held yesterday in the reform congregation, Temple Beth-El, and are being held today in orthodox and conservative synagogues. At these services, black ribbons symbolic of mourning are being distributed and special sermons of compassion are being delivered.

Religious schools of the various congregations will hold Children's Memorial Services on Sunday, May 16, at 11 a. m., and the Providence Emergency Committee on European Jewish Affairs will sponsor a meeting on the night of May 16 in the auditorium of the R. I. School of Design, Market Square.

Mourning Period Begun For Victims Of Nazis

NEW YORK—Memorial services, opening a six-week period of mourning for the Jewish victims in Nazi Europe, were held in many synagogues throughout the country in accordance with a call issued by the Synagogue Council of America which represents Conservative, Orthodox and Reform Jewry in America——both rabbis and congregations. A special prayer, distributed by the Council to synagogues in all parts of the country, was delivered during the services. A call issued by the Council to all Jews in the United States urges that the six-week period of mourning be observed by limiting the occasions of amusement during this season; by keeping Mondays and Thursdays as partial fast days; by contributing generously to the United Jewish Appeal, which is engaged in rescue work; by reciting special prayers and observing moments of silence at home and in all public gatherings; by attending synagogues frequently and calling special assemblies, in order to demonstrate the stake of humanity and religion in the salvation of Europe's Jews, and by acting in every way to converge the religious opinion of America to the necessity for prompt action.

Top left: *Hartford Courant* - May 23, 1943
Right: *Providence Journal* - April 27, 1943
Bottom left: *National Jewish Ledger* - May 7, 1943

Rabbis Seek Release Of Nazi-Held Jews

New York Telegram - May 24, 1943

The release of Nazi-trapped Jews and the full opening of Palestine were asked today by several hundred rabbis from all parts of New York who attended a Rabbinical convocation summoned by the New York Board of Jewish Ministers to intercede for Jewish and non-Jewish victims in occupied Europe.

As part of the six-week mourning and intercession proclaimed by the Synagogue Council of America, the rabbis met in the synagogue of Congregation Kehillath Jeshurun, 117 E. 85th St., which was draped in black and its Holy Ark covered by a black banner bearing a quotation in English and Hebrew from the Book of Lamentations, "For these I weep."

Seek Aid of Roosevelt.

In a resolution sent to President Roosevelt and Prime Minister Churchill, the rabbis asked:

"1. That the governments of the United States and Great Britain pursue every means to effect the release of Jews from those Axis lands which are still in a position to exercise a measure of sovereignty.

"2. That Palestine, which is accessible not only by sea but also by land routes, be opened without political restrictions to all who

(Continued on Page Eight.)

Rabbis Would Free Nazi-Held Jews

(Continued from Page One)

can be rescued and for whom it is the nearest available refuge.

"3. That the United Nations provide financial guarantees to all such neutral states as have given or will give temporary refuge to Jews coming from Nazi-occupied territories, and provide for their feeding and maintenance and eventual evacuation.

Ask Food for Victims.

"4. That the United Nations take appropriate steps without delay to organize a system for the feeding of the victims of Nazi oppression who are unable to leave the jurisdiction and control of the Axis."

"No higher and holier task," said the rabbis, "has ever confronted civilized nations than that of doing all that may be done, however difficult and laborious, in order to rescue the imperiled Jews of Europe."

Yet, they said, the voices of protest have been "desultory" and the relief suggested by United Nations spokesmen "ineffectual."

"We cannot believe that Bermuda is the answer to the agonizing cry of the millions of innocent victims," said the resolution. "Evasion and helplessness must not be the way of the United Nations now, any more than concession and appeasement should have been the prewar policy of the democracies."

Wise Cites Need.

Rabbi Stephen S. Wise, chairman of the Joint Jewish Emergency Committee, said the Jews can be rescued "only if England and America take the lead, resourceful, courageous, far-visioning, in rescuing them from bondage, from danger and death."

"To withhold possible rescue and salvation from innocent human beings marked for extermination is a sin against both religion and humanitarianism," declared Rabbi Israel Goldstein, president of the Synagogue Council of America.

Rabbi Ahron Opher of Hebrew Tabernacle, chairman of the convocation committee, introduced the participants, who also included Rabbis Joseph H. Lookstein, president of the New York Board of Jewish Ministers; J. X. Cohen, Bernard Drachman, Israel Goldfarb, Louis I. Newman, David De Sola Pool, Max Raisin, Joseph Sarachek and Elias Solomon.

Sunday Day of Compassion

Two million Jews, unarmed, helpless men, women and children, have been murdered by the Nazis in Europe. Hundreds of thousands more have been and are being tortured in concentration camps and have been driven from their native lands. Previous history records nothing so fiendish as Adolf Hitler's effort to exterminate a race. Nero, Caesar, Borgia, none of the tyrants who have caused streets and countrysides to run red with human blood can approach in bestiality this monster, a product of modern "civilization."

The Christian religion, which sprang from a Jewish source and many of whose votaries anticipate an eventual return to Jerusalem and re-establishment as the chosen people of God for the people who gave Christ to the world. From Judaism, the religion of the one God, and Christianity, it ultimate development, have come all the great contributions to human progress. It is a tragedy of the ages that, after more than 3,000 years of Jewish blessings for humanity, an entire nation has been dedicated to destruction of the race and perhaps more disquieting many millions who profess the name of Christians cherish enmity against the race from whom their religion has come.

The plight of their European relatives has caused the Synagogue Council of America to proclaim a period of mourning and intercession from April 29 to June 8. Its proclamation recites the details of the horror and makes this challenge:

Christians and Jews dare not stand by while millions of innocent people are being slaughtered, without moving Heaven by prayer and earth by every human means to save those who linger in hopeless captivity. "Penitence, prayer and charity will remove the evil decree," through our own endeavors and with God's help.

Protestant Christians, acting through the Federal Council of Churches, have recognized their obligation of intercession to the one God for the Jewish people and also to urge that immediate steps be taken for aid and rescue.

This program comes home to Chattanooga Sunday in a special service at B'nai Zion Synagogue in a Day of Compassion "for the suffering of Nazi Europe," with addresses for the Protestants by Dr. James L. Fowle and Dr. Spencer J. McCallie and for the Jewish congregations by Rabbi Israel Gerstein. The service deserves the attendance, or at least the prayerful support, of every person who believes in peace and brotherhood, two essential fundamentals of the Christian faith, and of democracy.

Chattanooga News-Free Press - May 14, 1943

DAY OF COMPASSION PRAISED BY RABBIS

They Express Gratitude to the Church Council for Arranging for Christian Prayers Today

---

JEWS' LOT GROWS WORSE

Goldstein Says Nazis Intend to Destroy Them and Victory May Come Too Late

---

Rabbis yesterday expressed gratitude to churches affiliated with the Federal Council of the Churches of Christ in America for setting aside today as a Christian "Day of Compassion" for persecuted Jews in Europe.

Today is the first Sunday in a six-week period of mourning and intercession proclaimed by the Synagogue Council of America in behalf of the oppressed Jewry of Nazi-occupied countries.

"I am sure that if the message of this Christian Day of Compassion were to reach any of the tragic company of Jewish survivors in Nazi Europe who have survived only to await their turn to be exterminated," Rabbi Israel Goldstein said in Temple B'nai Jeshurun, Eighty-eighth Street, near Broadway, "that message would give them new strength and new hope.

"To understand the plight of Jews in Hitler's Europe is to understand that they are not merely another page in Hitler's voluminous catalogue of terror, like unto the Yugoslavs, the Greeks, the Poles, but that, unlike the others, their appointed lot is total and complete destruction.

"The other peoples, however decimated, will live to see the day of victory. As for the Jews, if a way is not to be found to rescue numbers of them, the victory of the United Nations will come too late to do them any good. They will be dead."

"Upon American Jewry falls the solemn responsibility of attempting to fulfill the lives of millions of Europe's Jews who have met the death of martyrs," Rabbi David de Sola Pool said in the Spanish and Portuguese Synagogue, Seventieth Street and Central Park West.

"The bloody uprooting from continental Europe of the learning, the culture and the piety that are rooted in the Old Testament has made American Jews into a new generation of Pilgrim Fathers called to tend and strengthen this ancient spiritual culture in the sunshine of free American democracy."

"The great Day of Intercession for the persecuted and massacred in countries under the yoke of the Nazis," Rabbi Louis I. Newman said in Temple Rodeph Sholom, 7 West Eighty-third Street, "should serve to awaken citizens of all faiths—Christian and Jew alike—to the enormity of the crimes which Hitler has perpetrated.

"If there be any persons who still doubt the accuracy of the reports from abroad, let them study only a minimum of the evidence available, and they must needs be convinced. The cooperation of many Christian churches in this enterprise of prayer and supplication is another proof of the fact that Hitler and Goebbels cannot divide us in our united endeavor to bring light and salvation to a stricken mankind."

"These days of intercession and mourning over the innocent victims of nazism," Rabbi Hyman J. Schachtel said in West End Synagogue, 160 West Eighty-second Street, "are prayerful hours directed not only to God but to the conscience of mankind."

Discussing the coal strike, Rabbi Herbert S. Goldstein in West Side Institutional Synagogue, 122 West Seventy-sixth Street, declared, "In the conflict between John L. Lewis and the President of the United States the people of the country are behind the President.

"The will of the people will be best expressed by the success with which the President's efforts will be crowned.

"John L. Lewis has demonstrated to the world that the United States of America is a true democracy even in time of war, wherein every citizen has the right to speak and to differ not only with the War Labor Board, the constituted authority concerning labor difficulties, but also with the President of the United States.

"Mr. Lewis would be imprisoned or shot if he acted similarly in Germany, in Italy or even in Russia. Of course the patriotism of the misguided miners and their leader, Mr. Lewis, will finally show itself to be paramount."

The reaction to Mr. Willkie's recent book was interpreted by Rabbi William F. Rosenblum in Temple Israel, 210 West Ninety-first Street, as reflecting "The American people's hope that after this war our nation will remain a nation indivisible with liberty and justice for all, while the world will become one world divisible yet with the assurance of liberty and justice for all peoples and an everlasting peace for mankind."

Post-war cooperation among the United Nations depends upon continuance of the unity of purpose that keeps them united during the war, Rabbi Samuel M. Segal said in Mount Neboh Temple, 130 West Seventy-ninth Street.

Above: *New York Times* - May 2, 1943

Below: *Brooklyn Jewish Examiner* - May 7, 1943

Milwaukee Churches Call on U. S., Allies to Open Doors to Refugees

MILWAUKEE, Wisc. (RNS)— The Milwaukee County Council of Churches has distributed a letter to all Jewish congregations in the city expressing sympathy for the persecuted Jews of Europe.

The letter was issued as part of the local observance of the "Day of Compassion" (May 2nd), designated as a period of "intercession for the Jewish people of Europe who are victims of persecution."

Text of the letter follows, in part:

"The Milwaukee County Council of Churches wishes to express to the Jewish congregations and people of Milwaukee our sympathy with you and your people throughout the world as they undergo these unspeakable persecutions, even unto death. Nothing more horrible or outrageous is to be found in the annals of history, certainly not in our modern, so-called civilized world.

"In addition to extending our sympathy and prayer we are urging that our government and other Allied governments, so far as possible within regular immigration quotas, open the way for other groups. It is also our hope that Great Britain will move with the Allied governments to keep Palestine open as a place where great numbers of additional Jewish people can find refuge and new life possibilities.

"May our God and Father, the Father of Abraham, Isaac, and Jacob, grant you continuing courage and blessing and speedy release of your own and other people from the devastating destruction which is being inflicted upon them."

201

'Day of Compassion'

A GUEST EDITORIAL

Editor's Note: This is one of a weekly series of guest editorials written by ministers of White Plains and neighboring communities on topics of their own selection.

By REV. GALEN E. RUSSELL
Pastor, First Congregational Church, Chappaqua

A "Day of Compassion" for the Jews of Europe will be observed tomorrow! Every Sunday ought to be a day of compassion. This action, on the part of the executive committee of the Federal Council of Churches designating tomorrow, is timely. "Bear ye one another's burdens, and so fulfill the law of Christ."

The Council invites all Christian people to join in constant intercession—and unitedly tomorrow—for the victims of racial and religious persecution. In our supplication to God let us pray; that God, in His mercy, may open the way for the deliverance of the Jewish people; that the hearts of all Christian people may be stirred to active compassion for the suffering Jews; that Christians in America may steadfastly oppose all tendencies to anti-semitism in our own country; that the spirit of racial good will and justice may be greatly strengthened among all men throughout the world.

This need is urgent for several reasons. There is well-documented material reaching us now that a deliberate policy of extermination of the Jews within the Third Reich is being carried out with diabolical cruelty. The words "beastlike" or "savage" are inadequate to illustrate such actions. In the name of Him who "loved little children" we should offer help, both material and spiritual.

This attack on the Jews is an attack on all religion. It is the spearhead of an attack on the Christian church. The church is suffering like consequences whenever or wherever it opposes inhuman practices.

We must exercise active compassion or we run into the danger of drying up the springs of sympathy. The numbers of victims are reaching such enormous proportions, the deeds are so barbarous, the situation is one step removed from our shores; that we close our eyes and shield our hearts lest they be shocked into a state of temporary paralysis.

The Christians of Great Britain, and their church leaders have demonstrated their concern on numerous occasions. In Holland, France and Norway the churches—Roman Catholic as well as Protestant—have shown their sympathy for the Jews at the cost of persecution. In Holland, where the Jews were compelled to wear arm bands to make them easily distinguishable for oppression, many members of the Christian Youth movement also wore arm bands. In France there has been open resistance to the Nazi plans and much quiet assistance to the victims.

Tomorrow is a good time for us to unitedly engage in intercession. Even if it proves impossible to rescue large numbers of Jews from those occupied countries, we can at least show that we care. That is something!

The Reporter Dispatch (White Plains, NY) - May 1, 1943

Nazi Barbarism Condemned By Pastor At Temple Service

A special service of prayer and intercession was held Sunday night at the B'nai Israel temple at which church leaders of the city condemned the extermination of 2 million European Jews and appealed for the government to take action to rescue as many as possible of those still in Nazi-dominated Europe.

Rev. Clyde H. Canfield, D.D., pastor of the United Presbyterian church, spoke in behalf of the East Liverpool Ministerial association, in place of Rev. J. Hubert Henderson, who was unable to attend.

The special program was in observance of a nationwide "Day of compassion for the Jewish victims of Nazi barbarism," proclaimed jointly by the Federal Council of Churches of Christ in America and the Synagogue Council of America.

Rev. Canfield declared: "The Christian people of America must join with our Jewish fellow-citizens not only in protesting this cruel and brutal persecution, but also in using every means in our power for putting an end to it.

Rabbi Harry Lasker, who conducted the prayer service, read a message from Very Rev. Fr. Francis J. Lavery, pastor of St. Aloysius Catholic church, who said:

"Rev. Fr. Oliver and myself join with you, Rabbi Lasker, and the ministers of the Protestant churches in condemning anti-Semitism and every other form of persecution as un-Christian and un-American, totally opposed to the teachings of the Almighty God, who is the Father of us all."

Express Sympathy for European Jews

Statesmen and Religious Leaders Send Messages on 6-Week Mourning Period

New York (WNS)—Leaders of the United Nations governments and many distinguished Americans, expressing their sorrow for the Jews suffering under Nazi rule in Europe, have sent messages of compassion and encouragement to the Jewish people on the occasion of the six-week period of mourning and intercession proclaimed by the Synagogue Council of America.

Cordell Hull, Secretary of State, declared that "of all the inhuman and tyrannical acts of Hitler and his Nazi lieutenants, their systematic persecution of the Jewish people — men, women, children—is the most debased. The fate of these unhappy people must be ever before us in the effort we are making today for the final victory. The United Nations will be prepared not only to redeem their hopes of a future world based upon freedom, equality and justice, but to create a world in which such a tragedy will not again occur. The Jews have long sought a refuge. I believe that we must have an even wider objective; we must have a world in which the Jews, like every other race, are free to abide in peace and in honor."

Haakon, King of Norway, said in a message: "I express the hope that the day may not be far off when the victory of civilization will put an end to the sufferings of European Jews."

Mrs. Franklin D. Roosevelt stated that "The only thing we can do is to pledge ourselves in this country never to allow the kind of prejudice to grow up which leads to oppression of minorities and to cruelty towards any group in our community."

אידען און קריסטען וועלען היינט אויסדריקען טרויער און פראטעסט איבער נאצי-אויסראטונג פון אידען אין אייראפע

אין אידישע שוהלען און אין פרא־
טעסטאנטישע קירכען וועלען היינט
אפגעריכט ווערען תפילות און עס וועל
לען געהאלטען ווערען רעדעם וועגען
דער טראגעדיע פון די אידען אונטער'ן
נאצי-יאך אין אייראפע און עס וועלען
געפאדערט ווערען באלדינגע רעטוננס
מיטלען פאר די אומגליקליכע אידען,
וואס מען קאן נאך ראטעווען.

דער "סינאגאג קאונסיל", וואס רע־
פרעזענטירט אלע דריי רעליגיעזע ריב־
בינים אין אידישען לעבן: אָרטאָ־
דאקסעם, קאנסערוואטיווע און רעפאר־
מער, האט ארויסגעשיקט דעם טעקסט
פון א ספעציעלער תפילה צו זאָגען
אין אלע שוהלען:

דער "פעדעראל קאונסיל אוו טשוירטש־
טשעס אוו קרייסט" האט ארויסגע־
שיקט דעם טעקסט פון א ספעציעלער
געבעט צו די פראטעסטאנטישע גייסט־
ליכע צוזאמען מיט אן אויפפאדערטנג
צו געבען הילף די ליידענדע אידען.

די אידישע נייט וועט אויך אויז
גערופען ווערען דורך דריי ראדיא־
בראדקעסטס, אין וועלכע עס וועלען

זיך באטייליגען אידישע און קריסט־
ליכע פארשטעהער. שבת אוועגט, 8:45
וועט בישאפ מאקקעי, פרעזידענט פון
"פעדעראל קאונסיל" רעדען פופצען
מינוט וועגען דער אידישער לאגע.
זונטאג, צוועלף ביטאג, וועלען גע־
הערט ווערען איבער'ן ראנעצען לאנד
דוד נעשאנאל בראדקעסטינג
קאמפאניע רעדעם פון אבא הלל סיל־
ווער, אין נאמען פון סינאנגאג קאונ־
סיל; לואי רצבער, פון "נעשאנאל קאונ־
סיל אוו קאטאליק מען" און רעוו. לי
פערט פון דעם פראטעסטאנטישען
קאונסיל. נאך א פראגראם וועט גע־
בראכט ווערען אויף דער "מעטעדוש
אוו אידזראעל" שטונדע.

אין פארשידענע שוהלען אין ניו
יארק וועלען אפנעריכט ווערען ספע־
ציעלע תפילות און ארויסטרעטונגען
פון א צאל ראביים. און אזוי וועט אין
דער סינאגאנג אויף 607 וועסט 161טע
סטריט רעדען נים נאר ראביי אהרן
עופר, דער ראביי פון דער שוהל, נאר
נאך פיר ראביים פון אנדערע שוהלען.
דאס אייגענע וועט פארקומען אין אנ־
דערע שוהלען.

Newark Rabbi Preaches at Memorial Rite

Ministerial Association Head Speaks; Ark is Draped

The Ark on the pulpit of the Brith Sholom Community Center was closed and the candelabra covered with black cloth as a symbol of mourning at the service last evening of memoriam and intercession for the two million victims of Hitlerism. Rabbi Mordecai L. Brill, spiritual leader of the congregation was in charge of the service assisted by Max Rajeck.

The guest speaker, Dr. Louis Levitsky, Newark, N. J., rabbi, used as his theme, "How Long, Oh Lord, How Long?" and told his listeners to have faith and courage and not to return hate for hate.

Dr. Levitsky related a story of two Jewish girls outside of Warsaw, Poland, who met death rather than be forced into German brothel, thereby living up to the highest idealism of Judaism, to die by sanctifying God's name.

Rev. Kenneth G. Hamilton, president of the Bethlehem Ministerial Association, in behalf of that group made a few remarks and in part said that "we are all one human family and what happens to one member concerns us all."

Mayor Robert Pfeifle, members of City Council, and members of the various college faculties were among the congregation gathered for the service.

Bethlehem (PA) Globe-Times -
April 30, 1943

VESPERS SERVICE HAS RABBI GOODY AS FIRST SPEAKER

Inter-Faith Meeting Held Under Auspices of Ministerial Association

TELLS OF SUFFERING OF JEWS UNDER AXIS

Suggests That U. S. Should Be Willing to Admit Many Refugees

"Behold and see if there is a pain like unto my pain!" from the book of Lamentations, was used last night by Rabbi Henry Goody as his text when he addressed a congregation composed of members of the Greensburg churches at a community inter-faith vesper service sponsored by the Greensburg Ministerial Association in the First Evangelical and Reformed Church.

Tells Of Suffering Of Jews

The text was used in connection with the suffering of the Jewish people in Europe today, especially those in German-held territory. Rabbi Goody elaborated on the text by citing the atrocities committed against the Jews in the Ghetto in Warsaw as an example of the kind of treatment being given to Jews throughout these areas. He told of the diet given the Jews, of their mass killings, and of the threat to the entire Jewish race. Rabbi Goody warned that the attack on the Jewish people is part of the inevitable assault on all religions.

Presents Proposals

The speaker presented a number of proposals for helping the Jewish refugees that are approved by religious groups throughout this country and in England. He said that the United Nations must formulate a plan of action to save the Jews who are still living in these subjugated areas. He suggested that the neutral countries of Europe be asked to give aid and comfort to these refugees. He pointed out that the United Nations should be willing to take a major share of the responsibility of giving them temporary refuge at least until after the war is over, and that they should be allowed to come to this country as immigrants.

Suggests Palestine

Rabbi Goody suggested that the appeasement policy set up by the British government against the immigration of Jews into Palestine be relaxed, and he stated that Palestine is the only one of the European nations that has asked for these refugees. The speaker put forth the suggestion that these people be treated as prisoners of war, and receive, through the International Red Cross, food and medicine.

Last night's service marked the the beginning of a series of community vesper services. Next Sunday night, under the auspices of the Ministerial Association, Rev. H. Glenn Carpenter, pastor of the First Christian Church, will give the address.

Dr. Spaugy In Charge

Rev. Dr. L. D. Spaugy, pastor of the First Methodist Church, was in charge of the invocation, the responsive reading, the litany of intersesion, and read the resolutions adopted by the executive committee of the Federal Council of Churches, that set aside yesterday as a day of special compassion for the Jewish peoples in Europe.

Methodist Choir Sings

The Senior and Young People's Choir of the Methodist Church, under the direction of Mrs. C. H. Walker, sang "Softly Now the Light of Day," by Geibel. Mrs. Walter M. Edge, the organist of the Methodist Church, played Mozart's "Deus Tibi" as prelude, "Andante Pastorale" by Rogers, as the offertory selection, and "Honour and Arms" from "Samey Handel, as postlude.

Greensburg (PA) Morning Review - May 3, 1943

205

Appendix Q
Program of Action from the JTS Student Committee to the Joint Emergency Committee, April 25, 1943 (see pp. 83-84)

‣ A PROGRAM OF ACTION ‣

To: Members of the Joint Emergency Committee on European Jewish Affairs.

Respectfully submitted by the European Committee of the Student Body of the Jewish Theological Seminary of America

כל רגע שמאחר לפדות השבוים היכא דאפשר
להקדים הוי כאלו שופך דמים -- רמב״ם

"When one delays even a moment in redeeming captives--whever it is possible to hasten-- he is considered as one who spills blood"
-Maimonides-

The Bermuda Conference is sad proof that our State Department is not yet ready to do everything possible to save European Jewry. Only a program of public enlightment, unprecedented in Jewish history, can force the hand of our government. The spending of hundreds of thousands of dollars and the utilizing of the full-time energy of thousands of communal leaders and workers throughout the nation is the only answer worthy of American Jewry.

Up to now, there have been delegations to Washington and mass meetings in many large cities. In the city of Detroit the Community Council arranged a month of mourning; similar programs have been conducted in many localities by many organizations. The Federal Council of Churches has designated May 2nd as a Day of Compassion to be observed at all the churches throughout the country. The Synagogue Council of America has declared the Sefirah days (from Passover to the Feast of Weeks) as a Period of Mourning and Intercession. Rabbis throughout the country have been urged to conduct special services in order to arouse their congregants to the need for saving lives. They have been requested to publicize the Twelve Point Program and to form permanent committees within their congregations to conduct a letter writing campaign to Washington. Each person is being asked to wear a black ribbon as a symbol of mourning and protest. National organizations and community councils have been advised of what the Synagogue Council is doing and have been asked to cooperate.

There is still lacking, however, a comprehensive program designed to place the full weight of the American Jewish community and the humanitarian forces within this country squarely behind the Twelve Points for Action.

We should, therefore, like to suggest ways in which the Twelve Point Program should be implemented:

A. National Activities
1. An Emergency Office with full-time staff must be set up immediately.
2. Contact must be made with all national organizations--political, religious, labor and fraternal. These organizations should be urged to pass resolutions, publicize our program in their magazines, instruct their local affiliates to take action.
3. The full weight of the Joint Emergency Committee should be

placed behind the period of Mourning and Intercession of the Syna
gogue Council.

4. National Radio Broadcasts several times weekly must be a
ranged. Prominent Hollywood names should be enlisted since they c
an audience.

5. Full page advertisements should be inserted in the newspapers throughout the country, in a coordinated national campaign
Remember, cigarettes are no more important than human lives.

6. There should be a "March on Washington". Prominent Jewi
and Christian citizens from each of the states of the Union shoul
converge on Washington simultaneously in order to see their Senat
and Congressmen and to urge them to advocate rescue activities.
steady stream of literature should pour into the Senate and House
fice Buildings.

7. A dramatic emergency conference of representatives of al
Jewish organizations in the Metropolitan Area should be immediate
convened to demand government action. Similar action should be t
in all cities.

8. An emergency conference of Orthodox, Conservative and Re
Rabbis should be called. Such action would be unprecedented in
synagogue history.

9. The forthcoming American Jewish Conference should place
problem at the top of its agenda. The local conferences in June
the National conference in July must be public demonstrations of
our determination to save European Jewry.

B. Local Activities

1. A Local Emergency Committee should be created in each cit
with a counterpart in each organization (e.g., local B'nai B'rith
Junior Hadassah, Temple Sisterhoods, etc).

2. A campaign operated with all the thoroughness and machin
of a Welfare Fund drive should be begun in every community urging
that letters be written to the White House, the State Department,
Congress. Form letters should be mailed to every person on the W
fare Fund list. There should be special rallies, telephone squad
canvassers, and the like.

3. All Yiddish, Hebrew, and Anglo-Jewish publications shoul
print form letters advocating the substance of the Twelve Point p
gram. These could be used as models or could be clipped and sent
Washington.

4. Black ribbons symbolizing mourning and protest should be
by all Jews in America until the holiday of Shavuoth.

5. Spot announcements over the local radio should be made m
times daily.

6. Leaflet campaigns on the city streets should be undertak

7. Every type of Christian and Non-sectarian organization--
litical, religious, social, labor, fraternal, and civic--should b
approached and urged to protest to Washington.

8. Hundreds of distinguished citizens in each community sho
be induced to make public statements and to write to their Congre
man and the White House.

9. State Legislatures and local City Councils should be ask
adopt resolutions and forward them to Washington.

10. The Joint Emergency Committee (national) should have fie
representatives cover the country--assisting and stimulating the
communities in their work.

207

-3-

For this tremendous job of propoganda and organization great resources are needed. Will the millions we are gathering for the United Jewish Appeal be of value if there are no Jews alive to receive United Jewish Appeal help? If sufficient funds are not available, United Jewish Appeal money should be used. Hitler is determined to blot out the Jew; we must be more determined to save him.

By day and by night--even on holidays--the Jewish community of America should be working. All other communal activity should be geared so that this problem takes precedence. Thousands of Jewish lives are being destroyed daily, and American Jewry has not yet found its soul.

Maimonides' dictum indicts us. We must act now!

> THE EUROPEAN COMMITTEE OF THE JEWISH
> THEOLOGICAL SEMINARY
> Noah Golinkin
> Reuben Katz
> Jerome Lipnick
> Bertram Sachs

April 25th, 1943

Appendix R
Leaflet Distributed by the JTS Students at the
Opening Session of the American Jewish Conference,
August 29, 1943 (see pp. 89-90)

PARDON OUR INTRUDING

...but since you are a member of the Executive Committee of the American Jewish Conference, we <u>had</u> to deliver this message to you:

It comes from Poland, and the man who wrote it was speaking on behalf of what used to be called the Warsaw Ghetto.

"Jewish leaders abroad won't be interested. At eleven in the morning, you will begin telling them about the anguish of the Jews of Poland, but at one o'clock they will ask you to halt the narrative so they can have lunch.... They will go on lunching at the regular hour at their favorite restaurant. So they cannot understand what is happening in Poland."

The person who wrote this letter will never hear of the forthcoming American Jewish Conference. He and his comrades of the Warsaw Ghetto have been wiped out, but there are hundreds of thousands of Jews in Rumania, Bulgaria, Hungary, and even Poland, who, though living in constant danger of death, are sustained by the hope that their brothers abroad are using every device to effect their rescue.

To them the Conference could only mean a large-scale attempt on the part of all Jews of America to urge their government to do what it failed to do at Bermuda. However, according to the publicized program, the Conference will deal with (1) the rights and status of Jews in the post-war world, and (2) our rights with respect to Palestine.

How can the Conference discuss the rights and status of Jews in the post-war world—we are sure the Jews of Poland would ask—when there may not be any post-war Jews?

How to move the United Nations to save the remaining Jews of Europe must be <u>item number one</u> on the agenda of the Conference.

What the Joint Emergency Committee for European Jewish Affairs has not fully succeeded in accomplishing until now, the Conference must try to achieve at once. It must utilize all the resources—financial, political, and moral—of the various national organizations which compose it, to influence our government to act immediately. To do this best, the Conference should organize a permanent agency to initiate and direct a program of activities dealing with this specific problem.

The spokesman from Warsaw must be proven wrong!

American Jewry cannot be out to lunch in the hour of crisis!

THE AMERICAN JEWISH CONFERENCE MUST SEE TO THAT!

Appendix S
Partial List of the 400 Rabbis Who Marched in
Washington D.C., October 6, 1943 (see pp. 97-102)

PARTIAL LIST OF RABBIS
IN PILGRIMAGE TO WASHINGTON

Leaders of Delegation:

Rabbis Israel Rosenberg, President Union of Orthodox Rabbis of U.S.;
Eliezer Silver, Co-President Union of Orthodox Rabbis of U.S. and
President Agudas Israel of America; Hiam I. Bloch, Vice-President
Union of Orthodox Rabbis of U.S.; Wolf Gold, Vice-President Union
of Orthodox Rabbis of U.S., and Honorary President Mizrachi Organiza-
tion of America and Chairman Executive Committee of World Mizrachi
Organization; Juda L. Seltzer, Executive Director Union of Orthodox
Rabbis of U.S.; Reuben Levovitz, Secretary Union of Orthodox Rabbis
of U.S.; Solomon N. Friedman, President Union of Grand Rabbis of U.S.

New York City delegates:

Isaac Adler	N. W. Friedman
Juda Altusky	Noah Garfinkel
David Amsel	Eser Ginsburg
Isaac Amsel	L. Glatt
B. Appelman	Abraham Goldgeil
Nathan Aranson	Israel Goldman
Benjamin B. Auerbach	G. Golshevsky
R. M. Barishansky	I.M. Gordon
Joseph Baumol	Simcha Gordon
Nahum Ben-Horin	A.J. Gottesman
Bernard Bergman	Samuel Gottesman
Lejba Berkowicz	Mordecai Gottlieb
Miron Berniker	Samuel Greimman
Joseph Bornstein	Isaac Grozalsky
Haim Bialik	S.Z. Gurary
Benion Bloch	Aron Halberstam
Moshe Bloch	Benjamin Halberstam
Jacob Bobrowsky	Chaskel Halberstam
Benjamin Book	J. Halberstam
Chaim M. Braun	Mendel Halberstam
D. Braun	Jacob Halberstam
Simon Brenner	M. Halpern
L. Brill	Markus Harlig
Jacob T. Buchbinder	I. Hellerstein
Isaac Bunin	Abraham Heschel
Aaron D. Burack	Abraham P. Hirmes
Joseph Burstein	H.J. Hirsch
Naphtali Carlebach	Solomon Frankel-Horowitz
Michel Jechiel Charlop	Maurice Idell
J. Chamodes	Ahron Jeruchem
A. Chinitz	Jehuda Leib Kagan
S. Chipkewitz	Leib Kagan
Noah Chodos	A.B. Kahan
Mendel Chodrow	Charles Kahane
Abraham Clinitz	Levy I. Kahane
Meyer Cohen	Chaim Kaplan
Aaron B. Dachowitz	M.A. Kaplan
H. Dachowitz	Hyman Karulitzky
Israel Dusowitz	Chaim Karlinsky
Abraham Eichenstein	Shaie Karlinsky
Mates Eichenstein	Abraham M. Karpel
R. Epstein	M. Kasher
Seidel Epstein	Moshe Katz
L. Ezrin	Samuel Katz
A. Faivelson	K. C. Klappholtz
Simon Federbusch	Hersch Kohn
J. Michel Feinstein	M. Kovalenko
Moses Feinstein	Kupietzky
M. Feinstein	Kushelevsky
Max Felshin	Hirsch Landau
Philip Flatau	Ira Langer
S. G. Flax	Isidor Lax
Abraham Frankel	Strul Lebovics
Benzion Frankel	Abraham Lehrman
S. Frankel	Benjamin Levitin
Arno Friedman	Mayer Leiter
Solomon Friedman	Moses Leiter

New York City delegates (continued)

O.N. Lovitzn
Abraham Levovitz
Reuben Levovitz
Isaac Lewin
Chaim Licht
David G. Light
H. Nathan Manuel
J.M. Margolics
Jacob Meskin
Israel Miller
Nissin Mindel
Samuel K. Mirsky
Isaiah Molotin
Israel L. Mopstein
Shimon Morduchowitz
Israel Moskowitz
David Mozeson
Benj. Notelewitz
Samuel Novick
Jacob Perlow
N.M. Perlow
I. Pogorelsky
Emanuel Pollak
Jacob M. Pomeranec
Leiger Predmesky
Joseph Price
Boruch Putterman
Eli Quint
Mordechai Rubin
I. Rabino
Baruch M. Rabinowitz
Isaac J. Rabinowitz
M. Rabinowitz
Salmon Reichman
I. Reiter
Isaac Ripko
L.J. Risikoff
Menachem Risikoff
B. Rokeach
H.M. Rokeach
Meyer Rosenbaum
Jacob Rosenblum
Samuel Rubin
S.B. Rubin
Benjamin Rothenberg-Halberstam
Isaac Safrin
Jakob Safrin
Abraham S. Samuels
Abraham Scheinberg
Jacob Schevelowitz
Moses Schneider
Isaac Shmidman
M.I. Sheinkop
Isaac Schneidman
Lazer Schonfeld
Abraham Selmanowitz
M. Sfard
Meyer Shapiro
Motel Shapiro
Moses Shatzkes
Chaim Shereskesky
Abaham Isaac Shisgal
Morris Shoulson
Mendel Shuk
Moishe Shulman
Aaron B. Shurin
M.M. Silverman
Moses K. Skindon
Isaac Soddon
Mordhi Soihetman
Samuel Solnica
J. Spiegel

Pincus E. Spiegel
L. Spira
Moses Tabachnik
David Talansky
Isaac H. Taub
David Taubenflogel
Naftali Teitelbaum
Osias Teitelbaum
Samuel Teitelbaum
Elchanan W. Teitz
Isaac Tendler
Joseph Thumin
Nathan Thumin
Solomon Tietelbaum
Baruch Trainin
Samuel Turk
Mordechai Turker
D. M. Tworkky
Israel Twersky
Isaac Twersky
Moses Schneerson Twersky
Isaac M. Wapner
Hyman S. Warshavsky
Irving N. Weinberg
Dr. Hillel Weiss
Baruch David Weitzman
Aaron Wertheim
Elja Girsh Wiernikowski
Alter Wilamowsky
B. Wolkowitz
M. Wulliger
Moses M. Yoshor
Moses Zimmerman
Aron Zlotowitz
Joseph Zweig

A. Perlow
Taub
M. Heschel
Alexander Teitelbaum
Ezra Lojbik

OUT OF TOWN DELEGATES:

Jos. H. Aronson	New Britain, Conn.
Chaim Bloch	Jersey City, N.J.
Bozalel Cohen	Paterson, N.J.
Meir Cohen	Philadelphia, Pa.
M. Etter	Harrisburg, Pa.
Jos. H. Feldman	Baltimore, Md.
Chaim Glatzer	Newark, N.J.
Morduch J. Golinkin	Worcester, Mass.
Aaron L. Gottesman	Jersey City, N.J.
H. Zvi Gottesman	Plainfield, N.J.
Isaac Greenblatt	Newark, N.J.
Leopold Greenwald	Columbus, Ohio
M. Hirschsprung	Columbus, Ohio
Zorach Hurwitz	Worcester, Mass.
Abram M. Kagan	Corona, N.Y.
Joshua Klavan	Washington, D.C.
Meyer Lieberman	Baltimore, Md.
Efraim Minsberg	Poughkeepsie, N.Y.
Ephraim Folcovitz	Bridgeport, Conn.
Pesach Raymon	New Brunswick, N.J.
Joseph Rosen	Passaic, N.J.
I. Rosenberg	Baltimore, Md.
I. Solomon Rosenberg	Hartford, Conn.
Jos. Segal	Chicago, Ill.
Menachem F. Shomin	Philadelphia, Pa.
Mosheh Shapiro	Atlantic City, N.J.

(More)

211

Appendix T
Title Page of the Report Drafted by U.S. Treasury Department Official Josiah E. Dubois, Jr.
December 25, 1943 (see pp. 104-105)

REPORT TO THE SECRETARY ON THE ACQUIESCENCE
OF THIS GOVERNMENT IN THE MURDER OF THE JEWS.

One of the greatest crimes in history, the slaughter of the Jewish people in Europe, is continuing unabated.

This Government has for a long time maintained that its policy is to work out programs to save those Jews of Europe who could be saved.

I am convinced on the basis of the information which is available to me that certain officials in our State Department, which is charged with carrying out this policy, have been guilty not only of gross procrastination and wilful failure to act, but even of wilful attempts to prevent action from being taken to rescue Jews from Hitler.

I fully recognize the graveness of this statement and I make it only after having most carefully weighed the shocking facts which have come to my attention during the last several months.

Unless remedial steps of a drastic nature are taken, and taken immediately, I am certain that no effective action will be taken by this Government to prevent the complete extermination of the Jews in German controlled Europe, and that this Government will have to share for all time responsibility for this extermination.

The tragic history of this Government's handling of this matter reveals that certain State Department officials are guilty of the following:

(1) They have not only failed to use the Governmental machinery at their disposal to rescue Jews from Hitler, but have even gone so far as to use this Government machinery to prevent the rescue of these Jews.

(2) They have not only failed to cooperate with private organizations in the efforts of these organizations to work out individual programs of their own, but have taken steps designed to prevent these programs from being put into effect.

212

Appendix U
Memorial Prayer Composed by Buddy Sachs for Use
at his Student Pulpit, September, 3, 1943 (see p. 111)

Oheb Zedeck Congregation
Pottsville, Pa.
Founded 1857

Jacob Hochman, Rabbi

MEMORIAL SERVICE

R. Brothers of ghettos, death chambers and concentration camps,

    C. We stand humble before you.

R. We have not been sharers of your suffering, nor have we been bearers of aid.

    C. We seek, however, to express our unshatterable sense of identity with your fate. (Repeat)

R. Your heroic resistance in the ghettos in the face of certain death has been a sanctification of the name of God and the name of Israel.

    C. May we also prove ourselves worthy of the example of fortitude and dignity which you have given to the world.

R. In Warsaw and Bialystock and Vilna, in Czestochowa, Bendzin, Tarnow, the Ghetto men fought and died. At Treblinka and Sobibor we destroyed our extermination centers.

    C. The spirit of the heroes of the ghettos is the symbol of the unconquerable will of a people which will survive Hitler and his accomplices in evil.

R. Let Jewry remember. Let Jewry mourn over the glory of its elders, over the flower of its manhood.

    C. Over the purity of its womanhood, over the wholesomeness of its youth, which have been desecrated and destroyed.

R. Let Jewry refuse to be silent and comforted in this crisis. Let not its mourning pass until the day of redemption of our people throughout the world.

    C. We solemnly pledge to do all possible to save those who can still be saved. We shall not cease from our labors until the Jew people has obtained full restoration in Europe and in Palestine. We shall not rest until victory is won, until Jewry once again takes its place in a world of justice and peace.

213

Appendix V
Announcement of a Rabbinic Rally at the End of the
SCA Sefira Campaign, at Kehilath Jeshurun,
New York City, May 24, 1943 (see pp. 75 and 141-147)

הקהלת רבנים לקינה ולתפלה

למען אחינו הקדושים
הנשחטים והנענים בארצות אירופה המנואצת

נקראה על ידי ועד רבני ניו יורק
בתשעה עשר יום לחדש אייר התש'ג
בבית הכנסת קהלת ישורון

על.פי דרישת מועצת בתי הכנסת של ארצות חברית דאמריקה

A RABBINICAL CONVOCATION OF PRAYER AND MOURNING

on behalf of the victims
of racial and religious persecution
in Nazi-scourged Europe

convened by
The New York Board of Jewish Ministers

in compliance with the Proclamation of
The Synagogue Council of America

Monday, May 24th at 10:30 A.M.
at
Congregation Kehilath Jeshurun
117 East 85th Street
New York City

214

ABBREVIATIONS USED

AJA   American Jewish Archives

AJCongress Papers
> American Jewish Congress Papers, American Jewish Historical Society, New York City

AJCP   American Jewish Committee Papers, YIVO Institute, New York City

AJH   *American Jewish History*

AJHQ   *American Jewish Historical Quarterly*

CW   *Congress Weekly*

CZA   Central Zionist Archives, Jerusalem

DGP   David Golinkin Papers, Jerusalem

FDRL   Franklin D. Roosevelt Papers, Franklin and Eleanor Roosevelt Library, Hyde Park, New York

IGP   Israel Goldstein Papers, Central Zionist Archives, Jerusalem

JTA   *Jewish Telegraphic Agency Daily News Bulletin*

JEC   Joint Emergency Committee for European Jewish Affairs

MSP   Moshe "Buddy" Sachs Papers, The David S. Wyman Institute for Holocaust Studies, Washington, D.C.

MZ   Metzudat Ze'ev (Jabotinsky Institute), Tel Aviv

NP   *New Palestine*

NGP   Noah Golinkin Papers, The David S. Wyman Institute for Holocaust Studies, Washington, D.C.

NYT   *New York Times*

SCA   Synagogue Council of America Papers, American Jewish Historical Society, New York City

SD-NA State Department Records, National Archives

SSW-AJA Stephen S. Wise Papers, American Jewish Archives, Cincinnati

SSW-AJHS
> Stephen S. Wise Papers, American Jewish Historical Society, New York City

Voss   Carl Herman Voss, ed., *Stephen S. Wise, Servant of the People – Selected Letters* (Philadelphia, 1970)

Wyman, *Abandonment of the Jews*
> David S. Wyman, *The Abandonment of the Jews: America and the Holocaust 1941-1945* (New York, 1984)

Wyman, *Paper Walls*
> David S. Wyman, *Paper Walls: America and the Refugee Crisis 1938-1941* (Amherst, 1968)

215

NOTES

1   Noah Golinkin interview with Rafael Medoff, 28 February 1996.

2   James MacDonald, "Himmler Program Kills Polish Jews," *New York Times*, 25 November 1942, 1.

3   Wise to Mack, 15 April 1933, and Wise to Holmes, 1 June, 1933, in Voss, 184, 189.

4   Richard Breitman and Alan M. Kraut, *American Refugee Policy and European Jewry, 1933-1945* (Bloomington, IN, 1987), 18.

5   Wise to Mack, 18 October 1933, in Voss, 195.

6   Laurel Leff and Rafael Medoff, "New Documents Shed More Light on FDR's Holocaust Failure," *American Jewish World*, 30 April 2004, 5.

7   Jeffrey S. Gurock, "The Orthodox Synagogue," in Jack Wertheimer ed., *The American Synagogue: A Sanctuary Transformed* (Cambridge and New York, 1987), 63-4.

8   Jeffrey S. Gurock, "Yeshiva Students at JTS," in Jack Wertheimer, ed., *Tradition Renewed: A History of the Jewish Theological Seminary – Volume 1: The Making of an Institution of Jewish Higher Learning* (New York, 1997), 471-514.

9   See David Golinkin's entry on Mordechai Ya'akov Golinkin in the *Encyclopaedia Judaica*, second edition, Vol. 7, 740 and see below, 121-23. In the summer of 1939, the Danzig Jewish community shipped its renowned Judaica collection, including fifty-one Torah scrolls, to the Jewish Theological Seminary, in New York City, for safekeeping. Whether the contacts between JTS and Rabbi Mordechai Golinkin regarding the collection played any role in his son's subsequent decision to study at JTS is unclear. (Marsha L. Rozenblit, "The Seminary during the Holocaust Years," in Wertheimer, ed., *Tradition Renewed*, 283-4)

10 Noah Golinkin to the Director of the Yeshiva "Rabbi Isaac-Elhanan" of New-York [*sic*], 29 February 1937, and two letters from Rabbi Mordechai Ya'akov Golinkin to Rabbi Moshe Soloveitchik and one to Rabbi Bernard Revel, in Correspondence File, Bernard Revel Papers, Yeshiva University Archives, New York City.

11 Jeffrey S. Gurock, *The Men and Women of Yeshiva: Higher Education, Orthodoxy, and American Judaism* (New York, 1988), 58-66. Note Gurock's description of the friendly and sometimes collaborative relationship between a prominent Orthodox rabbi, Bernard Levinthal, and his son Israel, a leading Conservative rabbi [61-62]; Noah Golinkin likewise maintained a friendly relationship with his father despite Noah's choice of JTS. Also see Gurock, "Yeshiva Students at JTS" (above, note 8).

12 Gary Dean Best, "The Jewish 'Center of Gravity' and Secretary Hay's Roumanian Notes," AJA 32 (April 1980), 23-34; Evelyn Levow Greenberg, "An 1869 Petition on Behalf of Russian Jews," AJHQ 55 (March 1965), 278-295; Lloyd P. Gartner, "Romania, America, and World Jewry: Consul Peixotto in Bucharest, 1870-1876," AJHQ 58 (September 1968), 25-116.

13 Charles H. Stember *et al*, *Jews in the Mind of America* (New York, 1966), 53-55, 84-85, 121-128, 131-133.

14 The victim was Rep. E. Michael Edelstein, D-New York. See Edward S. Shapiro, "The Approach of War: Congressional Isolationism and Anti-Semitism, 1939-1941," AJH 54 (September 1984), 59-62.

15   Lloyd P. Gartner, "The Two Continuities of Antisemitism in the United
     States," in Shmuel Almog, ed., *Antisemitism through the Ages* (Oxford,
     1998), 317-318; Stember (above, note 13), 8, 210, 215; David S. Wyman and
     Rafael Medoff, *A Race Against Death: Peter Bergson, America, and the
     Holocaust* (New York, 2002), 5-6. At his peak, Coughlin displayed a
     frightening amount of political influence. In 1935, he played a key role in
     mobilizing the public outcry that blocked the Roosevelt administration's
     proposal for U.S. participation in the World Court (Coughlin regarded it
     as an attempt by "international bankers" – those with Jewish surnames
     were always highlighted in his speeches and literature – to rule the world.)
     Congressional candidates in Ohio and Michigan whom Coughlin targeted
     in 1936 were defeated due to a torrent of votes "directed to their
     opponents by Father Coughlin," according to the *New York Times*, and
     candidates associated with, or endorsed by, Coughlin did surprisingly
     well. "Senate Beats World Court, 52-36, 7 Less Than 2/3 Vote; Defeat for
     the President," NYT, 30 January 1935, 1; "Taft Captures 47 Seats, Borah 5;
     15 Coughlin Candidates Win in Ohio," NYT, 14 May 1936, 1.
16   JTA, March 14, 1933, 2; NYT, May 15, 1933.
17   Wise to Gottheil, April 17, 1933, Box 947, SSW-AJA.
18   Boycott advocates optimistically argued that an immediate, serious, and
     sustained boycott could bring about "ruin and disaster" for the German
     economy, "the end of German resources, and the end of all hope of the
     rehabilitation of Germany," and thus achieve their goal of "putting Adolf
     Hitler out of power." Whether the German economy in 1933 was indeed
     sufficiently fragile to be toppled by a foreign boycott continues to be
     debated by historians. See Moshe Gottlieb, "The Anti-Nazi Boycott
     Movement in the American Jewish Community, 1933–1941," Ph.D. diss.,
     Brandeis University, 1968, 442. Melvin Urofsky writes: "Hitler had
     promised to end the depression and unemployment, and his base of
     popular support would diminish unless he could produce some results. A
     foreign boycott of German goods could have serious effects on the
     economy, a fact the chancellor's economic advisers well knew." (Melvin
     Urofsky, *A Voice That Spoke for Justice: The Life and Times of Stephen S.
     Wise* [Albany, NY, 1982], 266.)
19   Memorandum by Stephen Wise and Bernard Deutsch, 28 April 1933,
     A405/83-A, Julian Mack Papers, CZA.
20   John Higham, *Strangers in the Land: Patterns of American Nativism 1860-
     1925* (New York, 1963).
21   Breitman and Kraut (above, note 4), 32.
22   Wyman, *Paper Walls*, 4.
23   Adler to Dickstein, 28 March 1933, reprinted in Michael N. Dobkowski,
     ed., *The Politics of Indifference: A Documentary History of Holocaust
     Victims in America* (Washington, D.C., 1982), 316.
24   "Rabbis Advocate Freedom of Ideas," NYT, 8 May 1933, 32.
25   Bat-Ami Zucker, "Frances Perkins and the German-Jewish Refugees,
     1933–1940," AJH 89 (March 2001), 40, 47.
26   "Dealing Responsibly with Poland" (editorial), *Opinion*, November 1936, 4.
27   Jerzy Tomaszewski, "Stephen S. Wise's Meeting with the Polish
     Ambassador in Washington, 1 April 1938," *Gal-Ed* 11 (1989), 103-15.

28   Allon Gal, *David Ben-Gurion and the American Alignment for a Jewish State* (Bloomington, IN, 1991), 40, 50–53.

29   Wise to Friedenwald, 12 October 1936, and Wise to Neumann, 13 October 1936, in Voss, 216-17; Urofsky (above, note 18), 284.

30   G.E.R. Gedye, "Nazi Terrorism in Austria Bared; Vienna Arrests Are Put at 34,000," NYT, 3 April 1938, 1.

31   State Department officials attributed the pressure to what they called "certain Congressmen with metropolitan constituencies." See Wyman, *Paper Walls*, 44.

32   *Ibid.*, 221.

33   The official numbers admitted under the German quota were 1,324 for 1933, 3,515 for 1934, 4,891 for 1935, 6,073 for 1936, and 11,127 for 1937.

34   Wyman, *Paper Walls*, 173; Wyman, *Abandonment of the Jews*, 6.

35   "The Refugee Conference" (editorial), *Opinion*, May 1938, 6.

36   Cited in Wyman, *Paper Walls*, 147.

37   Wise to Bakstansky, 27 June 1938, in Voss, 227.

38   Wyman, *Abandonment of the Jews*, 154.

39   See above, note 37.

40   Wise to Schneiderman, 31 March 1938, File: Immigration: Refugees, Evian Conference, Box 7, AJCP.

41   Wise to Frankfurter, 30 March 1938, Box 109, SSW-AJHS; Memorandum, Harry Schneiderman to Morris Waldman, "Subject: Proposed Immigration Legislation, April 5, 1938," File: Immigration 1936-39, Box 6, AJCP.

42   Abels to Waldman and Schneiderman, 29 April 1938, File: Immigration, 1936-39, Box 6, AJCP.

43   Cited in Wyman, *Paper Walls*, 50.

44   Golda Meir, *My Life* (New York, 1975), 159. Countries with vast amounts of unpopulated territory remained intransigent at Evian, but the tiny Dominican Republic announced that it would take up to 100,000 Jewish refugees. Less than one thousand arrived before the project was stalled, primarily due to pressure from State Department officials on the Dominican government to refrain from admitting refugees lest they turn out to be Nazi spies. In an episode that exemplified the paranoid mindset in Washington, FBI agents in 1941 believed they discovered refugees-turned-Nazi spies sending shore-to-sea signals from the Dominican beach front to German submarines in the region. The lights that were seen turned out to be from the flashlights of refugee settlers doing chores near the beach. The fact that no Jewish refugee, whether in North America or South, was ever found to have become a spy for the Nazis did not dissuade the Roosevelt administration from insisting that immigration needed to be severely restricted because of the danger of such spies. (Henry L. Feingold, *The Politics of Rescue* [New Brunswick, NJ, 1979], 121.)

45   Wyman, *Paper Walls*, 50.

46   "No Human Dumping" (editorial), *Opinion*, August 1938, 4; "Review of Events," *Contemporary Jewish Record*, September 1938, 42; Jonah B. Wise to Louis D. Brandeis, 26 August 1938, Reel 107, Brandeis Papers, Princeton University; Urofsky (above, note 18), 305.

47   Wyman, *Paper Walls*, 73.

48 Minutes of the General Jewish Council, 18 December 1938, AJCongress Papers.

49 Rosenman to FDR, December 5, 1938, personal correspondence, FDRL.

50 Feingold (above, note 44), 50; Wyman, *Paper Walls*, 97; Judith Tydor Baumel, *Unfulfilled Promise: Rescue and Resettlement of Jewish Refugee Children in the United States, 1934-1945* (Juneau, AK, 1990), 145.

51 Sarah A. Ogilvie and Scott Miller, *Refuge Denied: The* St. Louis *Passengers and the Holocaust* (Madison, WI, 2006), 24; Irwin F. Gellman, "The St. Louis Tragedy," AJHQ 61 (December 1971), 153.

52 V. O. Key Jr., *Public Opinion and American Democracy* (New York: Alfred A. Knopf, 1961), 277.

53 Justine Wise Polier and James Watterman Wise, eds., *The Personal Letters of Stephen Wise* (Boston, 1956), 235.

54 "Washington Sees Similarity Between Lindbergh's and Berlin's Anti-Jewish Propaganda," *JTA*, 14 September 1941, 1.

55 "Nazis Machine-Gun All Jews in Town Near Warsaw, Refugees Report," JTA, 8 December 1939, 1; "Nazis Machine-Gun 400 Jews in Polish Town on Sniping Charge" JTA, 14 December 1939, 1.

56 Cited in Alex Grobman, "What Did They Know? The American Jewish Press and the Holocaust, 1 September 1939-17 December 1942," AJH 68 (March 1979), 336-37.

57 "Thousands of Bukovina Jews Evacuated Into Soviet Interior," JTA, 8 July 1941, 1; "Thousands of Jews Killed by Nazi Bands in Zhitomir and Berditchev," JTA, 9 July 1941, 1; "Thousands of Jews Among Civilians Killed in Nazi-Soviet War; 500 Executed in Lublin," JTA, 10 July 1941, 1; "Nazis Force Jews in Minsk District to Dig Their Own Graves," JTA, 12 August 1941, 1; Grobman, 342-43. The JTA dispatch on the killings in Kiev referred to the massacre that took place in the Babi Yar ravine on September 29-30, 1941. An estimated 34,000 Jews were slaughtered on those two days, and additional thousands were killed in the ravine during subsequent months.

58 "Slaying of Jews in Galicia Depicted," NYT, 26 October 1941, 6.

59 "Zionism Underground in Polish Wasteland," *Hashomer Hatzair* [here-after HH] 9 (February 1941), 22-31; "Youth Amidst the Ruins," HH 9 (April 1941), 35-36; *Youth Amidst the Ruins* (New York: Hashomer Hatzair/Scopus, 1941); Moshe Sachs interview with the author, 29 February 1996 [hereafter Sachs interview]. Cf. below, note 263.

60 Jonathan D. Sarna, *JPS: The Americanization of Jewish Culture, 1888-1988* (Philadelphia, 1989), 186-87.

61 Sachs interview.

62 "What Jews Must Remember" (editorial), *Congress Weekly*, 1 May 1942, 3; "Accounts of Nazi Pogroms in Occupied White Russia Related at Moscow Jewish Rally," JTA, 25 May 1942, 3.

63 The text of the report was reprinted in Yehuda Bauer, "When Did They Know," *Midstream*, April 1968, 57-58.

64 Walter Laqueur, *The Terrible Secret: Suppression of the Truth about Hitler's 'Final Solution'* (Boston, 1980).

65 Wise to Frankfurter, 16 September 1942, Box 109, SSW-AJHS.

66 Wise to Korn, 9 September 1942, in Voss, 250.

67 Wise to Frankfurter, 16 September 1942, Box 109, SSW-AJHS.

68 Wise to Frankfurter, 4 September 1942, Box 109, SSW-AJHS; Wise to Korn, 9 September 1942, text reprinted in Voss, 249-250; Wise to Frankfurter, 16 September 1942, Box 109, SSW-AJHS; Stephen S. Wise to James Waterman Wise, 16 February 1943, text reprinted in Voss, 257.

69 Noah Golinkin interview with Rafael Medoff, 9 May 1996 [hereafter Golinkin interview].

70 Moshe Goldblum interview with Rafael Medoff, 29 February 1996; Kassel Abelson interview with Rafael Medoff, 29 February 1996; Reuben Katz interview with Rafael Medoff, 6 March 1996; Bernard Lipnick interview with Rafael Medoff, 28 April 1996.

71 Rabbi Wilfred Shuchat, "Rabbi Jerome Lipnick z"l," *Proceedings of the Rabbinical Assembly* XXXIX (1977), 115.

72 Golinkin interview; Reuben Katz interview with Rafael Medoff; Wilfred Shuchat interview with Rafael Medoff, 30 April 1996.

73 "Minutes of Meeting of Sub-Committee of Special Conference on European Affairs, Held at the Office of the American Jewish Congress, Monday, November 30, 1942," 1-2, AJCongress Papers.

74 Samuel Margoshes, "News and Views," *Der Tog*, 16 December 1942, 1.

75 "Fasting is Not Enough," (editorial), *The Reconstructionist*, 25 December 1942, 4; Golinkin interview.

76 Wise to Roosevelt, 2 December 1942, File: Correspondence Between FDR and Wise, 1929-1945, SSW-AJHS.

77 Wise to Niles, 9 December 1942, Box 181, SSW-AJHS.

78 Adolph Held, "Report on the Visit to the President," 8 December 1942, Part 3, Section 1, #15, Jewish Labor Committee Archives, text reprinted in David S. Wyman, ed., *America and the Holocaust – Volume 2: The Struggle for Rescue Action* (New York, 1990), 72-74.

79 Cited in Wyman, *Paper Walls*, 147.

80 Minutes of the Jewish Agency executive meeting, 28 September 1944, 10, CZA.

81 JIR was a non-denominational rabbinical school founded by Wise in 1922, whose graduates became Reform, Conservative, and Orthodox rabbis. See Morton M. Berman, "Jewish Institute of Religion," *The Universal Jewish Encyclopedia* 6 (New York, 1942), 132. After Wise's death in 1949, JIR merged with HUC in 1950 and its name was changed to HUC-JIR. JIR faculty members who did not agree with that merger later founded The Academy for Jewish Religion in 1956, which continued to ordain rabbis for *Klal Yisrael* – see www.ajrsem.org under History; personal communication from AJR Rabbi in Residence Jeff Hoffman to David Golinkin, 1 October 2010.

82 Weiner later authored several notable books, including *The Wild Goats of Ein Gedi* (New York, 1961) and *Nine and a Half Mystics: The Kabbala Today* (New York, 1969).

83 Gordon later was one of the founders of the Union of Orthodox Jewish Congregations of America (see Victor Geller, *Orthodoxy Awakens: The Belkin Era at Yeshiva University* [New York, 2003]). Cf. below, note 128.

84 Golinkin to Lookstein, 4 July 1986, NGP and DGP.

85 Golinkin interview.

86   Noah Golinkin interview with David Golinkin, 28-29 May 1986, DGP.
87   Roosevelt to Ickes, 18 December 1940, President's Official File 3186, FDRL.
88   Wise to Otto Nathan, 17 September 1940, text reprinted in Voss, 242.
89   "Alaska Colonization Essential for National Defense, Ickes Tells Senate Group," JTA, 14 May 1940, 1-2.
90   Harold L. Ickes, *The Secret Diary of Harold L. Ickes, Volume 3: The Lowering Clouds 1939-1941* (New York, 1954), 56-57.
91   Wise to Frankfurter, 17 October 1939, SSW-AJHS.
92   "New Frontiers in Alaska" (editorial), *Jewish Frontier*, May 1940, 3-4; Gerald S. Berman, "Reaction to the Resettlement of World War II Refugees in Alaska," *Jewish Social Studies* (Summer-Fall 1982), 271–82.
93   See Appendix A.
94   "Memorandum for Dr. Stephen S. Wise – December 17, 1942," MSP and DGP. See Appendix A.
95   Stephen S. Wise, *Challenging Years: The Autobiography of Stephen Wise* (New York, 1949), 268-69.
96   Abraham I. Karsh, ed. *Scroll of Agony: The Warsaw Diary of Chaim A. Kaplan* (Bloomington, IN, 1999), 347.
97   "Yeshiva Students Are Not Blameless" (editorial), *The Commentator*, March 1943, 4.
98   Rafael Medoff, "Conflicts between American Jewish leaders and dissidents over responding to news of the Holocaust: three episodes from 1942-1943," *Journal of Genocide Research* 5 (September 2003), 439-450; Jacobs to Smertenko, 6 December 1943 and Smertenko to Jacobs, 19 January 1944, File: Gillette-Rogers Resolution, Bergson Group Collection, The David S. Wyman Institute for Holocaust Studies, Washington, D.C.
99   There were also anti-Nazi protests when German representatives visited campuses such as Columbia and Harvard in the 1930s. See Stephen H. Norwood, *The Third Reich in the Ivory Tower: Complicity and Conflict on American Campuses* (New York, 2009).
100 Patti McGill Peterson, "Student Organizations and the Antiwar Movement in America, 1900-1960," *American Studies* 13:1 (1972), 141-42.
100a See Bickel (below, note 103).
101 Edward Alexander, "Irving Howe and the Holocaust: Dilemmas of a Radical Jewish Intellectual," AJH 88:1 (March 2000), 95-114.
102 Charles L. Arian, "Zionism, Socialism, and the Kinship of Peoples: Hashomer Hatzair in North America," rabbinical thesis, Hebrew Union College-Jewish Institute of Religion, 1986, 97-99.
103 Alexander Bickel, "Zionism at City College," *Furrows* 1:9 (July-August 1943), 2; Allon Gal, "Brandeis' Social-Zionism," *Studies in Zionism* 8:2 (Autumn 1987), 207-09; Samuel Grand, "A History of Zionist Youth Organizations in the United States," Ph.D. dissertation, Columbia University, 1958, 89-131.
104 "Views and News," *Furrows* I:2 (December 1942), 17; "Views and News," *Furrows* I:11 (October 1943), 4; Shalom Wurm, "When the Leaders Fail," *Furrows* II:3 (January 1944), 14-16; Saadia Gelb, "The Conference to the Rescue," *Furrows* II:2 (December 1943), 9; "Views and News," *Furrows* I:5 (March 1943), 6-7; "Views and News," *Furrows*, I:4 (February 1943, 14); "Views and News," *Furrows* I:2 (December 1942), 17.

105 "After Madison Square Garden: What Now?" (editorial), *Hamigdal* III:4 (April 1943), 3; "The Fate of a Million Jews" (editorial), *Hamigdal* IV:5 (May 1944), 4; "Who Is Guilty?," (editorial), *Hamigdal* III:2 (January 1943), 12-13; "Anti-Refugee Conference" (editorial), *Hamigdal* III:5 (May 1943), 3.

106 Benzion Netanyahu interview with Rafael Medoff, 20 March 1997; Sim Rosenberg interview with Rafael Medoff, 2 January 1996; David Krakow, "The Modern Epic of Betar: The American Betar," privately published.

107 Wyman, *Abandonment of the Jews*, 75.

108 Reams to Atherton and Hickerson, 9 December 1942, 740.00116 European War/694, SD-NA.

109 Golinkin interview.

110 "Governing Council meeting held Thursday, December 10, 1942 at 8:30 P.M. – Congress Offices," 2-3, AJCongress Papers.

111 The text of Greenberg's Yiddish article, "Bankrupt," may be found in English translation in Shlomo Katz, "6,000,000 and 5,000,000 (Notes in Midstream)," *Midstream* 10 (March 1964), 3-14. Cf. below, note 264.

112 Ben-Gurion to Shertok ["Moshe"], 8 July 1942, text reprinted in Aharon Kleiman, ed. *American Zionism – Volume 8* (London, 1991), 80. For the earlier period, note Frederick Lazin's comment that in the spring of 1939 – including during the crisis over the refugee ship *St. Louis* – the American Jewish Committee could not hold meetings of its leadership on Sundays "because in the spring so many of the members went to the country for weekends." (Frederick A. Lazin, "The Response of the American Jewish Committee to the Crisis of Germany Jewry, 1933-1939," AJH 68 [March 1979], 304.)

113 Memo of conversation between Dr. Nahum Goldmann and Bernard Meltzer, Acting Chief of the Division of Foreign Funds Control, State Department, 14 July 1943, State Department 840.48 Refugees/4063, SD-NA.

114 Silver to Neumann, 22 August 1944, A123/315, CZA; Emanuel Neumann, *In the Arena* (New York, 1976), 189.

115 Rozenblit (above, note 9), 274-78.

116 *Ibid.*, 278-79.

117 Interviews with Noah Golinkin, Reuben Katz, Wilfred Shuchat, Moshe Goldblum, Kassel Abelson, and Bernard Lipnick (above, notes 69-70).

118 Rozenblit (above, note 9), 273-308.

119 *Ibid.*, 298.

120 For the conference program, see Appendix B. The number 167 was cited by Brautigam in J. H[erbert]. B[rautigam]., Jr., "On Implementing Brotherhood," *The Union Review* IV:2 (March 1943), 2-3 – see Appendix F. This is the only extant source that refers to a specific number of attendees. Several weeks after the conference, JTS President Louis Finkelstein sent copies of a booklet, *Beliefs and Practices of Judaism*, to one student from each of the seminaries represented at the conference. While some students were sent one copy, others were sent larger quantities – for example, Dr. Finkelstein sent 41 copies to Brautigam, 30 to Gerald Stucky of the Biblical Seminary of New York, and 12 to JIR student Usher Kirshblum. If the quantities were determined according to the number of students from each seminary who attended the conference,

then one could conclude that 109 students from seminaries other than JTS took part. In all likelihood, the figure of 109 plus JTS student-attendees would add up to a number similar to Brautigam's estimate of 167. In any event, Dr. Finkelstein's booklet distribution project happens to provide the only identification of any individual student participants in the conference, aside from Brautigam. In addition to the aforementioned Gerald Stucky and Usher Kirshblum, they were: Earl R. Shay of the Moravian Theological Seminary; Douglas MacDonald of the New Brunswick Theological Seminary; Chilton McPheeters of the Drew Theological Seminary; Irwin Gordon of Yeshiva College; J. Ralph Deppen of General Theological Seminary; (Ms.) Ivol Godby of Yale Divinity School; and Theodore Gill of Princeton Theological Seminary. An additional participant was Richard Beving, a student at the New Brunswick Theological Seminary. Several weeks before the conference, Beving reported on the upcoming event at a meeting of the seminary's student council. (Finkelstein to Shay et al, 16 March 1943, File: "Inter-Seminary Committee, Inter-Seminary Conference," Louis Finkelstein Papers, Ratner Center for the Study of Conservative Judaism, Jewish Theological Seminary of America, New York City; Minutes of the Student Society of Inquiry, 2 February 1943, New Brunswick Theological Seminary Library; Janet Beving interview with Rafael Medoff, 31 January 2010.)

121　The original documents contain three similar but not identical lists of Seminaries. *The Challenge*, February 1943, 1 lists nine; *The Challenge*, March 1943, 6 lists eleven; the press release of the Religious News Service, 25 February 1943, which was dictated to them on the phone by Jerry Lipnick, lists ten. All three documents are in DGP. We have therefore made a composite list of all seminaries mentioned.

122　"Digest of the Speeches Delivered at the Interseminary Conference," *The Challenge*, March 1943, 2, NGP and DGP.

123　See Andy Marino, *A Quiet American: The Secret War of Varian Fry* (New York, 1999).

124　See above, note 122.

125　Goldblum interview (above, note 70).

126　Golinkin interview.

127　See above, note 122.

128　"Worship Service, Inter-Seminary Conference, February 22, 1943, NGP and DGP – see Appendix C. Irwin Gordon is mentioned as the author of this service by Golinkin to Lookstein, 4 July 1986, NGP; Golinkin to David Golinkin, 1 July 1986, DGP; handwritten note on top of the Worship Service in Appendix C: "Irwin Gordon, who this person was I don't remember" – DGP, received from Buddy Sachs, 19 June 1986. Cf. above, note 83.

129　For the complete text of the resolutions, see Appendix D and cf. note 130.

130　"Metropolitan Interseminary Conference Called to Discuss the Plight of European Jewry Today – February 22, 1943 – Report of the Resolutions Committee," NGP.

131　"Resolution Adopted at 'Stop Hitler Now' Demonstration – Madison Square Garden – March 1, 1943," File: American Jewish Congress, PPF 5029, FDRL.

132 "Another Evian?" (editorial), *Philadelphia Jewish Exponent*, 12 March 1943, 4.

133 Untitled and undated (late 1943 or early 1944) memo on U.S. refugee policy, NGP and DGP. Noah Golinkin wrote at the bottom of the DGP copy: "This must have been written after Rosh Hashanah 5704 (1943). We may have intended to submit it for publication in the newspaper *P.M.*, which printed Long's statements extensively."

134 Ben Hecht, *A Child of the Century* (New York, 1954), 554-57 .

135 "Administrative Committee, Minutes of Meeting, Tuesday, March 13, 1934 – 8:30 P.M.," 6-7, File: I-J77, AJCP.

136 Isaac Neustadt-Noy, "The Unending Task: Efforts to Unite American Jewry from the American Jewish Congress to the American Jewish Conference," Ph.D. dissertation, Brandeis University, 1976, 114.

137 Trager to Rosenblum, 1 February 1943, File: War and Peace: Jewish Army 1940-1943, Box 15, AJCP; David S. Wyman and Rafael Medoff, *A Race Against Death* (above, note 15), 35-36.

138 "The Conference is Not Over," *The Challenge*, March 1943, 1. See Appendix E.

139 Brautigam (above, note 120), 2-3. See Appendix F.

140 "T.A. Joins In Protest," *The Commentator*, 4 March 1943, 2; "Students Condemn Nazi Atrocities; Demand Action," *The Commentator*, 4 March 1943, 2; "Student Leaders Act," *The Commentator*, 4 March 1943, 2 (see Appendix G); "Action–Not Pity Can Save Millions Now!" (advertisement), NYT, 8 February 1943, 8. In an internal State Department memo in May 1943, Robert C. Alexander, assistant to Assistant Secretary of State Breckinridge Long, traced what he claimed was the secret history of "the slogan 'action–not pity,' which has become the watchword of the pressure groups who are interested only in a particular class of refugees." According to Alexander, Hitler accused the West of "moralizing – not acting" with regard to Jewish refugees. That, Alexander explained, was the same as saying "action – not moralizing," and "action – not moralizing" is "now known as 'action – not pity.'" (Alexander to Long, 7 May 1943, File: "Refugee Movement and National Groups, 1943," Box 203, Breckinridge Long Papers, Library of Congress.)

141 G. Schechter to Lipnick, 26 February 1943, DGP; Proskauer to Golinkin, 26 April 1943, NGP; Secretary to Dr. Wise to Lipnick, 27 April 1943, NGP; Heller to Lipnich [*sic*], 27 April 1943, NGP; Pool to Lipnick, 3 May 1943, NGP; Montor to Sachs, 4 May 1943, NGP; Alpert to Golinkin, 28 April 1943, NGP [see Appendix H]; Alpert to Rafael Medoff, 12 April 1996.

142 "Jerome Lipnick – March 7, 1943 – Zachor," Folder 22: Homiletic Class of Seminary, 1940s, Ratner Center for the Study of Conservative Judaism, Jewish Theological Seminary of America, New York City. See Appendix I.

143 Noah Golinkin, Jerome Lipnick, and N [*sic*]. Bertram Sachs, "Retribution Is Not Enough," *The Reconstructionist* IX/2 (March 5, 1943), 19-21, which is reproduced below in Appendix J. The reference is to Deuteronomy 21:7, concerning the community's responsibility for the corpse of an unknown homicide victim.

144 "Save European Jewry Now!" (editorial), *The Reconstructionist* IX/2 (March 5, 1943), 8, 24. See Appendix K.

145 The only Orthodox synagogues affiliated with the SCA were modern, or Americanized, Orthodox. European-style Orthodox synagogues (what today might be described as *haredi*) did not participate because they did not want to be seen as accepting the theological legitimacy of the non-Orthodox.

146 Goldstein to Lipnick, 26 March 1943, NGP; Synagogue Council of America Minutes, 10 March 1943, SCA. The minutes suggest the decision to create the committee was made in response to a memorandum presented by the [Conservative] Rabbinical Assembly; but it is evident from Goldstein to Lipnick, 26 March 1943, NGP, that the memorandum in question was, in fact, prepared by the JTS rabbinical students. The later letter quoted is Goldstein to Lipnick, 19 April 1943, DGP.

147 Opher to Lookstein, 16 May 1943, SCA; Ahron Opher interview with Rafael Medoff, 19 March 1996. See Appendices L and M and note 148.

148 "Synagogue Council of America Proclaims a Six-Week Period of 'Mourning and Intercession' for Europe's Jews; Jews Urged to Join Christian Observance May 2 as Day of Compassion," News Release, Synagogue Council of America, 9 April 1943, SCA; "Suggested Program for Synagogue or Organization Meeting," NGP; "Prayer to be Used at Meetings During the Period of Mourning and Intercession, Followed by Minute of Silence," NGP; "Home Prayer to be Recited Daily After the Main Meal," NGP; "Tell Them That We Are All Dying," NGP and "Sample Letter," SCA; Opher to "Dear Colleague," 14 April 1943 SCA; Opher to "Dear Colleague," 19 April 1943, NGP; "Suggestions for Service of Intercession," 2 May 1943, NGP; Opher to "Dear Rabbi," 8 April 1943, SCA; "Memorial Prayer for Concluding Day of Passover, 5703," SCA; Opher to "Dear Colleague," 28 April 1943, SCA. For Jerry Lipnick's letter and sermon about the black ribbon, see below, pp. 132-135, notes 268-270, and Appendix O.

149 See Appendix N.

150 These two prayers were published in Zvi Yehudah Rabinovitz, ed., *Yalkut Hamo'adim*, Vol. 2 (Buenos Aires, 1943), 1377. The prayers were not signed by Golinkin, but he told his sons that he wrote the prayers; he wrote this at the bottom of his copy (DGP); and he wrote to Rabbi Haskel Lookstein (Golinkin to Lookstein, Lag Ba'omer 5746): "I was the author of these two prayers (even though no credit was given to me)."

151 See Appendix N.

152 "Prayer to be Used at Meetings During the Period of Mourning and Intercession, Followed by Minute of Silence," SCA; "Home Prayer to be Recited Daily After the Main Meal," SCA: "Memorial Prayer for the Concluding day of Passover, 5703," SCA.

153 For example, see *American Hebrew* 151:52 (30 April 1943), 6; *Baltimore Jewish Times* 48:8 (30 April 1943), 27; *Brooklyn Jewish Examiner* 29:15 (16 April 1943), 1; *Jewish Forum* 26:4 (May 1943), 24; CW 10:16 (16 April 1943), 2; CW 10:19 (14 May 1943), 2; CW 10:21 (28 May 1943), 2; *Aufbau* 9:17 (23 April 1943), 9; *Hadoar*, 14 May 1943; *Forverts*, 25 April 1943; *Morgen Zhurnal*, 25 May 1943. See Appendix P for ads and press clippings.

154 "A People in Mourning" (editorial), *The Jewish Spectator*, January 1943, 4.

155 For examples, see "Vacation + Health," (advertisement), *NP* 35:11 (16

March 1945), 149; "The St. Charles" (advertisement), *NP* 35:3 (17 November 1944), 38; "Bazaar and Carnival" (advertisement), *CW* 11:5 (4 February 1944), 15; "Annual Dance and Entertainment" (advertisement), *CW* 11:10 (10 March 1944), 17; and "Installation Evening and Concert" (advertisement), *CW* 11:20 (26 May 1944), 13. Also see "No-Luxury Week," *Hamigdal* 3:4 (April 1943), 16.

156 Rebbitzin Miriam Teitz interview with Rafael Medoff, 7 March 2006.

157 Michael Zylberman, "Concern From Afar: The Participation of 'Yeshiva' Students and Faculty in World War II Service and Holocaust and Relief Efforts, 1936-1947" (unpublished research paper, Yeshiva College, 2000), 16.

158 Known as the Emergency Committee for Zionist Affairs at its inception in 1939, it added the word "American" in the wake of Pearl Harbor to underline its contention that Zionism did not conflict with the American war effort. In 1943, it would change its name, as a sign of its intended reinvigoration, to the American Zionist Emergency Council.

159 Joint Emergency Committee minutes, 15 March 1943, Box 8, AJCP.

160 Long to Lipnick, 14 May 1943, NGP.

161 Berle message cited in Monty Noam Penkower, *The Jews Were Expendable: Free World Diplomacy and the Holocaust* (Urbana and Chicago, 1983), 330, note 37.

162 "Bermuda Conferees Agree to Another Conference," *Independent Jewish Press Service*, 30 April 1943, 3; "Failure in Bermuda" (editorial), *Opinion*, May 1943, 4 ; "The Mockery at Bermuda," address by Dr. Israel Goldstein, 28 April 1943, A364/235, 2, IGP.

163 "Minutes of the Meeting of the Joint Emergency Committee for European Jewish Affairs, May 24, 1943," File: Joint Emergency Committee for European Jewish Affairs, Box 8, AJCP.

164 "We Turn to Our Spiritual Leaders for Guidance" (editorial), *Jewish Tribune* (Passaic, NJ), 29 April 1943.

165 Opher to "Dear Colleague," 7 May 1943, SCA.

166 "Mourning for Nazi Victims," *Herald* (Los Angeles), 26 April 1943; "Mourning Day Planned Here By Synagogues," *Richmond Times-Dispatch*, 1 May 1943; "Memorial Services Held by Isle Jewish Congregation for Victims of Hitler; United Nations Urged to Act for Relief," *Galveston Tribune*, 26 April 1943; "Local Synagogues To Hold Services Monday," *Hebrew Watchman* (Memphis), 27 May 1943; "Memorial Service Planned for 10:30 A.M. Today at Synagogue," *Charleston Courier*, 26 April 1943; "State Rabbis To Offer Prayers For Victims of Nazis," *Hartford Courant*, 23 May 1943; "Oheb Sholom Services," *Harrisburg* [PA] *News*, 30 April 1943; "Yizkor Service Opens Six-week Mourning Period," *Easton* [PA] *Express*, 26 April 1943; "Persecutions Are Recalled," *Reading* [PA] *Eagle*, 26 April 1943; "Jewish Suffering Awakens U.S., Governor Says Here," *Tulsa Daily World*, 12 May 1943; "Jews to Honor War Victims," *Youngstown Vindicator*, 24 April 1943; "Jews to Begin Mourning Rite," *Charlotte Observer*, 26 April 1943; "Jewish Spirit Undaunted As Nazi Victims Mourned," *Buffalo Courier-Express*, 3 May 1943; "Jewish Day of Mourning at 2 Services," *Newburgh* [NY] *News*, 30 April 1943; "Jews to Hold Memorial," *Elmira* [NY] *Star-Gazette*, 29 April 1943; "Sons of Israel Service Sunday," *Albany*

Times, 30 April 1943; "The Jewish Morning [*sic*] Services" (editorial), *Nassau County* [NY] *Daily Review*, 1 May 1943; Jews to Mourn Dead and Living Hitler Victims," *Chicago News*, 26 April 1943; "Prayers Slated For Nazi Victims," *St. Paul Dispatch*, 11 May 1943; "Prayer Service for Jews Friday," *Omaha Evening World-Herald*, 20 May 1943; "Worshipers [*sic*] Will Mourn 2,000,000," *Hudson [NJ] Dispatch*, 1 May 1943; "Martin M. Brody Will Be Confirmed," *Trenton Times*, 7 May 1943; Schotz to "Dear Friend," 4 May 1943, publicity scrapbook, SCA; "Resort Jewry Sets Sunday for 'Day of Prayer-Intercession'," *Jewish Record* (Atlantic City), 30 April 1943. See Appendix P for ads and press clippings.

167 Opher to Goldstein, 7 May 1943, SCA; The European Committee of the Jewish Theological Seminary, A Program of Action," NGP. See Rabbi Haskel Lookstein, below, pp. 141-47 and Appendix V.

168 "Denver Jewry Prays for Rescue of Nazi Victims," *Intermountain Jewish News*, 7 May 1943; "Faiths Observe Jewish Plight," *Des Moines Register*, 1 May 1943; "Local Synagogues To Hold Services Monday," *Hebrew Watchman* [Memphis, TN], 27 May 1943.

169 "Temple School Children Plan Closing Exercises," *Home News* [Bronx, NY], 2 May 1943; "All Sects To Protest Nazi Massacre of Jews," *Nassau County Leader*, 29 April 1943; "Prayers Set For Jewish Nazi Victims," *Richmond News-Leader*, 30 April 1943; "Sisterhood Will Aid at Service," *Nassau Daily Review*, 29 April 1943; "Jewish Group Pledges War Bond Purchases," *Newport* [RI] *News*, 28 April 1943; "Jewry to Pray For Oppressed," *Knickerbocker News* [Albany, NY], 30 April 1943.

170 For news coverage of Christian participation in Jewish-organized events, see "Hitler Victims To Be Honored at B'nai Zion," *Chattanooga News-Free Press*, 15 May 1943; "Jews Mourn Persecutions," *Sentinel* (Norwalk, CT), 29 April 1943; "Denver Jewry Prays for Rescue of Nazi Victims," *Intermountain Jewish News*, 7 May 1943; "Newark Rabbi Preaches at Memorial Rite," *Bethlehem Globe-Times*, 5 May 1943; Nazi Barbarism Condemned By Pastor At Temple Service," *East Liverpool* (OH) *Review*, 3 May 1943; "Raleigh Club Council Urges Observance, *Jewish Examiner* (Brooklyn, NY), 30 April 1943. For news reports about Christian-organized events, see "Special Services Will Honor Jews," *Chattanooga News-Free Press*, 12 May 1943; "Not Peace At Any Price" (editorial), *Chattanooga Times*, 16 May 1943; "To Offer Prayers For Jews Sunday," *Florence* [AL] *Times*, 1 May 1943; "Interfaith Service on Sunday Here," *Greensburg* [PA] *Evening Tribune*, 30 April 1943; "The Jewish Period of Mourning" (editorial), *Youngstown Vindicator*, 1 May 1943; "All Faiths Join in Plea To Save Jews," *Newburgh News*, 3 May 1943; "Christians Take Action on Jews' Plight in Europe," *Jamestown* [NY] *Post-Journal*, 23 May 1943; "All Sects To Protest Nazi Massacre Of Jews," *Nassau County Leader*, 29 April 1943; "Day of Compassion" (editorial), *Reporter Dispatch* [White Plains, NY], 1 May 1943; "Sunday's Prayers" (editorial), *Indianapolis News*, 1 May 1943; "Service of Compassion" (advertisement), *Detroit Jewish Chronicle*, 4 June 1943; "Prayers Slated For Nazi Victims," *St. Paul Dispatch*, 11 May 1943; "Pilgrim Church Holds Joint Services," *Home News*, 3 May 1943; "Milwaukee Churches Call on U.S., Allies to Open Doors to Refugees," *Jewish Examiner*, 7 May 1943. Also see Appendix R.

171 Wyman, *Abandonment of the Jews*, 102.

172 Wyman, *Paper Walls*, 78, 105.

173 Robert W. Ross, *So It Was True: The American Protestant Press and the Nazi Persecution of the Jews, 1933-1945* (Minneapolis, 1980), 280.

174 See above, notes 120 and 139 and Appendix F. The May 1944 issue of *The Union Review* included a symposium with exiled German church leader Frederick Forell and World Council of Churches secretary Henry Leiper on the suffering of the Protestant Church under Hitler in the May 1944 issue. They made no mention of the suffering of the Jews under Hitler. (See Frederick J. Forell and Henry Leiper, "A Symposium: The Protestant Church in Germany," *The Union Review* 5:2 [May 1944], 13-19.)

175 Wyman, *Paper Walls*, 74, 118; Wyman, *Abandonment of the Jews*, 412-413, note 25.

176 Wyman, *Abandonment of the Jews*, 65-66.

177 Haim Genizi, *American Apathy: The Plight of Christian Refugees from Nazism* (Ramat Gan, 1983), 172-214.

178 Susan Elisabeth Subak, *Rescue & Flight: American Relief Workers Who Defied the Nazis* (Lincoln, NE, 2010). Also see Genizi, *American Apathy*, 215-244. In 2007, the Sharps became only the second and third Americans to be recognized by Yad Vashem as "Righteous Among the Nations." Regarding Varian Fry, who was the first, see above, notes 123-124.

179 For information on the attitudes of American Catholic educational institutions to Nazi Germany in the 1930s, see Stephen H. Norwood, *The Third Reich in the Ivory Tower: Complicity and Conflict on American Campuses* (New York, 2009), 199-204.

180 Wyman, *Abandonment of the Jews*, 319.

181 Genizi (above, note 177), 149-171; Wyman, *Abandonment of the Jews*, 319.

182 The text of the resolutions appears in "American Catholic Responses to the Holocaust: An Exchange Between David S. Wyman and Eugene J. Fisher," *Journal of Ecumenical Studies* 40 (Fall 2003), 385-389.

183 "The Church Appeals for the Resolution," in *Save Human Lives: Report of Activities and Financial Statement of the Emergency Committee to Save the Jewish People of Europe* (New York, 1944), 18, in File: Emergency Committee to Save the Jewish People of Europe – The March of 500 Rabbis, Correspondence, Invitations, Speeches, Reports, Clippings, 2/11/11-chet, MZ.

184 "Sponsors of the Emergency Conference to Save the Jewish People of Europe," File: Emergency Conference to Save the Jewish People of Europe – Resolutions, 1/7/1-11 chet, MZ.

185 Wyman, *Abandonment of the Jews*, 144.

186 "A Chicago Chapter of the Emergency Committee," *Emergency Committee to Save the Jewish People of Europe Circular Letter* II:8 (17 January 1944), 1; "Local Chapters," in File: Emergency Committee to Save the Jewish People of Europe – Other Members of the Emergency Committee, Correspondence, 1/7/1-11 chet, MZ.

187 For more on the controversies that the Bergson ads often ignited, see Ben Hecht (above, note 134), 565, and Wyman and Medoff (above, note 15), 65–69, 241, note 16.

188 "Quick Aid is Asked for Europe's Jews," NYT, 21 July 1943; "Jews' Rescue

229

Seen in Red Cross Help," NYT, 22 July 1943; "Plan is Outlined for Feeding Jews," NYT, 23 July 1943; "Ships Seen Ample for Rescuing Jews," NYT, 24 July 1943; "U.S. Help for Jews Asked by Alfange, NYT, 25 July 1943; "President Pledges Aid to Save Jews," NYT, 26 July 1943. For a detailed study of the Times's coverage of the Holocaust, see Laurel Leff's *Buried by The Times: The Holocaust and America's Most Important Newspaper* (New York, 2005).

189 Proskauer to Held, 29 June 1943, File: Proskauer Emergency Committee, AJCP, text reprinted in David S. Wyman, ed., *America and the Holocaust – Volume 5: American Jewish Disunity* (New York, 1990), 137.

190 "Meeting of the Steering Committee of the Joint Emergency Committee for European Jewish Affairs, Held at the Harmonie Club, April 2 [1943], at 3 PM," AJCP.

191 "Minutes of the Meeting of the Joint Emergency Committee for European Jewish Affairs, Held at the Harmonie Club, April 18, [1943] at 5:00 P.M.," File: Joint Emergency Committee for European Jewish Affairs, Box 8, AJCP.

192 Wise to Goldmann, 22 April 1943 and 23 April 1943, Box 1001, SSW-AJHS.

193 See above, note 183.

194 "Meeting of Emergency Committee on European Jewish Affairs Held at Hotel Commodore, Monday, May 24, 1943, at 12:30 P.M.," File: Joint Emergency Committee on European Jewish Affairs, Box 8, AJCP.

195 The students attributed the quote to Maimonides; it is actually from *Shulḥan Arukh, Yoreh De'ah* 252:3.

196 In addition to Golinkin, Lipnick, and Sachs, this particular document was also signed by a fourth student, Reuben Katz. See "A Program of Action," 25 April 1943, MSP, which is reproduced below in Appendix Q.

197 Proskauer to Lipnick, 26 April 1943, NGP.

198 See above, note 189.

199 Jaffe to Wise, 2 June 1943, Leib Jaffe Papers, CZA.

200 Minutes of Executive Committee Meeting, June 8, 1943, 1943 Folder, Box 6: Executive Committee 1916-49, AJCongress Papers.

201 "Minutes of the Meeting of the Joint Emergency Committee for European Jewish Affairs, July 15 1943," File: Joint Emergency Committee for European Jewish Affairs, Box 8, AJCP; Jaffe to Goldmann, 22 July 1943, S5/733, CZA; Jaffe to Keren HaYesod, 19 August 1943, S5/773, CZA.

202 "Joint Emergency Committee for European Jewish Affairs, Meeting held Tuesday, August 10, 1943, at the Congress Office," File: Joint Emergency Committee for European Jewish Affairs, Box 8, AJCP.

203 Stephen S. Wise, "As I See It: 'The Jewish Vote'," *Opinion*, November 1932, 15; "Rabbi Stephen S. Wise Sees No 'Jewish vote'," NYT, 2 November 1936, 12; "No Jewish Issue" (editorial), *Opinion*, September 1937, 9.

204 Isaac Lewin, "Indeed, Your Blood, of Your Souls, I Shall Seek" (Hebrew), *HaPardes* 17:9 (1943), 31.

205 "National Assembly to Fix Jewish Attitude on War and Peace," *Independent Jewish Press Service*, 25 January 1943, 3-4; "Call for the American Jewish Conference," CW, 23 April 1943, 24; "Platform of the Delegates of the American Jewish Congress to the American Jewish Conference," CW, 4 June 1943, 20.

206 Stephen S. Wise, "The American Jewish Conference: A Forecast," *Opinion*, August 1943 , 5.

207 Wyman, *Abandonment of the Jews*, 162; Minutes, Executive Committee Meeting, American Jewish Conference, Waldorf-Astoria Hotel, 14-15 July, 1943, 9, File: American Jewish Conference 1943-1948, SSW-AJHS.

208 Grossman to Goldstein, 26 May 1943, and "Statement on the American Jewish Conference by Dr. Israel Goldstein," 364/1951, 1, IGP.

209 Golinkin interview.

210 Philip Rubin, "Will Zionists Rise To Their Responsibility?," *National Jewish Ledger*, 12 August 1943, 6; A. S. Lyrique, "Trust the Common Man," CW, 18 June 1943, 5.

211 Baerwald to Wise, Monsky, and Goldstein, 7 December 1943, 364/1952, IGP.

212 "Rumor Washington Urging Delay in American Jewish Conference," *Independent Jewish Press Service*, 16 August 1943, 1.

213 The statement from the Warsaw Ghetto first appeared in the New York City newspaper *P.M.* on May 18, 1943, describing the suicide in London of exiled Polish Jewish leader Szamul Zygielbojm. His suicide note explained his act as a protest against the apathetic response of the Allies to the Holocaust. Zygielbojm was one of those who had met with the Polish courier, Jan Karski, earlier that year and heard the anguished message Karski bore from Warsaw. That message lambasted the Allies' silence, urged Diaspora Jewish leaders to stage hunger strikes to the death in front of American and British government offices, and commented sarcastically on Jewish leaders' lunch routine. The Labor Zionist journal *Jewish Frontier* reprinted the entire Warsaw message in its June edition. The Jewish Telegraphic Agency distributed a truncated version, in which it noted that the message "expressed doubt that Jewish leaders would do anything to help the Jews in Poland."

Perhaps not surprisingly, news articles about the Zygelbojm suicide that appeared in the publications of the American Jewish Congress, American Jewish Committee, and B'nai B'rith did not mention the embarrassing 'lunch' barb. But it seems likely that between *P.M.* and the *Jewish Frontier*, the organizers of the American Jewish Conference heard about it. See Frederick Kuh, "Grieving Polish Leader Suicide," *P.M.*, 18 May 1943, 9; "The Last Stand" (editorial), *Jewish Frontier*, June 1943, 4; "Zygelbjojm Inquest Adjourned for Three Weeks," JTA, 19 May 1943, 3; "Rollcall of Martyrs," CW 10:22 (4 June 1943), 6; "Poland-in-Exile," *Contemporary Jewish Record* 6:4 (August 1943), 410; "Compassion?" (editorial), *National Jewish Monthly* , July-August 1943, 352; and cf. above, pp. xiii-xv.

214 "Pardon Our Intruding" (leaflet), NGP, which is reproduced below in Appendix R.

215 Entry for 10 March 1944, John Morton Blum, ed. *The Price of Vision: The Diary of Henry A. Wallace 1942-1946* (New York, 1973), 313.

216 Monty N. Penkower, "The 1943 Joint Anglo-American Statement on Palestine," in Melvin Urofsky, ed., *Herzl Year Book, Vol. 8: Essays in American Zionism* (New York, 1978), 212-241.

217 Minutes of the Office Committee of the American Emergency Committee for Zionist Affairs, 12 August 1943, SSW-AJHS; Menahem Kaufman, *An*

Ambiguous Partnership: Non-Zionists and Zionists in America, 1939-1948 (Detroit, 1991), 132-33; Morris D. Waldman, *Nor By Power* (New York, 1953), 262.

218 Leff, *Buried by The Times* (above, note 188), 214-215.

219 Waldman, *Nor By Power*, 258.

220 Phineas J. Biron, "Strictly Confidential," *Philadelphia Jewish Exponent*, 22 October 1943, 5; Phineas J. Biron, "Strictly Confidential, *Philadelphia Jewish Exponent*, 5 November 1943, 5.

221 "Appeal to Save European Jewry: Address by Dr. Israel Goldstein," *The Conference Record*, 31 August 1943, 3 and cf. *The Reconstructionist* article, above, note 143 and Appendix J.

222 Golinkin interview.

223 "Oil & the Rabbis," *Time*, 18 October 1943, 21.

224 Rafael Medoff, "The Day the Rabbis Marched," *Hamodia*, 11 October 2005, 4; Rafael Medoff, "New Documents Reveal Impact of the 1943 Rabbis' March," *Hamodia*, 12 September 2008, 1; Efraim Zuroff, "The Evolution of American Orthodox Relief and Rescue Efforts During the Holocaust: Two Documents," *Journal of Ecumenical Studies* 40 (Fall 2003), 450-56.

225 See above, note 196 and Appendix Q.

226 See above, note 191.

227 "Partial List of Rabbis in Pilgrimage to Washington," issued as part of a news release from the Emergency Committee to Save the Jewish People of Europe, 6 October 1943, in File: Emergency Committee to Save the Jewish People of Europe – The March of 500 Rabbis, Correspondence, Invitations, Speeches, Reports, Clippings, 2/11/11-chet, MZ. See Appendix S.

228 Letter from Eri Jabotinsky to supporters, 1 October 1943, File: Emergency Committee to Save the Jewish People of Europe, MZ.

229 See above, note 223.

230 William D. Hassett, *Off the Record with F.D.R. 1942-1945* (New Brunswick, NJ, 1958), 209.

231 "Propaganda by Stunts" (editorial), *Opinion*, November 1943, 4.

232 Press accounts cited in "The Washington Pilgrimage," *The Answer* 1:12 (November 1943), 6-10.

233 Rafael Medoff interview with Cantor Ben Zion Shenker, Brooklyn, NY, 14 January 2009; Rafael Medoff and Martin Ostrow interview with Rabbi Levi Horowitz, Boston, MA, 5 December 2006; Arthur Hertzberg, "Marching with the Bergson Group: A Memoir," *Journal of Ecumenical Studies* 40:4 (Fall 2003), 390-93.

234 Wyman, *Abandonment of the Jews*, 153.

235 See "Establishment of a Commission to Effectuate the Rescue of the Jewish People of Europe," in *Problems of World War II and Its Aftermath – Part 2: The Palestine Question, Problems of Postwar Europe* (Washington, D.C., 1976), 15-249 (La Guardia's testimony is on 147-156; Wise's is on 217-243); Rogers to Goldstein, Monsky, and Wise, 8 February 1944, A364/1954, IGP.

236 Wise to Goldmann, 23 April 1943, SSW-AJA, Box 1001; "Jewish Labor Committee Brands Joint Emergency Body as 'Do-Nothing,' " *Independent Jewish Press Service*, 23 August 1943, 1; Joint Emergency Committee minutes, 5 November 1943, Box 8, AJCP.

237 *Problems of World War II*, 171.

238 Frederick R. Barkley, "580,000 Refugees Admitted to United States in Decade," NYT, 11 December 1943, 1.

239 "Statement by the Commission on Rescue of the American Jewish Conference," 27 December 1943, 364/152, IGP; Wyman, *Abandonment of the Jews*, 197-98.

240 Cited in Wyman, *Abandonment of the Jews*, 99.

241 Rafael Medoff, *Blowing the Whistle on Genocide: Josiah E. DuBois, Jr. and the Struggle for a U.S. Response to the Holocaust* (West Lafayette, IN, 2009), chapters 3 and 4.

242 *Congressional Record – Senate*, 78th Congress, 1st Session, 9305.

243 Medoff, *Blowing the Whistle on Genocide*, 53-64. The first page of the abbreviated report is reproduced below in Appendix T.

244 Wyman, *Abandonment of the Jews*, 66, 285.

245 Noah Golinkin, "How Should We Commemorate the Shoah in Our Homes?," *Moment*, June 1989, 30-35. For additional bibliography about Noah Golinkin, see below, note 252.

246 Cited in Lipnick, *From Where I Stand* (below, note 268), 13. For additional information about Jerry Lipnick, see below, 132-36 and Shuchat (above, note 71), 114-118.

247 Shuchat, 114, 116.

248 Davis to Hanin, 9 July 1943, File: "M. Bertram Sachs," Louis Finkelstein Papers, JTS; Buddy Sachs notes for Oheb Zedeck service, 3 September 1943, MSP – this service is reproduced below in Appendix U.

249 Dean Kotlowski, "Breaching the Paper Walls: Paul V. McNutt and Jewish Refugees to the Philippines, 1938-39," *Diplomatic History* 33:5 (November 2009), 865-896.

250 Moses B. Sachs and Elisha Mallard, eds., *Under Siege and After: Life in Jerusalem 1947-1949* (Jerusalem, 2006).

251 Moses B. Sachs, ed., *Brave Jews: Conversations with Soviet Jewish Activists, 1972-1974* (Jerusalem, 2007).

252 This essay is based on David Golinkin, *Insight Israel: The View from Schechter* (Jerusalem, 2003), 157-167; Rafael Medoff, *Encyclopaedia Judaica*, second edition, Vol. 7, 740-741, s.v. Golinkin, Noah; Noah Golinkin interviews with David Golinkin, undated; ca. 1977-1978; 28-29 May 1986; 13 January 1990; Noah Golinkin interview with Abe Golinkin, November 2001; Noah Golinkin to Meyer Goldstein, December 2000.

253 Concerning the Petlyura massacres, see *Encyclopaedia Judaica*, second edition, Vol. 16, p. 17, s.v. Petlyura, Simon.

254 See above, 97-102.

255 See David Golinkin, *Encyclopaedia Judaica*, second edition, Vol. 7, p. 740, s.v. Golinkin, Mordechai Ya'akov.

256 This town was immortalized in 1901 in a poem by Bialik *"Mee yodea ir Lishtina?"* (see Avner Holzman, *Hayyim Nahman Bialik: Hashirim*, Or Yehudah, 2004, 208-209). Daniel Persky once wrote in *Hado'ar* that this was a fictitious town. My father wrote to him that it was very real – it had saved the lives of my father and his family! It might be the town of Ludza/Luchin/Liutchin east of Riga – see Chester Cohen, *Shtetl Finder* (Los Angeles, 1980), 51.

257 For a vivid description of the relentless antisemitism in Vilna in 1938-1939,

see Lucy Davidowicz, *From That Place and Time: A Memoir 1938-1947* (New York and London, 1989), 64, 69, 75, 103, 164-185.

258 Cf. Dawidowicz, pp. 167-169. For a detailed description of the campaign to seat Jewish students on the left and to evict them from the University of Vilna and of the physical violence against Jews on that campus, see Yisrael Klausner, *Vilna, The Jerusalem of Lithuania: Recent Generations 1881-1939,* Vol. 1 (Hebrew; Beit Lohamey Hagetaot and HaKibbutz Hameuhad, 1983), 288-306.

259 See above, note 10.

260 Eliyahu Yosef Golinkin, a teacher and principal, fled with his wife Miriam to Kazakhstan where he succumbed to disease on 21 Iyar 5704 (14 May 1944). His wife Miriam made aliyah after the Holocaust and became a beloved teacher in Herzliyah where she passed away on 12 Adar 5751 (26 February 1991).

261 Haskel Lookstein, *Were We Our Brothers' Keepers? The Public Response of American Jews to the Holocaust, 1938-1944* (New York, 1986). Cf. his article below, 141-47.

262 Email from Noam Zion to David Golinkin, 12 August 2009. Cf. Rabbi Wilfred Shuchat (above, note 71, 115-116): "Rabbi Golinkin's response was that what hurt them most in those years was the feeling and the conviction that after it was all over, not a single Jewish life was saved as a result of this super-human effort. This hurt lingered on through the years."

263 See above, note 59.

264 See above, note 111.

265 See above, note 143 and Appendix J.

266 See above, 43-50.

267 See above, 89-90 and Appendix R.

268 Bernard Lipnick, ed. *From Where I Stand: From the Writings of Jerome Lipnick* (St. Louis, 1986).

269 This letter was printed by Wilfred Shuchat (above, note 71) and photographed in *From Where I Stand,* 23-24. It is reproduced below in Appendix O.

270 Lipnick, *From Where I Stand,* 87-89.

271 See above, note 143 and Appendix J.

272 See above, Chapter 3.

273 "Period of Mourning and Intercession," *Kehilath Jeshurun Bulletin,* 30 April 1943, 1.

274 Ahron Opher, "New York Board of Jewish Ministers – Committee for Rabbinical Convocation," 10 May 1943, SCA.

275 Minutes of the Kehilath Jeshurun Board of Trustees, 20 May 1943, Kehilath Jeshurun Archives, New York City. Cf. above, p. 75 and Appendix V for an announcement of the May 24th meeting.

276 For example, that phrase appeared in "Rabbis Urge Aid for Jews," *New York Journal-American,* 24 May 1943; but it did not appear in "Rabbis Plead for Aid to Stricken People," NYT, 25 May 1943.

277 This essay can be found in Ismar Schorsch, *From Text to Context: The Turn to History in Modern Judaism* (Hanover and London, 1994), 118-132.

278 This speech is reprinted in Shmuel Katz, *Lone Wolf: A Biography of Vladmir (Ze'ev) Jabotinsky* (New York, 1966), Vol. II, 1522.

279 For a description of this episode involving Hildesheimer and Hirsch, see David Ellenson, *Rabbi Esriel Hildesheimer and the Creation of a Modern Jewish Orthodoxy* (Tuscaloosa, AL, 1990), 110ff.

280 For a brief synopsis of the situation that prompted Hildesheimer's words, see *ibid.*, 97-98.

281 David Ellenson, " 'Our Brothers and Our Flesh': Rabbi Esriel Hildesheimer and the Jews of Ethiopia," *Judaism* 35:1 (Winter 1986), 63-65.

282 This article was not part of the symposium in 2008. It has been added here as a bibliographical postscript.

283 Lookstein, *Were We Our Brothers' Keepers?* (above, note 261), 125-26.

284 Rafael Medoff, *The Deafening Silence: American Jewish Leaders and the Holocaust* (New York, 1987), 110-11.

285 Rafael Medoff, " 'Retribution Is Not Enough': The 1943 Campaign by Jewish Students to Raise American Public Awareness of the Nazi Genocide," *Holocaust & Genocide Studies* 11 (Fall 1997), 171-89.

286 Rozenblit (above, note 9), 289-91.

BIBLIOGRAPHY

BOOKS CITED

Baumel, Judith Tydor. *Unfulfilled Promise: Rescue and Resettlement of Jewish Refugee Children in the United States, 1934–1945.* Juneau, AK: The Deli Press, 1990.

Blum, John Morton, ed. *The Price of Vision: The Diary of Henry A. Wallace 1942-1946.* New York: Houghton Mifflin, 1973.

Breitman, Richard and Kraut, Alan M. *American Refugee Policy and European Jewry, 1933-1945.* Bloomington, IN: Indiana University Press, 1997.

Dobkowski, Michael N. ed., *The Politics of Indifference: A Documentary History of Holocaust Victims in America.* Washington, D.C.: University Press of America, 1982.

Ellenson, David. *Rabbi Esriel Hildesheimer and the Creation of a Modern Jewish Orthodoxy.* Tuscaloosa, Alabama: University of Alabama Press, 1990.

Feingold, Henry L. *The Politics of Rescue.* New Brunswick, NJ: Rugers University Press, 1970.

Gal, Allon. *David Ben-Gurion and the American Alignment for a Jewish State.* Bloomington, IN: Indiana University Press, 1991.

Genizi, Haim. *American Apathy: The Plight of Christian Refugees from Nazism.* Ramat Gan: Bar-Ilan University Press, 1983.

Gurock, Jeffrey S. *The Men and Women of Yeshiva: Higher Education, Orthodoxy, and American Judaism.* New York: Columbia University Press, 1988.

Hassett, William D. *Off the Record with F.D.R. 1942-1945.* New Brunswick, NJ: Rutgers University Press, 1958.

Hecht, Ben. *A Child of the Century.* New York, Simon & Schuster, 1954.

Higham, John. *Strangers in the Land: Patterns of American Nativism 1860-1925.* New York: Atheneum, 1963.

237

Ickes, Harold L. *The Secret Diary of Harold L. Ickes, Volume 3: The Lowering Clouds 1939-1941*. New York: Simon and Schuster, 1954.

Karsh, Abraham I., ed. *Scroll of Agony: The Warsaw Diary of Chaim A. Kaplan*. Bloomington and Indianapolis: Indana University Press, 1999.

Kaufman, Menahem. *An Ambiguous Partnership: Non Zionists and Zionists in America, 1939-1948*. Detroit: Wayne State University Press, 1991.

Kleiman, Aharon, ed. *American Zionism – Volume 8*. London: Taylor & Francis Group, 1991.

Laqueur, Walter. *The Terrible Secret: Suppression of the Truth about Hitler's 'Final Solution.'* Boston: Little, Brown, 1980.

Leff, Laurel. *Buried by* The Times: *The Holocaust and America's Most Important Newspaper*. New York: Cambridge University Press, 2005.

Lipnick, Bernard, ed., *From Where I Stand: From the Writings of Jerome Lipnick*. St. Louis: Rabbi Lipnick Education and Charity Foundation, 1986.

Lookstein, Haskel. *Were We Our Brothers' Keepers? The Public Response of American Jews to the Holocaust, 1938-1944*. New York: Hartmore House, 1986.

Marino, Andy. *A Quiet American: The Secret War of Varian Fry*. New York: St. Martin's Press, 1999.

Medoff, Rafael. *Blowing the Whistle on Genocide: Josiah E. DuBois, Jr. and the Struggle for a U.S. Response to the Holocaust*. West Lafayette, IN: Purdue University Press, 2009.

Meir, Golda. *My Life*. New York: G.P. Putnam's Sons, 1975.

Neumann, Emanuel. *In the Arena*. New York: The Herzl Press, 1976.

Norwood, Stephen H. *The Third Reich in the Ivory Tower: Complicity and Conflict on American Campuses*. New York: Cambridge University Press, 2009.

Ogilvie, Sarah A. and Miller, Scott. *Refuge Denied: The* St. Louis *Passengers and the Holocaust*. Madison, WI: University of Wisconsin Press, 2006.

Penkower, Monty Noam. *The Jews Were Expendable: Free World Diplomacy and the Holocaust.* Urbana and Chicago: University of Illinois Press, 1983.

Rabinovitz, Zvi Yehudah, ed., *Yalkut Hamo'adim*, Vol. 2. Buenos Aires, 1943.

Ross, Robert W. *So It Was True: The American Protestant Press and the Nazi Persecution of the Jews, 1933-1945.* University of Minnesota Press: Minneapolis, 1980.

Sachs, Moses B. and Mallard, Elisha, eds., *Under Siege and After: Life in Jerusalem 1947-1949.* Jerusalem, 2006.

Sachs, Moses B., ed., *Brave Jews: Conversations with Soviet Jewish Activists, 1972-1974.* Jerusalem, 2007.

Jonathan D. Sarna, *JPS: The Americanization of Jewish Culture, 1888-1988.* Philadelphia: Jewish Publication Society of America, 1989.

Schorsch, Ismar. *From Text to Context: The Turn to History in Modern Judaism.* Hanover and London: Brandeis University Press, 1994.

Stember, Charles H. et al, *Jews in the Mind of America.* New York: Basic Books, 1966.

Subak, Susan Elisabeth. *Rescue & Flight: American Relief Workers Who Defied the Nazis.* Lincoln, NE: University of Nebraska Press, 2010.

Urofsky, Melvin. *A Voice That Spoke for Justice: The Life and Times of Stephen S. Wise.* Albany, NY; State University of New York Press, 1982.

Urofsky, Melvin, ed., *Herzl Year Book, Vol. 8: Essays in American Zionism.* New York: Herzl Press, 1978.

Waldman, Morris D. *Nor By Power.* New York: International Universities Press, 1953.

Wertheimer, Jack, ed., *Tradition Renewed: A History of the Jewish Theological Seminary of America.* New York: Jewish Theological Seminary of America, 1997.

Wertheimer, Jack, ed., *The American Synagogue: A Sanctuary Transformed.* Cambridge and New York: Cambridge University Press, 1987.

Wise, Stephen S. *Challenging Years: The Autobiography of Stephen Wise*. New York: Putnam's Sons, 1949.

Wyman, David S., ed., *America and the Holocaust*. New York: Garland, 1990.

Wyman, David S. *Paper Walls: America and the Refugee Crisis 1938-1941*. Amherst, MA: University of Massachusetts Press, 1968.

Wyman, David S. and Medoff, Rafael. *A Race Against Death: Peter Bergson, America, and the Holocaust*. New York: The New Press, 2002.

Wyman, David S. *The Abandonment of the Jews: America and the Holocaust, 1941-1945*. New York: Pantheon, 1984.

Voss, Carl Hermann, ed. *Stephen S. Wise, Servant of the People – Selected Letters*. Philadephia: Jewish Publication Society of America, 1970.

SELECTED BIBLIOGRAPHY
ALLIED GOVERNMENT RESPONSES TO THE HOLOCAUST

Abella, Irving and Harold Troper. *None is Too Many: Canada and the Jews of Europe, 1933–1948*. New York: Random House, 1982.

Abzug, Robert H. *America Views the Holocaust, 1933–1945: A Brief Documentary History*. Boston and New York: Bedford/St. Martin's, 1999.

Bartrop, Paul. *Australia and the Holocaust, 1933–1945*. Melbourne: Australian Scholarly Publications, 1993.

Bauer, Yehuda. *Jews for Sale? Nazi-Jewish Negotiations, 1933–1945*. New Haven and London: Yale University Press, 1994.

Breitman, Richard. *Official Secrets: What the Nazis Planned, What the British and America Knew*. New York: Hill and Wang, 1998.

Breitman, Richard and Alan M. Kraut. *American Refugee Policy and European Jewry, 1933–1945*. Bloomington and Indianapolis: Indiana University Press, 1987.

Ephraim, Frank. *Escape to Manila: From Nazi Tyranny to Japanese Terror*. Urbana and Chicago: University of Illinois Press, 2003.

Feingold, Henry L. *Bearing Witness: How America and Its Jews Responded to the Holocaust*. Syracuse, NY: Syracuse University Press, 1995.

Feingold, Henry L. *The Politics of Rescue: The Roosevelt Administration and the Holocaust, 1938–1945.* New Brunswick, NJ: Rutgers University Press, 1970.

Friedman, Saul S. *No Haven for the Oppressed: United States Policy Toward Refugees, 1938–1945.* Detroit: Wayne State University Press, 1973.

Fry, Varian. *Surrender on Demand.* Boulder, CO: Johnson Books, 1997.

Genizi, Haim. *American Apathy: The Plight of Christian Refugees from Nazism.* Ramat Gan, Israel: Bar-Ilan University Press, 1983.

Gilbert, Martin. *Auschwitz and the Allies.* New York: Holt Rinehart and Winston, 1981.

Hirschmann, Ira A. *Life Line to a Promised Land.* New York: Vanguard Press, 1946.

Jackman, Jarrell C. and Carla M. Borden. *The Muses Flee Hitler: Cultural Transfer and Adaptation, 1930–1945.* Washington, D.C.: Smithsonian Institution Press, 1983.

Laqueur, Walter. *The Terrible Secret.* Boston and Toronto: Little Brown, 1980.

Laqueur, Walter and Richard Breitman. *Breaking the Silence.* New York: Simon and Schuster, 1986.

Lowenstein, Sharon R. *Token Refuge: The Story of the Jewish Refugee Shelter in Oswego, 1944–1946.* Bloomington: Indiana University Press, 1986.

Marino, Andy. *A Quiet American: The Secret War of Varian Fry.* New York: St. Martin's Press, 1999.

Morse, Arthur D. *While Six Million Died: A Chronicle of American Apathy.* New York: Random House, 1967.

Penkower, Monty Noam. *The Holocaust and Israel Reborn: From Catastrophe to Sovereignty.* Urbana and Chicago: University of Illinois Press, 1994.

Penkower, Monty Noam. *The Jews Were Expendable: Free World Diplomacy and the Holocaust.* Urbana and Chicago: University of Illinois Press, 1983.

Perl, William R. *The Four-Front War: From the Holocaust to the Promised Land.* New York: Crown, 1978.

Smith, Sharon Kay. "Elbert D. Thomas and America's Response to the Holocaust." Ph.D. dissertation, Brigham Young University, 1992.

Thomas, Gordon and Max Morgan Witts. *Voyage of the Damned.* New York: Stein and Day, 1974.

Vrba, Rudolf and Alan Bestic. *I Cannot Forgive.* New York: Grove Press, 1964.

Wasserstein, Bernard. *Britain and the Jews of Europe, 1939–1945.* New York and Oxford: Oxford University Press, 1979.

Weisberg, Alex. *Desperate Mission.* New York: Criterion Books, 1958.

Wood, E. Thomas and Stanislaw M Jankowski. *Karski: How One Man Tried to Stop the Holocaust.* New York: John Wiley and Sons, 1994.

Wyman, David S. *The Abandonment of the Jews: America and the Holocaust, 1941–1945.* New York: Pantheon, 1984.

Wyman, David S. *America and the Holocaust.* 13 vols. New York: Garland, 1993.

Wyman, David S. *Paper Walls: America and the Refugee Crisis, 1938–1941.* Amherst: University of Massachusetts Press, 1968.

Wyman David S., ed. *The World Reacts to the Holocaust.* Baltimore: Johns Hopkins University Press, 1996.

Zucker, Bat-Ami. *In Search of Refuge: Jews and U.S. Consuls in Nazi Germany, 1933–1941.* London and Portland, ME: Vallentine Mitchell, 2001.

AMERICAN MEDIA COVERAGE OF THE HOLOCAUST

Leff, Laurel. *Buried by* The Times*: The Holocaust and America's Most Important Newspaper.* New York: Cambridge University Press, 2005.

Lipstadt, Deborah E. *Beyond Belief: The American Press and the Coming of the Holocaust, 1933–1945.* New York: The New Press, 1986.

Shapiro, Robert Moses, ed. *Why Didn't the Press Shout? American and International Journalism During the Holocaust.* New York: Yeshiva University Press, 2003.

AMERICAN CHRISTIAN RESPONSES

Ross, Robert W. *So It Was True: The American Protestant Press and the Nazi Persecution of the Jews.* Minneapolis: University of Minnesota Press, 1980.

Subak, Susan Elisabeth. *Rescue & Flight: American Relief Workers Who Defied the Nazis.* Lincoln, NE: University of Nebraska Press, 2010.

AMERICAN JEWISH RESPONSES

Arad, Gulie Ne'eman. *America, Its Jews, and the Rise of Nazism.* Bloomington and Indianapolis: Indiana University Press, 2000.

Bauer, Yehuda. *American Jewry and the Holocaust: The American Jewish Joint Distribution Committee, 1939–1945.* Detroit: Wayne State University Press, 1981.

Bauer, Yehuda. *My Brother's Keeper: A History of the American Jewish Joint Distribution Committee, 1929–1939.* Philadelphia: Jewish Publication Society of America, 1974.

Baumel, Judith Tydor. *The "Bergson Boys" and the Origins of Contemporary Militancy.* Syracuse, NY: Syracuse University Press, 2005.

Ben-Ami, Yitshaq. *Years of Wrath, Days of Glory: Memoirs from the Irgun.* New York: Shengold, 1983.

Berman, Aaron. *Nazism, the Jews, and American Zionism.* Detroit: Wayne State University Press, 1990.

Gottlieb, Moshe. "The Anti-Nazi Boycott Movement in the American Jewish Community, 1933–1941." Ph.D. dissertation, Brandeis University, 1967.

Grobman, Alex. *Battling for Souls: The Vaad Hatzala Rescue Committee in Post-War Europe.* Jersey City, NJ: Ktav, 2003.

Hecht, Ben. *A Child of the Century.* New York: Simon & Schuster, 1954.

Korff, Baruch. *Flight from Fear*. New York: Elmar, 1953.

Lookstein, Haskel. *Were We Our Brothers' Keepers? The Public Response of American Jews to the Holocaust, 1938–1944*. New York: Hartmore House, 1985.

Medoff, Rafael. *The Deafening Silence: American Jewish Leaders and the Holocaust*. New York: Steimatzky-Shapolsky, 1987.

Medoff, Rafael. *Militant Zionism in America: The Rise and Impact of the Jabotinsky Movement in the United States, 1926–1948*. Tuscaloosa: University of Alabama Press, 2002.

Neuringer, Sheldon Morris. "American Jewry and United States Immigration Policy, 1881–1953." Ph.D. dissertation, University of Wisconsin, 1969.

Neustadt-Noy, Isaac. "The Unending Task: Efforts to Unite American Jewry from the American Jewish Congress to the American Jewish Conference." Ph.D. dissertation, Brandeis University, 1976.

Nurenberger, M.J. *The Scared and the Doomed: The Jewish Establishment vs. the Six Million*. Ontario: Mosaic Press, 1985.

Rafaeli, Alex. *Dream and Action: The Story of My Life*. Jerusalem: Achva, 1993.

Rapoport, Louis. *Shake Heaven and Earth: Peter Bergson and the Struggle to Rescue the Jews of Europe*. Jerusalem: Gefen, 1999.

Wolk, Kenneth. "New Haven and Waterbury, Connecticut Jewish Communities' Public Response to the Holocaust, 1938–1944." Ph.D. dissertation, New York University, 1995.

Wyman, David S. and Rafael Medoff. *A Race against Death: Peter Bergson, America, and the Holocaust*. New York: The New Press, 2002.

Zuroff, Efraim. *The Response of Orthodox Jewry in the United States to the Holocaust: The Activities of the Vaad-ha-Hatzala Rescue Committee, 1939–1945*. New York: Yeshiva University Press, 2000.

OTHER AMERICAN RESPONSES

Norwood, Stephen H. *The Third Reich in the Ivory Tower: Complicity and Conflict on American Campuses.* New York: Cambridge University Press, 2009.

PHOTO CREDITS

We thank the following individuals and libraries for permission to use the photograhs appearing in this volume.

The Brautigam Family: 44 bottom

The Central Zionist Archives: 47 middle

Congregation Beth El, Houston, Texas: 48 right

Foss, Miriam: cover photo, 8, 28, 109

General Theological Seminary Library: 50 top left

The Godby Family: 50 top right

The Golinkin Family: cover photo, 2, 27, 98, 107

Gordon, Shifra: 32

The Lookstein Family: 75

New Brunswick Theological Seminary Library: 50 bottom left

The Ratner Center for the Study of Conservative Judaism at the Jewish Theological Seminary: 1, 44 top, 48 left, 49, 51,

The Sachs Family: cover photo, 8, 27, 111

The Shay Family: 50 bottom right

World Council of Churches: 47 left

The David S. Wyman Institute for Holocaust Studies: 3, 4, 16, 34, 38, 46, 47 right, 55 left, 55 right, 67, 81, 85, 92, 97, 99, 100 (both), 101

The Yeshiva University Library and Archives: 60 left and center

Zuroff, Efraim: 60 right

INDEX

Abelson, Joan Lipnick, 135

Adath Jeshurun synagogue (Minneapolis, MN), 109

Adler, Cyrus, 45

Adler, Stella, 58

Agnon, S.Y., 112

Agudath Israel, 72, 82, 88

Ahmadinejad, Mahmoud, 152

Al Domi (Do Not Be Silent), 117-118

Alaska refuge plan, 34-35, 77

Alexander, Robert C., 225 n. 140

Alfange, Dean, 80

Alpert, Carl, 61

America, 78

American Civil Liberties Union, 3

American Council for Judaism, 45, 48-49, 130-131

American Federation of Labor, 30

American Friends Service Committee, 48, 78

American Jewish Committee: 6, 19-20, 72, 91;
and anti-Hitler rallies, 11, 53;
and boycott of Nazi Germany, 11;
conflicts with other Jewish organizations, 57;
and immigration to the United States, 14, 18;
and Evian conference, 19;
and Zionism 10, 14

American Jewish Commission on the Holocaust (Goldberg Commission), 155

American Jewish community: 6; and "business as usual" mood, 70-71, 113, 112;
charge of warmongering, 21;
knowledge of the Holocaust, 22;
protests for Jews overseas, 9-10;
response to news of the Holocaust, 30, 42-43, 93-95, 113, 141, 155

American Jewish Conference, 84, 88-96, 103, 130, 231 n. 213

American Jewish Congress: 3, 6, 55-56, 72, 82, 86, 87, 88, 92, 117, 119;
and boycott of Nazi Germany, 11, 218 n. 18;
conflicts with other Jewish organizations, 57;
and anti-Hitler rallies, 11, 53;
responses to news of the Holocaust, 42;
women's division, 11;
and Zionism, 10

American Jewish Joint Distribution Committee, 18, 24, 78, 89

American Jewish World Service, 135

American Zionist Emergency Council, 43, 92-93

Anglo-American joint statement on Palestine, 90-92

Antisemitism:
among Allied leaders, xiv;
in the United States in the 1930s, xii, 10, 11, 113

Arbeiterring (Workmen's Circle), 56

Arendt, Hannah, 47

Arens, Moshe, 40

Aronson, Shlomo, 122

Associated Synagogues of Massachusetts, 122

Atkinson, Henry, 78

Auschwitz, x, xi, xii, 2, 106

Avuka, 39-40

Baerwald, Paul, 89

Baldwin, Rep. Joseph, 102

Belzec (Nazi death camp), xiii, 2

Ben-Gurion, David, 32, 43

Bergson Group: 38, 54-58, 60, 65, 72, 81, 86, 96, 113, 114, 146, 155;
Christian supporters, 79;
Emergency Conference to Save

247

the Jewish People of Europe
(1943), 80, 89, 96;
Emergency Conference to Save
the Jewish People of Europe
(1944), 80;
Jewish army campaign, 55, 65,
117;
newspaper advertisements, 80, 91,
96;
rabbis' march in Washington,
D.C., 97-102;
rescue resolution in Congress, 98,
102-103;
We Will Never Die, 55, 57, 79, 96;
also see Committee for a Jewish
Army of Stateless and Palestinian
Jews; Emergency Committee to
Save the Jewish People of Europe
Bergson, Peter (Hillel Kook), 54-55
Berkeley Theological Seminary, 46
Berle, Adolph, 73
Berlin, Meyer, 86
Bermuda conference, 72-74, 82, 95, 98
Bernstein, Philip, 46-47
Betar, 40
Beth Shalom synagogue (Columbia,
MD), 107
Beving, Richard, 224 n. 120
Bialik, Hayyim Nahman, 29 n. 256
Biblical Seminary, 46
Birnbaum, Jacob, x
Bloom, Rep. Sol, 73, 82, 99, 102-103
B'nai B'rith: 6, 10, 30, 55, 72, 88;
conflicts with other Jewish
organizations, 57
B'nai B'rith Youth Organization, 109
Boston Globe, 123
Boston Redevelopment Authority,
123
Brautigam Jr., J. Herbert, 44-46, 59, 77,
223-224 n. 120
Brodetzky, Moshe, 40
Brooklyn Jewish Examiner, 18
Browne, Duncan, 79
Brownville, C. Gordon, 80

Buchenwald (Nazi death camp), 23
Bund, Jewish Socialist, xiii, 24
Bureau of Immigration, 78

Cannon Jr., James, 79
Capper, Sen. Arthur, 80
Catholic Committee for Refugees, 78
Celler, Rep. Emanuel: and Anglo-
American joint statement on
Palestine, 91;
criticism of Bermuda conference,
73;
proposal to liberalize immigration
(1938), 18
Chagall, Marc, 47
Chelmno (Nazi death camp), 24
Christian Century, 77-78
Church Peace Union, 78
Churchill, Winston, xiii, 91
The Churchman, 79
Citizens Association of Greater Utica,
109-110
Clark University, 27
Coffin, Henry Sloane, 79
The Commentator, 37, 59-60
Committee for a Jewish Army of
Stateless and Palestinian Jews:
117.
Also see Bergson Group
Commonweal, 78
Communist Party USA 38
Congregation Beth El (Utica, NY), 109
Congregation Beth Jeshurun
(Houston, TX), 109
Congregation Beth Shalom
(Wilmington, DE), 109
Congress of Industrial Organizations,
30
Congress Weekly, 89
Coolidge, Grace, 20
Coughlin, Father Charles, xii, 11, 218
n. 15

Dachau (Nazi death camp), 23

The David S. Wyman Institute for
    Holocaust Studies, 142

Davis, Moshe, 111

Day of Compassion, 76-77, 83, 86

Deppen, J. Ralph, 224 n.120

Der Tog, 22, 30

Der Yiddisher Kemfer, 42, 130

Dickens, Charles, 151

Dickstein, Rep. Samuel: criticism of
    Bermuda conference, 73;
    proposal to liberalize immigration
    (1933), 13;
    proposal to liberalize immigration
    (1938), 18

Dieffenbach, Albert C., 80

Drew Seminary, 46

Dubois Jr., Josiah E., 104-105

Edelstein, Rep. E. Michael, 217 n. 14

Eden, Anthony, xiv, 72

Einsatzgruppen, 22, 24

Emergency Committee for Zionist
    Affairs, 3, 57, 72, 227 n. 158

Emergency Committee to Save the
    Jewish People of Europe (Bergson
    Group), 117

Emergency Rescue Committee, 47

European Committee of the Student
    Body of the Jewish Theological
    Seminary, 28-29, 35-37, 44, 46, 49,
    59, 62-65, 73, 117, 118, 129, 131,
    134, 137-140, 149, 156, 226 n. 146

Evian conference, 15, 18, 72, 219 n. 31,
    219 n. 44

Federal Council of Churches, 48, 77

Federation of Jewish Men's Clubs,
    108, 137

Fein, Helen, xiv

Feingold, Henry, 154

Feinstein, Moshe, 99

Fellowship of Reconciliation, 38

Finkelstein, Louis, 45, 51-52, 223-224
    n. 120

Forverts, 101

Free Synagogue (New York City), 3

Friedman, Solomon, 99

Fry, Varian, 47-48, 78

Furrows, 38, 40

Gelb, Saadia, 38

General Jewish Council, 19, 57, 82

General Theological Seminary, 46, 79

Gill, Theodore, 224 n. 120

Gillette, Sen. Guy, 102-104

Godby, Ivol, 224 n. 120

Goldblum, Moshe, 28, 49

Goldfarb, Morris, 56

Goldmann, Nahum, 32, 43, 82, 92, 98

Goldstein, Herbert, 143-145

Goldstein, Israel, 68, 73, 82, 88, 140,
    147

    speech at American Jewish
    Conference, 93-95

Golinkin, Devorah (Dolly) Perlberg,
    107, 138

Golinkin, Mordechai Ya'akov, 8, 98-
    99, 102, 121-122, 217 n. 9, 217 n. 11

Golinkin, Noah, x, xi, 1, 5, 7, 26, 30,
    55, 98, 126-128, 131, 137-140, 152,
    155, 156;
    biographical information, 8-9, 27,
    107-108, 217 n. 11;
    black ribbon idea, 69;
    civil rights activism, 108, 125;
    contacts with UTS students, 44;
    essay in *The Reconstructionist*, 62-
    65, 93, 118-119, 130, 139, 140;
    and Inter-Seminary Conference,
    45, 51, 56;
    learns of the Holocaust, 2-4;
    meeting with Stephen Wise, 33,
    37, 42;
    meetings with other Jewish
    leaders, 61;
    meeting with leaders of the
    Synagogue Council of America,
    68;
    Sefira campaign, 67-70, 96;
    Soviet Jewry activism, 108, 125-126

Golinkin, Rachel, 8, 124-125
Golinkin, Rivka, 8, 124-125
Gone with the Wind, 55
Gordis, Robert, 45, 48-49
Gordon, Irwin, 32, 52, 60, 223-224 n. 120, 224 n. 128
Graetz, Heinich, 152
Grayzel, Solomon, 23
Greenberg, Hayim, 42, 60, 129
Greenberg, Irving (Yitz), ix
Gross, Louis, 18
Gruenewald, Rabbi Max, 24, 27, 129
Gutman, Israel, xiii

Habonim, 40, 112
Hadassah, 103, 124
Hadassah Magazine, 123
Haganah, 112
Hamigdal, 40
Harper, Fowler, 98
Hart Jr., Henry M., 32
Hart, Moss, 58
Hartman, Lewis O., 79-80
Hashomer Hadati, 40
Hashomer Hatzair, 23, 39, 129
Hashomer Hatzair (magazine), 23
Hassett, William D., 101
Havenner, Rep. Franck, 35
Hearst, William Randolph, 80
Hebrew Literacy Campaign, 108, 126, 137-138
Hebrew Union College, 3
Hebrew University, xii, 112
Hecht, Ben, 55-58, 118
Held, Adolph, 30-31
Heska Emunah synagogue (Knoxville, TN), 108
Hildesheimer, Esriel, 151-152
Himmler, Heinrich, 2
Hirsch, Samson Raphael, 151-152
Hitler, Adolf, 4, 5, 9, 21, 39, 47, 51, 141
Holmes, John Haynes, 117

Holocaust and Genocide Studies, 120, 155
Hoover, Herbert, 80
Houghteling, Laura Delano, 20
Hull, Cordell:
    criticizes Jewish members of Congress, 17;
    and Evian conference, 15

Ickes, Harold, 34, 35, 80
Immigration (to the United States):
    quotas enacted, 12-13;
    quotas not filled, 16, 53-54, 219 n. 33
Independent Jewish Press Service, 89
Institute of Jewish Affairs, 117
Inter-Seminary Conference, 45-54, 56, 58-60, 62, 64, 65, 96, 130, 120
Irgun Zvai Leumi, 54

Jabotinsky, Vladimir Ze'ev, 33, 54, 55, 150-152
Jacksonville (FL) Jewish Center, 109
Jaffe, Leib, 85-86
Jewish Agency for Palestine, 32, 86
Jewish Community Council of Greater Washington, D.C., 107
Jewish Frontier, 42, 74, 129-130, n. 213
Jewish Institute of Religion, 3, 32, 33, 37-38, 46, 49, 130, n. 81
Jewish Labor Committee, 30-31, 57, 72, 81, 82, 85, 88
Jewish Publication Society of America, 23
Jewish Spectator, 71
Jewish Telegraphic Agency, 22, 24, 26, 231 n. 213
Jewish Theological Seminary of America: 1, 23, 29, 37, 61, 68, 111, 117, 119-120, 129, 134, 141, 148, 155, 156, 217 n. 9;
    aids German Jewish refugee scholars, 45;
    campus life during the Holocaust, 45-46;

established, 7;
hosts Inter-Seminary Conference, 45-53
Jewish Theological Seminary of Breslau, 152
Jewish War Veterans of America, 100
Jewish Welfare Board, 46
Johnson Immigration Act, 12
Johnson, Willard, 48
Joint Consultative Council, 57
Joint Emergency Committee on European Jewish Affairs, 72-74, 81-86, 97-98, 103
Junior Hadassah, 76

Kalmanowitz, Avraham, 82
Kaplan, Chaim, 37
Karski, Jan, xiii-xv, 231 n. 213
Katz, Reuben, 230 n. 196
Kehilath Jeshurun synagogue (New York City), 75
Keren ha-Yesod (Palestine Foundation Fund), 85
Kershner, Howard, 48
King, Sen. William, 11, 35
King-Havenner legislation, 77
Kirshblum, Usher, 49, 223-224 n. 120
Knox, Frank, 20
Koestler, Arthur, 118
Kohler, Max, 13
Kook, Abraham Isaac, 55
Kook, Hillel: see Bergson, Peter
Korff, Samuel, 123
Kristallnacht, 19, 34, 77
Ku Klux Klan, 12
Kubowitzki, A. Leon, 60

La Guardia, Fiorello, 102
Labor Action, 39
Labor Zionists of America, 37, 38, 40, 42, 61, 74, 86, 98, 112, 129, 231 n. 213
Landon, Alf, 20

League of Nations, 14
Lehman, Herbert, 31
Lehman, Irving, 5
Leifman, Morty, 119
Leiper, Henry Smith, 48
Leventhal, Bernard Dov, 99, 217 n. 11
Lewin, Isaac, 82, 88
Lieberman, Saul, 29
Lindbergh, Charles, 21
Lipnick, Bernard, 132-133
Lipnick, Jerome (Jerry): x, xi, 4, 73, 125-128, 131, 137-140, 152, 155;
biographical information, 7-8, 27-28, 109-110, 132;
black ribbon idea 133-135;
civil rights activism, 110, 125, 132, 133-134;
contacts with UTS students, 44;
essay in *The Reconstructionist*, 62-65, 93, 118-119, 130, 139, 140;
and Inter-Seminary Conference, 45, 49, 51, 56, 60;
meeting with Rabbi Stephen Wise, 33, 37, 150;
meeting with leaders of the Synagogue Council of America, 68;
meetings with other Jewish leaders, 61;
notes from Homiletics class, 61-62;
Sefira campaign, 67-70, 96;
Soviet Jewry activism, 110, 125, 132
Lodge, Sen. Henry Cabot, 125
Long, Breckinridge: 73, 225 n. 140;
relationship with President Roosevelt, 17;
seeks to curtail immigration, 16;
testifies against rescue resolution in Congress, 103-104, n. 133
Look, 123
Lookstein, Haskel, x, 126
Lookstein, Joseph, 75, 142, 145-147

MacDonald, Douglas, 224 n. 120

McConnell, William J., 79
McCormack, Rep. John, 124
McDonald, James, 17, 31-32
McIntyre, Marvin, 101
McNutt, Paul, 111-112
McPheeters, Chilton, 224 n. 120
March of the Living, ix
Meir, Golda, 18, 219 n. 44
Messersmith, George, 15
Messinger, Ruth, 135
Meyerhof, Otto, 47
Ministerial Association of Arlington, 125
Minkoff, Isaiah, 82
Mizrachi movement, 122
Monsky (Montor), Henry, 30, 82, 88, 98
Moravaian Theological Seminary, 46
Morgen Zhurnal, 1
Morgenthau, Jr., Henry M.: 5, 26; and Anglo-American joint statement on Palestine, 91; presses FDR on rescue issue, 103-105
Morse, Arthur, 154
Moss, Louis, 13
Muni, Paul, 58

National Association for the Advancement of Colored People (NAACP), 3, 80
National Catholic Welfare Conference, 78, 79
National Conference of Christians and Jews, 48, 125
National Jewish Ledger, 89
Neumann, Emanuel, 43
New Brunswick Theological Seminary, 46
New Palestine, 61
The New Republic, 47
New York Board of Jewish Ministers, 142, 144, 145
New York Times, 1-2, 15, 20, 22-23, 26,

103, 118, 141, 146, 147, 155
New York Times Magazine, 118
New Zionist Organization of America, 40, 91
Newman, Louis I., 146
Newsweek, 18, 123
Niebuhr, Reinhold, 44
Niles, David, 31

Oheb Zedeck Congregation (Pottsville, PA), 111
Okun, Sam, 59
Opher, Ahron, 68, 74, 142-145
Oxnam, G. Bromley, 80

Partisan Review, 39
Pat, Jacob, 81, 82, 85
Peel Commission (1937), 151
Pehle, John, 105
Pergola, Sergio Della, xii
Perkins, Frances, 14
Petlyura, Simon, 122, 123
Pets Magazine, 20
Philadelphia Jewish Exponent, 54, 93
P.M., 225 n. 133, 231 n. 213
Poalei Zion (Labor Zionists of America), 35
Polish Government in Exile, xiii, xv
Polish National Council, xiii
Pool, David de Sola, 143-146
Pope Pius XII, 26, 41
Presidents Advisory Committee on Political Refugees, 16, 31, 48
Princeton Theological Seminary, 46
Proskauer, Joseph, 72, 81, 83, 85
Protestant Theological College, 79

Rankin, Rep. John, 10
The Reconstructionist, 30, 62, 67, 70, 93, 111, 119, 130, 139, 140, 155
Redler-Feldman, Yehoshua (Rabbi Binyamin), 118
Reichsvertretung der deutschen

Juden, 24

Reit, Hyman, 13

Religious News Service, 60

Revel, Bernard, 124

Revisionist Zionist movement, 33, 40, 91

Riegner, Gerhart, 24-26

Robbins, Howard Chandler, 79

Robinson, Edward G., 58

Rogers, Rep. Edith, 20

Rogers Jr., Rep. Will, 102-104

Roosevelt, Eleanor:
and Wagner-Rogers legislation, 20;
and *We Will Never Die*, 58

Roosevelt, Franklin D.: xiv;
and Anglo-American joint statement on Palestine, 90-91;
and Alaska refuge plan, 35;
declines to meet delegation of rabbis, 101;
creates Presidents Advisory Committee on Political Refugees, 16-17;
and Evian conference, 15-16;
and immigration policy, 19-20;
Jewish criticism of, 101-102, 147;
Jewish electoral support for, 87;
relationship with Stephen S. Wise, 3, 150;
response to plight of European Jewry, 5, 31-32, 34, 126;
and the S.S. St. Louis, 20-21;
and Wagner-Rogers legislation, 20

Roosevelt administration: x;
and boycott of Nazi Germany, 11;
downplays Jewish identity of Nazis' victims, 17;
halts Varian Fry's rescue mission, 47;
and Palestine, 15;
"rescue through victory" policy, 98;
response to *We Will Never Die*, 57-58;
restricts immigration, 53-54, 219 n. 44;

role in 1942 Allied Declaration on mass murder, 41;
urged to rescue European Jewry, 64-65

Rosenberg, Israel, 30, 99

Rosenman, Samuel: and Anglo-American joint statement on Palestine, 91;
and immigration policy, 19-20;
and rabbis' march in Washington, D.C., 101

Rothenberg, Morris, 87

Rozenblit, Marcia, 156

Rustin, Bayard, 134

Sachs, Moshe (Buddy): x, xi, 4, 37, 125-127, 137-140, 152, 155;
biographical information, 7-8, 27-28, 128;
civil rights activism, 112, 125, 128;
contacts with UTS students, 44;
essay in *The Reconstructionist*, 62-65, 93, 111, 118-119, 130, 139,140;
and Inter-Seminary Conference, 45, 51, 56;
learns of the Holocaust, 23-24, 129;
meetings with Jewish leaders, 61;
Sefira campaign, 67-70, 96;
Soviet Jewry activism, 112, 125, 128;
Zionist activism, 112, 125

Samuel, Maurice, 60

Scarface, 55

Schachtel, Hyman, 48-9

Schorsch, Ismar, 148

Schulte, Edward, 25

The Screamers, 117-118

Sharp, Martha, 78, 229 n. 178

Sharp, Waitstill, 78, 229 n. 178

Shay, Earl R., 224 n. 120

Shearith Israel (the Spanish and Portugese Synagogue, New York City), 75, 143-144

Sherman, Carl, 82

Shipler, Guy Emery, 79
Shuchat, Wilfred, 29, 110
Shultz, Lillie, 82, 87
Silver, Abba Hillel, 43, 92-93, 96
Silver, Eliezer
Silverman, Sidney, 25
Silverstein, Baruch, 45
Sidney, Sylvia, 59
Smith, Alfred E., 42
Sobibor (Nazi death camp), 2
Social Justice, 11
Soloveitchik, Joseph B.
Stefan Batory University, 27, 123
Stevens, W. Bertrand, 79
S.S. St. Louis, x, 20-2, 154, 223 n. 112
St. Vladimir's Theological Seminary, 46
St. Louis Park synagogue (Minneapolis, MN), 112
Stone, I.F., 106
Stucky, Gerald, 223-224 n. 120
Student Struggle for Soviet Jewry, xv
Synagogue Council of America, 57, 72, 73, 82, 88, 93, 95, 113, 144, 145, 226 n. 145;
and Sefira campaign, 67-70, 74-77, 96, 130, 140, 142

Talmudical Academy (New York City), 59
Taylor, Myron, 82
Teplitz, Saul, 45-46
Thomas, Sen. Elbert, 80, 104
Tillich, Paul, 44
Time, 100
Treblinka (Nazi death camp), xiii, 2
Tucker, Henry St. George, 79

Union of Grand Rabbis, 99
Union of Orthodox Rabbis, 30, 72, 82-83, 88, 99
The Union Review, 59, 77, 229 n. 174

Union Theological Seminary, 44, 45, 46, 58, 59, 60, 77, 79, 130, 155
Unitarian Service Committee, 78
United Palestine Appeal, 3, 57, 82, 87, 98
United States Holocaust Memorial Museum, xiv, 155
United Synagogue of America, 7, 13
Untermeyer, Samuel, 11
Utica Daily Press, 110

Va'ad ha-Hatzala, 98
Va'ad Hayeshivot, 122
Virgin Islands refuge plan, 34, 64-65
Voyage of the Damned, 154

Wagner, Sen. Robert, 20
Wagner-Rogers legislation, 20, 77
Walker, Jacob, 60
Wall Street Journal, 123
Wallace, Henry, 91, 100
Wallenberg, Raoul, 106
War Refugee Board, 105, 126
War Relief Services, 79
Warren, George, 47
Warsaw Ghetto, xi, xiii, 37, 73, 74, 86, 89, n. 213
Washington Times-Herald, 101
We Will Never Die, 55, 57, 79
Weill, Kurt, 58
Weiner, Herbert, 32, 38
Weisgal, Meyer, 86
Weitzmann, Baruch David, 71
Welles, Sumner, 15, 25-26, 72
Werfel, Franz, 47
Wertheim, David, 86
West Side Institutional Synagogue (New York City), 75, 143
White Paper (British Palestine policy), 95-96
Who Shall Live, Who Shall Die, 154
Wiesel, Elie, 148

Winslow, Fred Adams, 80

Wise, Jonah, 18

Wise, Stephen S.: 7, 38, 72, 81, 83, 85, 86, 88, 117, 146, 149, 151; and Alaska refuge plan, 35; and Anglo-American joint statement on Palestine, 91-92; and anti-Nazi boycott, 11-12; and Bermuda conference, 74; biographical information, 3; and charge of warmongering, 21; conflicts with Abba Hillel Silver, 93; conflicts with the Bergson Group, 38, 79; and Evian conference, 16-17,19; health problems, 17, 37; and immigration to the United States, 18; and Jewish emigration from Europe, 14; and Jewish votes, 87; learns of the Holocaust, 2, 9, 24-25, 55, 78, 141; and Palestine immigration, 15; and Pope Pius XII, 26; meeting with President Roosevelt (1942), 30-31; meeting with rabbinical students' delegation, 32-33, 35-37, 41, 44, 59, 139; relationship with Franklin D. Roosevelt, 4-5, 34, 113, 150; and rescue resolution in Congress,102-103; responses to news of the Holocaust, 42-43;

and the Roosevelt administration's refugee policy, 26; and the S.S. St. Louis, 20-21; support for England, 15; and Virgin Islands refuge plan, 34; and Wagner-Rogers legislation, 20; withholds news of the Holocaust, 25

World Council of Churches, 229 n. 174

World Jewish Congress, 3, 24, 32, 43, 54, 60, 82

Wyman, David S., 154

Yale Divinity School, 46

Yeshiva College (Yeshiva University), ix, 8, 32, 33, 37, 46, 52, 59-60, 71, 124

Yeshiva College Student Organization, 60

Yeshivat Hakhmei Lublin, 122

Young Zionist Action Committee, 125

Youth Committee Against War, 38

Zionist Organization of America, 3, 39

Zirelson, Judah Leib, 122

Zygielbojm, Shmuel, xiii, xv, 231 n. 213

Zuroff, Abraham, 60

ABOUT THE AUTHORS

Dr. Rafael Medoff is founding director of The David S. Wyman Institute for Holocaust Studies, based in Washington, D.C., which focuses on America's response to Nazism and the Holocaust (www.WymanInstitute.org). He is the author of 12 books about the Holocaust, Zionism, and American Jewish history, and has contributed to the *Encyclopaedia Judaica* and many other reference volumes. He has also taught Jewish history at Ohio State Unversity, Purchase College of the State University of New York, and elsewhere, and served as associate editor of the scholarly journal *American Jewish History*.

Rabbi Prof. David Golinkin is the President and Jerome and Miriam Katzin Professor of Jewish Studies at the Schechter Institute of Jewish Studies in Jerusalem. He is the author or editor of over 40 books and almost 200 articles, including: *The Responsa of the Va'ad Halakhah, Responsa in a Moment, Women in Jewish Law: Responsa, Ginzey Rosh Hashanah,* and *The Shoah Scroll*, which is used throughout the world on *Yom Hashoah*.